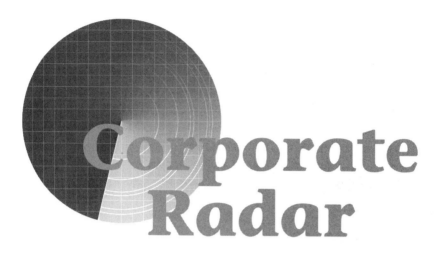

Corporate
Radar

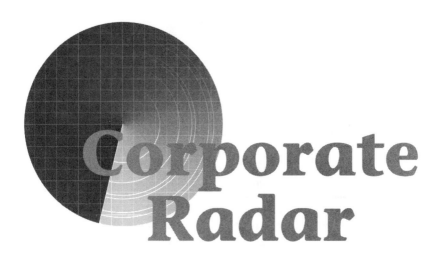

Corporate Radar

Tracking the Forces That Are Shaping Your Business

Karl Albrecht

AMACOM

American Management Association

New York • Boston • Chicago • Kansas City • San Francisco • Washington, D.C.
Brussels • Mexico City • Tokyo • Toronto

Special discounts on bulk quantities of AMACOM books
are available to corporations, professional associations,
and other organizations. For details, contact Special
Sales Department, AMACOM, an imprint of AMA
Publications, a division of
American Management Association,
1601 Broadway, New York, NY 10019
Tel.: 212-903-8316   Fax: 212-903-8083

This publication is designed to provide accurate and
authoritative information in regard to the subject matter
covered. It is sold with the understanding that the publisher is not engaged in rendering legal, accounting, or
other professional service. If legal advice or other expert
assistance is required, the services of a competent professional person should be sought.

Library of Congress Cataloging-in-Publication Data

Albrecht, Karl, 1941-
    Corporate radar : tracking the forces that are shaping your
business / Karl Albrecht.
        p.   cm.
    Includes bibliographical references and index.
    ISBN 0-8144-0504-5 (hc.)
    1. Business intelligence.   I. Title.
    HD38.7.A42   1999   99-30448
    658.4'7--DC21   CIP

Printing number
10 9 8 7 6 5 4 3 2 1

Contents

Preface ix

1: Extinction Is Forever 1

The Treacherous Business Environment 1
Managing the Blind Side 4
Would You Invest in Your Company? 5
Tuning up Your Corporate Radar 7
Boundaries and Ground Rules for This
Discussion 9
The Americentric View of Business 11

2: The Environmental Scan: Your Corporate Radar 14

Environmental Intelligence: The Key to
Your Survival 14
Your Eight Strategic Radar Screens 15
Connecting the Dots 21

3: The New Realities of Business 23

The Business Environment, Pre-1980s:
Managing Growth 23
The Business Environment, Post-1980s:
Hypercompetition 25
Price Wars and Collective Suicide 26

v

Points of Inflection 29
Long Waves, Short Waves, and Choppy Seas 32

4: Surfing the Third Wave 34

A New Species of Human 34
A New Wave 35
The Global-Tribal Paradox 36
The Bell Curve 37
What's Driving the Third Wave? 38
Impacts of the Third Wave 40
Using What We Know 43

5: How to be Your Own Futurist—Without Getting Lost in the Ozone 44

The Future: Gee Whiz or Gee Won't? 44
Thinking Strategically and Futuristically 49
Liars Figure: Beware of Bogus Data 51
The S-Curve: Avoiding Premature
    Extrapolation 59
Drivers, Dominos, and Wildcards 63

6: Your Customer Radar 69

Markets or Customers? 69
The "Molecular Customer" 70
Demographics: The Great Engine of Marketing 72
Whatever Happened to Customer Service? 77
The Myth of Customer Loyalty 81
Understanding Customer Value: The "Need
    Context" 85

7: Your Competitor Radar 92

Who Is Your Competition? 92
The Enemy of Your Enemy Might or Might Not
    Be Your Friend 94
Which Companies Will Dominate? Ask Your
    Broker 96

Consolidation: The David and Goliath Scenario   99
Is There a Merger in Your Future?   102
Branding: The Endless Battle for Mindshare   108
The Struggle for Differentiation   115

8: Your Economic Radar   118

The Big Shift: Intangible Economies   118
Economics as a Behavioral Science   122
Domino Economics: The Knee Bone's
    Connected to...   126
Death-Row Economics: Industries Slated
    for Destruction   128
Economic "Weather" Factors: How They Affect
    Your Business   133
How Currency Exchange Rates Affect Business
    Performance   135
The Euro: The Great Equalizer?   141

9: Your Technological Radar   144

Spotting Winners: Corporate
    Binoculars or Blindfolds?   144
Technology Is Selective in Its Effect   150
The Age of Cheap Information   150
Y2K: The Biggest Wildcard of
    Them All?   155
    Scope of the Problem   157
    Severity of the Potential Impact   159
    Economic Effects   159
    Social Effects   161
    Possible Legal Impacts   162
    Y2K and You   162
Dehumanizing the Customer Interface:
    The Digital Moat   163
Internet Mythology: What the Internet Will
    and Won't Do   167
CyberPolitics: The Battle for Control of the
    Desktop   176

10: Your Social Radar   180

Cultural and Social Factors That Shape
  Customer Intention   180
The American Culture: Prototype for the New
  World Order?   186
Social Values: Rising, Declining, Conflicting   192
Cultural Imperialism and Protectionism   200

11: Your Political Radar   204

There's More to Politics Than Politics   204
The Heavy Hand of Government:
  Unanticipated Consequences   207
The Age of Agendas and Dilemmas   211
Anti-Corporate Politics   215

12: Your Legal Radar   219

Trade: Laws and Lawlessness   219
Liabilities, Lawsuits, and Legal Nightmares   223
Regulations: Defining the Playing Field   224
Contracts: How Not to Victimize Yourself   226

13: Your Geophysical Radar   231

Infrastructure and You   231
Natural and Unnatural Disasters   234
Geopolitics: The Power of Place   235
Geo-Economics: World Supply and Demand   239

14: What Good Is a Radar If You Can't Read the Screen?   243

Bifocal Vision   243
Assembling the Radar Data: The Basic Annual
  Strategic Estimate   244
Interpreting the Big Picture: The Annual
  Strategic Retreat   246
Refining the Business Strategy   249

Index   253

Preface

On Thursday, October 24, 1861, workers completed the last link of the transcontinental telegraph system across the United States. Forty-eight hours later, California's famous Pony Express mail service declared bankruptcy. In nineteen months of operation, it became a legend but never returned a profit to its investors.

In 1997, Hayes Electronics, the company that pioneered the personal-computer modem, went into bankruptcy and never came out. It closed its doors leaving $40 million in debt, at a time when modem sales were setting new records.

Meanwhile, McIlhenny & Company, the small Louisiana firm that makes Tabasco sauce and other condiments, completed its 129th year in business.

Picking winners and losers in the game of business has always been a risky occupation, and it's becoming more so.

Irving Thalberg, business adviser to the legendary Hollywood producer Louis B. Mayer, advised him to turn down a certain movie project he considered a guaranteed failure. "Forget it, Louis," he counseled. "No Civil War picture has ever made a nickel." Mayer passed up *Gone With The Wind* and his rival David O. Selznik brought the film to the silver screen.

Who knows how to recognize the next Pony Express or the next *Gone With The Wind*? Who can predict the real payoff of information technology, genetic engineering, or investments in the infrastructure of a developing country?

The "environmental scan," the careful and thoughtful study of the business environment, has become a critical part of the management thinking process. I call it using your "corporate radar," the sensing system that provides you with the evidence on which to base your decisions about the very destiny of your enterprise.

Will the business you're in ten years from now be the same business you're in now? This is a question that hangs above the head of every strategist. The American writer and humorist Mark Twain advised, "When everybody is out digging for gold, the business to be in is selling shovels." There is actually quite a grain of wisdom in that wisecrack. What is the figurative "shovel" that everybody will need tomorrow?

Success in business seems to be largely a matter of getting a few critical things right, and then applying that success model in the face of the challenges and changes of the business environment. But many times the changes are too complex, too subtle, or too profound to allow the leaders of an enterprise to make simple course corrections. Continuous change, i.e., the steady unfolding of recognized trends, presents one kind of challenge. But discontinuous change, which brings an enterprise to a fork in the road, presents another kind of challenge altogether.

Technological change, for example, has often confused and confounded even the best and brightest leaders in business and government. In their thought-provoking and amusing book *The Experts Speak*, Christopher Cerf and Victor Navasky offer a surprising inventory of confident judgments by highly qualified people that went wide of the mark.[1]

In 1921, the U.S. Secretary of War was so convinced that airplanes had no real future in warfare that he offered to stand on the bridge of a ship while General Billy Mitchell, the chief promoter of military air power, tried to sink it by dropping bombs on it from a plane.

As early as 1921 and as late as 1940, no less than the *New York Times* and *Scientific American* magazine declared that

---

[1]Cerf, Christopher and Victor Navasky. *The Experts Speak: The Definitive Compendium of Authoritative Misinformation.* New York: Villard Books, 1998.

rocket flights outside the Earth's atmosphere were theoretically impossible. They and others dismissed Dr. Robert Goddard's concepts, which later became the theoretical foundation of modern space exploration, as "too far-fetched to be considered."

Ironically, Thomas Edison declared flatly that his favorite invention, the phonograph, had no commercial possibilities. As early as 1937, Walt Disney's brother Roy proposed to retire Mickey Mouse as a character and a commercial product that had seen its day. None other than the CEO of Digital Equipment Corporation, the respected computer engineer Ken Olson, asserted in 1977 that no person had any reason to have a computer in his or her home.

The economic sector is also prone to serious misjudgment by intelligent people. Immediately after the great crash of the U.S. stock market in 1929, many noted economists and financial experts declared that economic growth and prosperity would resume within a matter of months. The U.S. economy did not return to full strength until well into World War II. Conversely, many of the same experts predicted a long and painful depression in America following the war. What actually happened was an unprecedented phase of consumer-led growth that lasted for nearly a decade.

For many business leaders, the real fascination of strategic thinking is in the very *uncertainty* that lies at the core of the process. It presents the ultimate intellectual challenge, a kind of cognitive sport with high risk and high consequences. To peer into the future, knowing that the payoff of your decisions depends on the wisdom—or luck—that guides you to your conclusions, is a very sobering experience.

Over the past two decades I've been fortunate to observe, and sometimes participate in, the strategic thought processes of some of the brightest business leaders on the planet. I've learned a great deal about the various ways they conceptualize the future of their enterprises. From those experiences and observations I've evolved a relatively simple model for managing the daunting intellectual challenges involved in the environmental scan. By conceiving of the business environment in terms of eight figurative sectors, in which events and trends are acting to shape the options open to the firm, we can describe and think about the forces at work there.

By using our figurative "radar" to scan these eight environmental sectors, we can compile a useful picture of the particular business environment facing a particular organization. The most valuable aspect of these eight key radar screens lies in the way they enable the leaders of the business to discuss, debate, interpret, and assimilate the lessons the environment has to teach. Out of this understanding, which must be continually updated and refreshed, they can commit energy, attention, talent, and resources for the greatest strategic value.

This is not really a "futures" book, in the generally accepted sense. It has less to say about what may happen in general than it has to say about *how to figure out* what may happen in particular. In covering a wide range of possibilities that may affect many businesses, it is not possible to specialize in the particular problems of any one. However, I have tried to sketch out the elements of common concern, and to point out ways to explore them further in order to build the strategic estimate for a particular business.

To all who are kind enough to invest their valuable time in reading these precepts: I hope you find value here, and I wish you the best of success—and a bit of luck—in your ventures. This is a great time to be in business.

Karl Albrecht
San Diego, California
albrechtintl.com

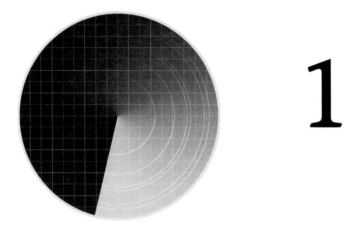

Extinction Is Forever

*There is a tide in the affairs of men, which, taken at the
flood, leads on to fortune. Omitted, all the voyage of their
life is bound in shallows and in miseries. On such a full
sea are we now afloat, and we must take the current
when it serves, or lose our ventures.*
— *Marc Antony, "Julius Caesar"*

The Treacherous Business Environment

Bill Marriott, Sr., founder of the Marriott Corporation and
chairman of that enterprise for many years, often said
"Success is never final." He believed that staying at the top of
the competitive heap was even harder than getting there. Dr.
Peter Drucker also commented dryly in an interview, "Whom
the gods would destroy, they first grant forty years of business
success." He believed that sooner or later, time will turn your
most precious assets into liabilities, and that the most powerful competitive advantage may eventually be neutralized by
the shifting structure of the business environment. Intel's
chairman Andy Grove agreed, with his now-famous remark,
"Only the paranoid survive."

When we study the changing fortunes of companies over
periods of twenty years or more, we are forced to the conclusion

that there is no final answer, no permanent solution to the problem of long-term survival and growth. Management skill can make a big difference, but there are times when the tide just turns against you. Success in business is becoming more and more a matter of "riding the waves," i.e., anticipating and capitalizing on the fundamental changes in the business environment that can turn winners into losers and create new winners.

You don't have to look far for illustrations of trends and events in the business environment that can radically change the success formula for various lines of business. Horizon Health Corporation, for example, a leading provider of mental health and rehab services under outsource contracts to hospitals, lost its footing when the U.S. federal government abruptly changed its policies for reimbursement of the firm's client hospitals for such services. Many hospital executives decided it was unfeasible to continue offering the services and began canceling or not renewing their contracts. Through no fault of its own, the company found itself with radically declining revenues, crushed profit margins, and a share price chopped to one-third of its peak.

In the vaunted high-tech sector, Applied Magnetics Corporation, one of the leading makers of read-write heads for computer hard drives, got caught in a timing squeeze as the technology for making the products shifted. The company's leading position in inductive thin-film magnetic technology suddenly lost its value as magnetoresistive technology became the preferred concept within a matter of months. The firm's revenues dropped by over half and it had to embark on a year-long crash program of heavy investment and retooling to refocus its products. Shareholders saw the market price of their certificates drop from twenty-seven dollars per share to less than four.

Even more ironically, Hayes Corporation, the company that pioneered the electronic modem used by personal computers to send data over telephone lines, ran into trouble keeping its product line current. Other firms copied its products, improved upon them, and left it behind. It filed for bankruptcy protection and recently closed its doors with $40 million in debts, at a time when modem sales were setting new records.

All of Japan's biggest banks went into financial crisis at about the same time, when it became evident that their five-year lending binge had created an unprecedented number of ill-advised and unrecoverable loans. The domino effect of the banking crisis caused a credit shortage that crippled other capital-dependent firms such as exporters and others seeking to grow their operations. The result was a near melt-down of the Japanese economy, resulting in the worst recession in fifty years.

Indonesia suffered a similar banking crisis, for similar reasons, although the impact was far worse due to the colossal waste and mismanagement of capital by the members of President Suharto's extended family and others who were part of that country's "crony capitalism" structure.

Boeing Aircraft Corporation, America's largest single exporter, found itself in the rare position of posting record losses on record orders from its customers. A combination of factors created the dilemma: deep discounts given to acquire the biggest orders, high operating expenses inflicted by an antiquated production system desperately in need of re-engineering, declining demand from the Asian markets, and cutbacks in orders from previously secure customers. The company had to resort to massive layoffs and production cutbacks, as well as revamping its production systems. Of course, many of the firms supplying parts and materials to the company felt the domino effect, including Northrop Grumman, with twelve percent of its revenues coming from Boeing.

Callaway Golf Company, the leading maker of high-performance and prestige golf equipment, saw its impressive sales growth flame out under the double-barreled effects of declining demand from the Asian markets and price cuts by its ever-more aggressive competitors. Falling demand, overcapacity, and price wars are a sure-fire recipe for the destruction of profit. The firm's earnings dropped to zero, and its share price fell to one-third of its peak.

Motorola Corporation, once the darling of Wall Street, became a pariah when its delay in switching to the new digital technology for its cellular phones cost it a major chunk of market share.

Smith-Corona Corporation held the dominant position in the market for typewriters for decades. The company filed for bankruptcy in 1995, leaving many industry observers to wonder why it didn't transform its business to adapt to the personal computer age. After all, they reasoned, why shouldn't the leader in typewriters be the natural candidate for leader in the printer market?

These and countless other examples dramatize the need to be ever more watchful for events, trends, and forces in your business environment that can threaten your existence. It is no longer enough to relegate the strategic review of the environment to the annual executive planning retreat or the annual management conference. It is no exaggeration to say that executives must scan the business horizon every single day for telltale signs of significant change.

Managing the Blind Side

While we're tuning up our sensitivity to events and trends in the business environment, let's not overlook the obvious threats. It's not always a devious competitor or a capricious customer that can cause you harm. There are plenty of mundane ways a firm can lose money, lots of it, that don't seem at first thought like part of the big picture of grand strategy.

While a company is fighting its competitors with finely tuned maneuvers to gain an extra sliver of market share, a significant labor strike could inflict far greater damage on its profits than the amount the share war might capture. A major strike by the United Auto Workers against General Motors in 1998 cost the company over *$1 billion in profit*. Are your union and its political parents part of your business environment? The question answers itself.

What about a major product disaster that creates enormous liability costs? Should such an event be considered in a review of the hypothetical legal environment? Certainly. Consider that Foodmaker Incorporated, operator of over 1,000 Jack-in-the-Box hamburger restaurants, incurred costs of over $40 million in 1993 caused by an episode of food poisoning involving beef tainted with *E. coli* bacteria. Several customers died and others became seriously ill. Even though the episodes were limited and local, the firm's brand image took a major blow. Lawsuits by customers, as well as franchisees who claimed their investments were devalued, distracted company management for over a year.

Corporate security expert Steve Albrecht refers to these types of episodes as "blind side" events. A major lawsuit for sexual harassment or racial discrimination can take a significant nick out of the bottom line. Episodes of employee violence, if not properly managed, can trigger major legal liabilities. Even the kidnapping or death of a key executive by foreign criminals has to be part of the list of possibilities.

Albrecht points out that "A company's executive team can be concentrating so closely on the customers, competitors, economic trends, and technological issues, that they overlook the potentially lethal threats right under their noses. Dealing with all strategic contingencies has to include managing the 'blind side' as well as the frontal threat."

In his book, *Crisis Management for Corporate Self-Defense*, Albrecht says:

> No matter what product or service you sell, no matter what your industry, market, or type of organization, you may face a serious corporate emergency at some point in the near future. If nothing significant has happened to you or your firm to date, consider yourself lucky. But just because you don't hear examples of modern-day disasters doesn't mean they aren't going on around you.[1]

This is not to say that the executive team should be frightened into immobility by the unlimited number of possible threats that could arise in the environment. But a thorough scan of the business environment must include these kinds of possibilities in addition to the more commonplace issues.

Would You Invest in Your Company?

One way to think about the future of your business, in terms of its opportunities and problems, is to stand back and look at it dispassionately as if you were a potential buyer of the business or an investor. How would you decide whether this firm will be a good investment over the next five years? What are the key factors that will drive its growth and profitability?

In the language of strategic planning, this process of searching the business environment is known as the "environmental scan," and it's the first key step in formulating, revising, or verifying the overall competitive strategy. Scanning the business environment has become an essential habit for senior executives and thinking managers at all levels. Of course, it is necessary to transform the discoveries that come from the environmental scan into policies and actions; there is little point in knowing you're heading for an iceberg if you don't know how to steer around it.

Certainly, you'll want to consider the "internals," i.e., the talent and knowledge of the senior management team and the various assets of the firm. A strong CEO and a well-qualified team of executives can never hurt. But in some cases, management quality may be far overshadowed by the "externals," such as a steadily declining demand for the product or service, a takeover of the market by a few deep-pocket competitors, or a technological change that undermines the added-value proposition of the firm's offering. Conversely, sometimes a firm rides to glory on an environmental wave, regardless of—or in spite of—the capabilities of the leadership team.

Management skill may be important, but it is often not decisive in predicting the success of the firm when all key driving factors are considered. The celebrated mutual-fund investment guru Peter Lynch likes to say, "I want to invest in a company that can be run by any fool, because sooner or later it will be."

This is not to disparage the management team of any enterprise but merely to point out that executives need to consider the environmental forces over which they have little or no control and prepare the firm to adapt to them in any way possible.

Of course, we have to understand the primary business parameters: What's happening to the total market demand for our value package? What is the structure of the competition? Which competitors are favored by the structure of the industry, brand power, capital strength, and access to the customer? What are the unique strategic issues for a firm of our particular size, capabilities, and style of operating? Most executive teams are very familiar with these basic truths of their business, and it isn't necessary for this book to dwell on what everyone already knows.

The trick, however, in scanning the business environment is to reach beyond the standard business parameters and explore the variables and relationships that present real threats or opportunities. These may always not be obvious, even to the experts who manage the firm on a day-to-day basis. Making your firm a good investment means aligning its strengths with the possibilities presented by the business environment that is unique to your particular enterprise. And that requires an intimate understanding of those possibilities.

Most executive teams could benefit by devoting more time and attention to the environmental scan, and especially to discussing the implications of the findings. Not all executives are equally up to date on what's happening in the business environment. Most are probably aware of the primary issues and events that affect their business, or at least their particular part of the business, but it is not at all uncommon for a whole team to lack a coherent concept of the environment.

As the overall business environment becomes ever more fluid and complex, it becomes more critical that every member of the management team, including middle managers, have a firm grasp of the basic dynamics that affect the firm itself. It is equally important that the leaders keep up a running dialogue on the meaning of the significant events and trends, and that they build some kind of consensus as a basis for setting or refining the direction and strategy of the business. Although the techniques for setting and implementing the business strategy are outside the scope of this book, we should keep in mind that the whole purpose of the environmental scan is to make that process more intelligent and more effective.

Tuning up Your Corporate Radar

To offer a useful metaphor: every business enterprise is a bit like a ship plowing through heavy seas, presumably to a well-chosen destination. Its crew must keep it on course when the course is right, and they must know when and how to rethink the course if circumstances change. The key to this consciousness of the correct course is knowing what's ahead of the ship. This is why the *Titanic* sank, and it's why ships today all have radar systems.

Every ship needs a physical radar, and every corporation needs a figurative radar. Your corporate radar is the disciplined process of investigating, studying, analyzing, and thinking about the various dimensions of your business environment. Your radar must be turned on and scanning full time.

About twenty-five years ago, the vogue in management thinking was long-range planning. Executives were supposed to think in terms of decades and to draw up growth plans reaching to the end of the century. Japanese firms claimed planning philosophies that extended outward for a hundred years or more.

Starting with the "oil shock" of 1972 and beyond, executives saw more and more change and upheaval in the business environment. At the same time, a wave of restructuring in business touched off mergers and de-mergers, acquisitions and spin-offs, partnerships, downsizing, delayering, and outsourcing, which shifted the emphasis in management planning to a very short-term mindset. "Long range" now typically meant "until the end of the year." Many executives began to feel that success depended on being able to react quickly to events and being willing to make drastic moves to cut costs, move products to market faster, and grow more aggressively. Time-based competition became the concept of choice in a number of industries, particularly the high-tech industries.

Now, however, the imperative for the longer view seems to be returning. It becomes more and more necessary to define and analyze the key events, trends, and forces in the business environment that will dictate the tactics of choice. This is not to say that the need to move quickly and manage resources more aggressively is diminished in any way. But business leaders are going to need a special brand of "bifocal vision," which is the ability to see and react to the immediate threats simultaneously with detecting the midterm changes that are not so obvious but which will shape the options for the new near term.

Intel Corporation's chairman Andy Grove speaks often of "points of inflection," which are points in the lifespan of a company or industry at which subtle but profound changes begin to make themselves felt. In his book *Only the Paranoid Survive*,[2] he contends that failing to perceive one of these key points of inflection can spell the difference between survival and extinction in some industries. He believes that the key role of the chief executive is to study the environment, learn from it, and help others interpret its messages. One reason he stepped down from his role as chief executive officer of Intel in 1998, aside from his battle with cancer, was to devote more of his time and attention to understanding, as he describes it, "a world with a billion connected computers."

In this book, I will offer a framework for learning the lessons the business environment has to teach; for getting useful insights into the structure and dynamics of a particular business sector; and for integrating a wide range of discoveries, findings, and conclusions into a unified tapestry. The purpose of this strategic tapestry is to give the leaders of the enterprise a shared concept of their likely future, and a framework for evaluating various strategic alternatives and initiatives in terms of their likely success.

Boundaries and Ground Rules for This Discussion

I seldom devote space in my books to "intellectual preliminaries," e.g. previewing the subject matter, profiling the reader, or setting out cautions and disclaimers. I prefer to get right to work. However, the task of understanding the business environment is quite vast, and reducing it to manageable proportions requires making key choices about the focus of the discussion, the extent of coverage of various topics, and a consciousness of the wide range of variation in readers, business sectors, and business environments in various countries and regions. In this case, it does seem advisable to set some boundaries and ground rules for the exploration.

The first step in tackling a mission such as that promised in this book is to get our ambitions under control. For example, it would be a futile exercise to try to catalog all the key events, trends, and forces that will shape the future of even one major industry or business sector, to say nothing of trying to do so for many. Such a result might be mind-boggling in its scope, and it's unlikely than any category would have greater depth of insight than already offered by experts who specialize in that particular industry or sector. So it is immediately clear that this discussion must focus on the thinking process itself, not solely on the content or inputs to the process.

Next, we will have to set some reference point for the level of knowledge expected of the reader in order to use this book properly, as well as the kind of business he or she is engaged in. Although some readers might be quite well-versed in various management topics, others may not. I don't want to write a book just for experts. Although expert readers might find a discussion of population demographics a bit boring, for example, it might not seem at all simplistic to a reader who has less formal training in marketing topics. If I have to choose, I'd prefer to bore the expert rather than baffle the novice.

On the other hand, this cannot be a primer on the basics of business, because we would never get to the techniques to be explored. I will assume, as a reference point for the reader of this book, a person with management responsibilities, ranging anywhere from middle management up through executive management, which includes owners or CEOs of small- to medium-sized firms. It seems fair to assume that this person has a reasonable grasp of business fundamentals, including at least the simple truths of economics, corporate finance, marketing, and the effects of information technology, but not necessarily an interest in highly analytical methods such as statistics and economic modeling.

We must also recognize that the possible responses to significant factors in the environment will be very different for different kinds of firms. In particular, the problems and possibilities facing the small- to medium-sized enterprise are very different from those facing the large firm. It seems only fair to entertain both perspectives to the extent possible, in hopes of discovering lessons of value to both kinds of businesses. The same reasoning applies to firms operating in different countries. What makes sense for a firm operating in a mega-economy such as U.S., Japan, or any of the other GATT nations, might not make sense for a firm in one of the "micro-tiger" economies such as Finland, Hong Kong, Israel, Singapore, or Taiwan.

Similarly, the issues presented to a firm in a strong developing economy such as Brazil could manifest themselves very differently in a less-developed country such as Vietnam.

Further, every discussion of the future necessarily proceeds from the particular worldview, personal biases, and base of knowledge of the person offering it. There can be no "objective" discussion of the future. This mandates that we consciously make note of these biases at the outset, and wherever possible account for their impact on the discussion. It also means that

I as your figurative tour guide should point out my own biases whenever possible.

The Americentric View of Business

Inasmuch as I am American by birth and acculturation, and most of my experience has been focused in the U.S. business environment, my reference points are the U.S. culture and economic system, and American—or at least Western—management thinking. I can only say that, having worked in various countries around the world for 20 years or more, I believe I have become reasonably alert to significant differences in point of view that can influence the discussion. I have no doubt, however, that my multinational and multicultural colleagues will take me to task if my Americanized worldview overshadows the discussion too much.

In this book, as in most of my other books, I have made a conscious effort to "de-Americanize" the discussion by invoking examples from various countries rather than dwelling on those best known to American readers. I've also tried to draw upon and credit the ideas of various management thinkers from other nations besides my own. But beyond that, if we're going to scan the business environment in this book, or at least think about how to scan it, we must start with the realization that the environment can be radically different for different countries in many ways.

To cite just a few examples: the American population is one of the most ethnically diverse on Earth, certainly for any sizable country. In contrast, the Japanese population is one of the most ethnically homogeneous. The process of building a brand concept, crafting a marketing message, and communicating it to prospective consumers is radically different under those different circumstances. Target marketing, although not unimportant in Japan, tends to be much more important in the U.S., because of its more differentiated population.

Similarly, building a powerful brand image for a certain product or service might be quite possible in a small country like New Zealand, with a population of about 3.6 million. But in a country like America, with 270 million people, it may not be economically feasible. It might make more sense to build a regional brand identity and compete in regional markets, rather than conceive of the whole country as a single market.

Conversely, it might be a mistake to assume that something that works in the U.S. would not work in a less-developed country, based on differences in educational level or economic status. For example, I have usually discovered that executives and professional people in the developing countries I have visited are just as up to date with computers, software, and information technology as their American counterparts. Indeed, when I lecture in various developing countries, I must be very careful to get an accurate profile of the level of knowledge of the attending audiences. It is easy, and painful, to underestimate their knowledge of contemporary business practices and management concepts. The same is true for journalists. Many of them are fully up to date on current business issues.

At the same time, we can acknowledge the value of extending certain business practices and management concepts developed in the U.S. to other business environments. For example, many of the social trends, demographic shifts, and technological directions taking place in the U.S. will probably extend to many other national cultures and business environments. People in those countries can get a sense of their own futures by observing the effects of these trends on the American culture. They can become more conscious of the choices to be made and begin thinking about the possible consequences of those alternative choices.

The sheer size of the American economy means that there will inevitably be more research and development, more experimentation, more trial and error, more entrepreneurial activity, and more published knowledge than in any other country, at least on an absolute scale. This enables business leaders from many other countries to monitor developments in the American environment and to selectively import those they find valuable. It's no accident that American book publishers find willing partners to translate business books into other languages. It's also no accident that any major industry conference in America will have a sizable contingent of people attending from all over the world.

One important characteristic of America and Americans in general, charitably stated, is their relative ignorance of what goes on in other countries. I am always startled to discover how much people in other countries I visit know about America, its politics, and the current scandals going on there. While many business executives in Australia, for example, can easily name not only the President of the United States, they also know the vice president, top congressional leaders, and key members of the President's cabinet. Conversely, few Americans could name the prime minister of Australia, and fewer still could identify any other national figures except famous golfers, athletes, and a few entertainers.

But for all of its agonies, its self-flagellation, and its soul-searching, America is still the place to go for ideas. Those who are in the business of importing ideas into other countries have learned how to sort through the raw material and make good use of those parts that do travel well across national cultures and business environments.

Notes

1. Albrecht, Steve. *Crisis Management for Corporate Self-Defense*. New York, AMACOM, 1996, p. 13.
2. Grove, Andrew S. *Only the Paranoid Survive: How to Exploit the Crisis Points that Challenge Every Company and Career*. New York: Doubleday, 1996.

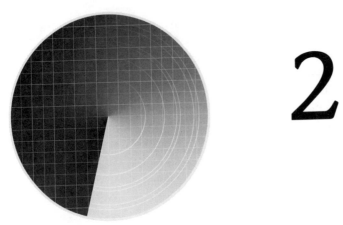

The Environmental Scan: Your Corporate Radar

There is nothing so frightening as ignorance in action.
— *Johann Wolfgang von Goethe*

Environmental Intelligence: The Key to Your Survival

Executive teams vary considerably in the discipline with which they study their environments. The more sophisticated of them devote continuous attention to what's happening outside their doors. Some organizations even have what amount to "environmental intelligence" units. They have people with no other job but to read the signals and alert the leaders to their implications.

Many organizations, however, are remarkably out of touch with the wider world. Their executives may be so preoccupied with near-field problems and issues that they feel they have no time to think about the far-field. These organizations tend

14

to be the sitting ducks who take the worst punishment when the shockwave hits. A major shockwave may come through a particular industry only once in a decade, and nine years of complacency can leave most of the players dangerously vulnerable.

But environmental intelligence has more value than just averting disasters. It is the very raw material for creating new opportunities as well. Indeed, it is the starting point for the whole strategy development process. The Environmental Scan, the first component of the model presented in my book *The Northbound Train*, gets us grounded in reality and may enable us to see what our competitors may not see. It is the figurative crystal ball of strategic thinking.

However, there is a lot going on in the environment of a typical business enterprise. Who can even define the environment comprehensively? Can anyone ever fully understand all of its dimensions and interpret all of its signals? Surely not.

But by thinking of the environment in terms of its major components, we can at least make the challenge less daunting. We need a way to subdivide the business environment into more manageable categorical components so we can begin to organize our knowledge of it.

Your Eight Strategic Radar Screens

Figure 2-1 shows a conceptual breakdown of the business environment into eight critical sub-environments. By studying the goings-on in each of them and connecting the lessons of all of them into a unified picture, we can build a solid basis in fact and a reasonable basis for speculation about what's going to happen to the players in the competitive arena.

Let's briefly visit the eight basic environments treated in the environmental scan:

- *Customer environment*—the identity, wants, needs, behaviors, habits, values, and life situations of those who do business with you. This category deals with both demographic and psychographic truths about customers. It also recognizes that the enterprise may deal with complex customer entities such as businesses, governments, and groups of people, as well as simply with individuals.

Figure 2-1. The Business Environment.

What are demographic changes doing to your customer environment? What demographic factors, such as gender, age, marital patterns, birthrates, education, economic situations, buying habits, religious patterns, mobility, and the like, have the biggest influence on your access to your customers? What psychographic changes are happening in your customer environment? How do social values, such as styles and trends, ecological awareness, health consciousness, attitudes toward institutions such as government, police, and corporations, family values, and gender relationships, condition the life environment of your customers? How do rising crime and violence influence their thinking? How are changes in the customers' own personal or business environments forcing them to change? Get yourself mentally inside their worlds and

learn what they're experiencing and how they are reacting to the changes in their worlds. By studying closely
what's happening to your customers you can better
understand and even anticipate what's happening with
them. Are there new issues facing them, and can you
translate these issues into the value premise of your
business? By the way, be sure to study the customers you
hope to do business with, not just the ones you're currently serving; you may discover important differences.

■ *Competitor environment*—the identity, motives, strengths,
weaknesses, current behavior, and potential behavior of the
other enterprises who compete for your customers'
resources. It's not necessary, and usually not advisable, to
build your strategic approach around what your competitors are doing; you just need to be clear about how they are
approaching the customers you want to do business with.
How do the competitors array themselves in your particular industry? Are there just a few big players? Is your
enterprise one of them? Or is it a "cats and dogs" industry
with no real dominant player? Are your competitors gang-
ing up? Are they forming alliances or co-ventures? Are they
searching for acquisitions that strengthen their customer
access? Are they aggressively bringing new offerings to the
market? Are they taking advantage of new technologies to
do more for the customer or to drive down costs, or both?
Are global competitors affecting you? Where are the other
players weak or inadequate? What gaps exist? What
blindspots might they have concerning customer value
that you might be able to exploit? Don't forget that in
some cases, your customers themselves may become
your competitors if they "in-source" things they have been
buying from you. In fact, your competitors aren't limited to
just the other enterprises that offer the same thing you do.
There may be other operators in your business world that
offer alternative solutions that could lead your customers
to do less business with you.

■ *Economic environment*—the dynamics of markets, capital, critical resources, costs, prices, currency, state of the
national economy, and the state of international trade, all
of which may affect the buying patterns of the customers,

the behavior of competitors, and the opportunities open
to your own enterprise. What are the few critical economic factors that most affect demand for what you provide? How recession-sensitive is your industry? How does
it behave in boom times? On the down slope? During the
comeback phase? Do global markets affect your business
directly? Are your prices or costs sensitive to foreign
exchange, interest rates, or investment yields? Do you
depend heavily on critical materials or processes that
fluctuate in price or availability? Is demand for your
products or services hostage to, or derived from, other
more primary economic activity? How will changes in tax
policy affect your customers or your business? What
shockwaves can you see coming, and how might they
affect you? If you depend on a few large customers for
most of your revenue, could losing one jeopardize your
survival? Are there economic changes in other industries
that can translate into advantage in your industry, i.e.,
can you "cannibalize" business from others who vie for
the customer's resources? The economic environment is a
very complex one, and it helps to sort the various
changes into primary and secondary effects so you can
keep the analysis to manageable proportions.

■ *Technological environment*—the range of technological
events, trends, and solutions available or on the way, that
can improve the capability of your enterprise for creating
value. This includes the study of the developers of new
technologies and their likely behavior, the technology
itself, and the trends associated with the application of
the technology. How are technological changes affecting
your customers, and how do those changes lead to new
threats or opportunities for your enterprise? Which technologies are coming fast, and which ones are dying? Are
you riding the developing ones or the dying ones? What
are the long-wave changes, the ones certain to drive
events for many years? What are the short-wave changes,
open to debate about their long term consequences? How
long will it take to build the most valuable of these technologies into your operation? Are there new products or
processes that can jeopardize the very existence of your

enterprise? What possible breakthrough, if achieved, could restructure your whole industry? What one technological capability could make the biggest difference in your ability to create value for your customers? Should you be investing your own resources in developing certain technologies for your needs?

■ *Social environment*—the cultural patterns, values, beliefs, trends, styles, preferences, heroes, villains, and conflicts that form the reference system of people's behavior. These may include the effects of national cultures, individual ethnic cultures within a country, and various social segments such as teenagers and people with various lifestyles. These parameters can strongly affect customer behavior as well as define the opportunities open for new market ventures. What broad social issues or changes in attitudes might make certain products less desirable, or others more in demand? What problems of public life, such as law and order, civil rights, questions of medical ethics, family values and relationships, moral issues, religious issues, the role of the media, and the rights of various special-interest groups, are changing your part of the business environment? What part does the issue of corporate social responsibility, i.e., good citizenship, play in your business? How do people feel about your kind of industry or your organization? What must you rethink, what must you re-evaluate, and what must you start doing differently to position your enterprise with the set of values you consider necessary?

■ *Political environment*—the processes of national, regional, and local governments, as well as various power groups that can affect the rules for doing business. This can include government intervention in particular industries, tax policies at all levels, government expenditures for certain causes, legislation aimed at implementing social policy, and regulation of various industries and trade practices. In some countries, it can even involve the basic stability or instability of the national government, effects of corruption, and the safety of the enterprise itself. Differences in laws and policies from one regional government to another can mean that doing business can be easy in one part of a country and a nightmare in another. It may even be advisable to relocate all or part of a business operation to eliminate the negative effects of political hostility. The political environment can also include the influence of informally organized pressure groups, activist organizations, associations representing people or organizations committed to various goals, and media interest in certain issues.

■ *Legal environment*—the pattern of laws, lawmaking activity, and litigation that can affect the success of the enterprise. This can involve legal considerations of patents, copyrights, trademarks, and other intellectual property; anti-trust considerations; trade protectionism; product liability; environmental liability; and employment law and litigation, including equal employment issues, sexual harassment, and the rights of employers to hire and fire at will. Clearly, some societies are more litigious than others; the United States, for example, has over twenty times more lawyers per 100,000 people than Japan. Some firms use litigation as part of their competitive strategy. The prospect of expensive or even catastrophic litigation requires that the leaders of the enterprise have a conscious risk-management approach suitable to the realities of their business.

■ *Geophysical environment*—the physical surroundings of the organization's facilities and operations, including the ecosystems and natural resources, availability of raw materials, transportation options, proximity to major population centers and sources of skilled talent, susceptibility to environmental disasters like earthquakes and hurricanes, and the effects of crime in the near environment. Changes in any of these factors can affect the success of the business. The location of the corporate headquarters may not be very significant, but the location of geographic offices and distribution centers to maximize customer access can be critical. Operating in a severely congested urban environment may make it more difficult to attract certain kinds of highly talented employees, who value other aspects of the quality of life. For businesses that depend on natural resources such as oil, minerals, wood, water, or land access, trends in the management of these assets by governments or other custodians can have a major effect on strategic options.

Connecting the Dots

At some point in our schooling, most of us had to learn about the constellations in the night sky with those exotic names such as *Orion, Cassiopia, Ursa Major,* and *Ursa Minor.* Children in the southern hemisphere had to learn about the *Southern Cross* and others. To see a constellation, you had to find a particular group of stars and then you had to imagine they were connected by lines to form a diagram or a drawing.

I always had trouble with *Orion,* the hunter. I knew how to find the three stars in his belt, but that hodgepodge of stars didn't really look like a person to me. Seeing a drawing of the constellation in an astronomy book, I could understand how the ancient stargazers created the picture, but it still seemed to me that they were stretching things a bit. Perhaps they saw a hunter because they wanted to see a hunter.

That's actually the way your environmental radar screen works. You see the constellation that your personal knowledge, history, and biases equip you to see. Your radar screen supplies the stars, the key events and trends, and your mind creates the constellation, the concept of what's happening. Each radar screen gives you a different "take" on the environment. There is no correct set of constellations, and no objective conclusion that is correct for all businesses. The technological constellation or the legal constellation for your enterprise is whatever you conclude that it is. You'll never know whether it's right or wrong in the objective sense, only whether it seemed to support the success of your business over the long term.

But without a fully functioning corporate radar, and a thoughtful analysis of the information it brings you, you can't even hope to approach the future of your business with the educated guesswork that it makes possible.

In using this environmental model, a note of caution is in order: it is important not to fall into the habit of thinking of these eight hypothetical environments as if they really were separate components. Indeed, they are not. In many cases, the most valuable insights come from discovering phenomena that weave through all of them or that transcend any imaginary intellectual dividing line between one and another. The only value in dividing them up is to make the process of analysis more manageable. The real value is ultimately in putting them back together.

Most executive teams could do a much better job of reading their environmental radar screens, and most could do a much better job of putting the information to use. It is quite common for the market research "eggheads" in an organization to have a wealth of information at their disposal, and for none of the leaders of the enterprise to even know what they have. And seldom do executives deploy market intelligence throughout the organization, or even one or two levels down to the managers who could benefit from a better understanding of the business challenges facing the enterprise.

If your leadership team has a periodic formal strategy retreat, say at least as often as once a year, it is a good idea to present everybody at the meeting with a written report of the environmental scan. This document should be a masterpiece of careful selection, digestion, and interpretation of the critical elements of environmental intelligence. It should not overwhelm them with data or too much information for them to process. But every leader should be expected to understand the operating environment in some depth and be prepared to capitalize on that knowledge in the strategy development process as well as in leading his or her own unit to meet its mission.[1]

Notes

1. This chapter is adapted from my book *The Northbound Train: Finding the Purpose, Setting the Direction, Shaping the Destiny of Your Organization*. New York: AMACOM, 1994, page 72.

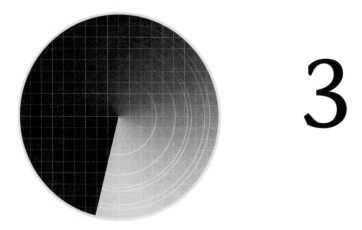

3

The New Realities of Business

Toto, I don't think we're in Kansas any more.
—Dorothy to her dog, in The Wizard of Oz

Beginning about the early 1980s, a subtle but significant change began to take place in the business environment for almost all of the developed countries. Most of the major Western economies, as well as the key Asian economies, began to experience a permanent shift in structure. This change has been intensifying ever since and has become the dominant reality for most business organizations. To understand better the new issues and new options presented to business leaders for the next decade or more, it is important to understand how this great shift took place and where it has brought us.

The Business Environment, Pre-1980s: Managing Growth

Many economists characterize the period from the end of World War II up through the late 1970s and early 1980s as one of increasing prosperity and rising demand. Especially in the U.S., but generally in the other developed economies as well, consumerism was on the rise. Very strong demand for new products and services, rising social aspirations, and rapidly increasing industrial productivity combined to launch a long period of dramatic economic growth.

Management thinking and business practices in general tended to reflect this sense of permanently rising demand. The business environment prior to the 1980s was generally characterized by the following assumptions:

1. Demand was generally running ahead of output. A company with a good product at a good price, and willing to sell it hard, could generally look forward to fairly steady growth.

2. Competition was relatively limited and largely local. There was little talk about global commerce, global markets, and global competition, even in primary industries such as oil, steel, and industrial commodities. Markets during that period were primarily the home markets. Certainly exports were on the rise, but most American products were designed primarily for the American market with export sales largely considered a bonus. Outside the U.S., it was more common for firms to try to target their products to the American market, but the reverse was seldom the case with American products.

3. Producers were, for the most part, in the driver's seat. With rising demand and falling production costs, many firms had little incentive to make radical increases in product quality. Consumers generally had a few primary choices in each category. Imported products were still relatively novel in America, in most cases.

4. Rising revenues were largely taken for granted. The assumption seemed to be that, if we can keep our costs under control, keep increasing productivity, and keep expanding our capacity, we can ride the sales curve to ever rising revenues and ever-rising profits. Most management books and courses implicitly dealt with the management of growth.

5. Management thinking and energy was largely devoted to production issues, i.e., to the operational systems in the organization that produced the product or delivered the service. Customer demand was taken largely for granted, and the customer experience was not generally considered a key element of the business formula to be managed.

6. Cost-oriented strategies tended to parallel the production focus. The prevailing management worldview, promoted by almost all well-known business schools, represented the business as basically an apparatus with resources and processes to be managed. This was the age of "Industrial Management."

The Business Environment, Post-1980s: Hypercompetition

Somewhere around the turn of the 1970s decade, the consumer growth boom began to top out, as the post-war baby boom generation began to mature past their intensive-consumption phase, birth rates began to decline, and people found themselves in possession of many of the things they had desired. Management thinking and business practices have been characterized by the stress of adapting to this changed reality:

1. Output began running ahead of demand. While demand was leveling off, the steady flow of capital invested in new production capacity in a wide range of industries created world overcapacity in many industries and intense pricing pressures.

2. Competition became more intense and much more global. With falling trade barriers, a strong dollar, and a quality revolution in Japan, the U.S. experienced unprecedented levels of imports at lower prices than many American firms could charge. Japanese firms virtually took over the market for consumer electronic products and began to make serious inroads into the U.S. car market. At the same time, many of the larger American firms began expanding aggressively overseas and branded fast-food products such as McDonald's hamburgers and Coca-Cola began adding to the influence of Hollywood films in exporting the American culture to all parts of the globe.

3. Customers were now in the driver's seat. With imported products from weak-currency countries underpricing those of the richer economies, consumers became more comfortable buying foreign-made products. Adding to the continuing oversupply of home-built products, this provided consumers with unprecedented buying power. The early- and mid-1980s saw a steady rise in price wars among car sellers, airlines, appliance makers, banks, insurance companies, fast-food merchants, and many others.

4. Revenues became increasingly uncertain. The steady-growth assumption came under intense fire as each recession did proportionally more and more damage to profits. "Diversification" was no longer the magic word for profit-building. As competition became ever more intense, many firms discovered the hard way that trying to invade markets in which they had no special advantages could be unhealthy for shareholder value.

5. Management thinking and energy began to shift from an internal focus, i.e., production issues, to an external focus, dealing with marketing, customer perception, and the selling of value.

6. Value-oriented strategies began to dominate. The "customer revolution," arising in the early 1980s, captured the attention of many executive teams as a concept for differentiating their companies from their competitors. A more intense focus on understanding the customer's conception of value, and focusing the energy of the organization on delivering it, replaced the previous attitude of taking the customer for granted. This became the era of "Service Management."

Price Wars and Collective Suicide

The shift from the "demand" economy to the "push" economy and the rise of hypercompetition in almost all sectors have given us an ugly and permanent truth:

The competitors in a crowded market tend toward collective suicide.

To see how this works, consider Figure 3-1, which shows how the competitive dynamics shift as an industry, sector, or product moves through its market lifecycle from infancy to maturity.

Developing Stage. When the market is new or developing, the competitive picture tends to be confused and unsettled. Suppliers have to innovate because there is not yet an accepted definition of what the product should look like. Competitive differentiation is high because each of the suppliers is searching for a winning solution. The basic competitive dynamic of this type of market is evolution toward a value package that the customers will respond to most enthusiastically. The early days of the personal computer and PC software saw this chaotic, formative state of affairs in the market. The

Figure 3-1. Product Evolution and Competition.

Market Life Cycle			
	Developing	**Maturing**	**Saturating**
Suppliers:	Innovators	Imitators	Predators
Differentiation:	High	Decreasing	Minimal
Dynamic:	Evolution	Positioning	Price Wars

World Wide Web went through much the same process on its way to commercialization.

Maturing Stage. As more and more competitors offer a wider range of choices, the customers vote with their purchases and certain kinds of value packages succeed while others fail. The surviving competitors quickly gravitate toward a narrower range of choices, and a particular "style" of the product or service emerges as the preferred design. At this stage, most of the suppliers become imitators. Differentiation decreases radically and the competitive dynamic becomes a matter of positioning, as competitors ply the customer with their favorite variations on the core design. Virtually all new products and services pass into this maturing stage. Automobiles now tend to look and operate just about the same, with various cosmetic differences. Even clothing designs gravitate toward basic structures, with stylistic variations. Personal computers have looked basically alike for a long time. The Internet has not yet passed completely into the second stage.

Saturating Stage. Once too many competitors have discovered a product or service and a core design has evolved, the market becomes a shoving contest, with competitors elbowing one another for a better shot at the customers. Innovation is virtually nonexistent, or at least seldom emphasized. Differentiation is limited to the standard choices that have emerged, such as price range, feature sets, or style variations. At the saturating stage, market share gets divided thinly, profit margins fall, and more competitors battle for the available revenues. Inevitably, one or more competitors, usually the larger ones, will start a price war with a predatory pattern of discounting and price-cutting in hopes of gaining market share by forcing others out of the game. For example, the personal computer is now a fully commoditized product, subject to fierce competition and enriched only by price-related feature options. The Internet went into the price war stage in record time, as self-styled marketing experts began to slash prices on Internet access almost as soon as the phenomenon became popular. Indeed, this "giveaway" mentality has probably doomed the Internet to the permanent status of a no-profit zone.

The movement of any product, service, industry, or sector through these three stages is almost inevitable. The competitive forces moving all players from innovation to cutthroat competition are almost irresistibly strong, like gravity pulling them down a slippery slope into the mud. When the product or service has lost all or most of its variability, and all suppliers look just about alike to the customer, then the customer gets to the point where he or she has no rationale for choosing one supplier over another except the lowest price.

Price wars tend to be rampant in mature industries such as airlines, retailing, and fast foods, as all players drift into a kind of collective suicide pact. Even those who try to resist giving away their gross margins feel the pressure as others slash prices below the point of profitable operation. It is sometimes said that, in a price-driven business, you're no more successful than your dumbest or most desperate competitor. In a number of saturated industries, well-capitalized mega-firms have jumped in, adding excess capacity and trying to buy customers with subsidized pricing. Like the big kid who cannonballs into the swimming pool, they make a big splash, annoy everyone there, and chase the smaller kids out of the pool.

The few firms that resolve to separate themselves from the self-destructive price wars usually find it very difficult. If virtually all of the suppliers in a particular line of business have spent years conditioning their customers to perceive price as the only variable that counts in their purchases, a maverick firm must find a way to offer genuinely superior value, make its message believable to enough customers, and work hard to help them perceive the difference. Years of commercial experience have shown that most customers will quickly gravitate toward the lowest price if they cannot detect a *significant and believable difference* in the value being offered. Regaining a valid level of differentiation in a saturated industry can be a very daunting challenge, although potentially very rewarding to the firm that can pull it off.

Points of Inflection

Intel chairman Andy Grove's concept of *points of inflection* involves a subtle but profound proposition: we must detect, or at least infer, the *beginnings* of major shifts in the business environment as early as possible, so we can position the enterprise to deal with them when they arise. Waiting until a trend becomes obvious means you probably won't have the range of options for reacting to it that you would have if you'd seen it coming. And your competitors will surely be reacting to it as well. To Grove's way of thinking, a point of inflection, or "flex point," is an early warning signal that can start you thinking.

What is a point of inflection? Grove has borrowed a concept from mathematics, but we don't have to delve into mathematical discussions to appreciate the value of the metaphor he is using. A point of inflection is a change in a change, or more specifically, a *change in a trend*.

For example, while government spending on defense may be increasing, each year's increase might be proportionally smaller than the one before. In other words, there is a slackening in the upward trend. If the *rate* of growth in the spending keeps declining, then at some point the rate of growth gets to zero and goes negative; spending will stop rising, level off, and eventually begin to fall. Figure 3-2 illustrates this inflection point, i.e., the point at which the trend begins to reverse itself.

To use an analogy from personal experience, suppose you're driving your car up a hill. If the hill has a uniform upward slope, you can hold the accelerator pedal at the same point and the car's speed will remain constant. You're on a constant upward trend, in this case in your altitude above sea level. Every additional mile you drive adds the same amount to your altitude as the previous mile.

Figure 3-2. The Point of Inflection.

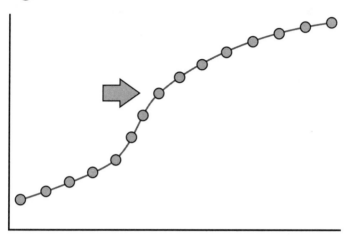

Now suppose you sense that the hill begins "leveling off." The car demands less and less gasoline to maintain its speed. You're still gaining altitude, but now each additional mile adds less altitude than the previous one. You've passed through an inflection point. Your altitude is still on an upward trend, but *the trend itself* is decreasing. If the slope of the hill keeps decreasing, you will eventually stop climbing, pass over the top of the hill, and begin going downhill.

This explanation could sound a bit tedious to some, but it encodes a very subtle idea. You don't have to wait until a trend completely dies, or reverses itself, to know something is going on. By watching changes in the trend itself over time, you might spot a point of inflection that could signal that the forces driving the trend are getting stronger or weaker.

Chairman Grove applies the concept of the inflection point to the growth of his particular business, the semiconductor industry. To him, an inflection point is any point in the life-span of a product, a company, or an industry that marks a change in its destiny. Just about all products that contain microchips have been on strong upward trends for about twenty years, with occasional short term variations. Presumably, this kind of trend should give Grove plenty of cause to sleep peacefully.

However, to paraphrase Grove, "The seeds of our destruction could be germinating at this very moment. Some new twist in chip design or manufacturing, or even some totally new concept for managing data might be getting started in some garage or research lab right now. If it is, we'd better be able to see the first signs of its effects before anybody else does, including our customers. There may be certain subtle signals in the marketplace or the technical environment that tell us the long-running success story of silicon is about to change."

Every executive and manager needs to watch for the points of inflection in his or her industry. What signals might you be receiving from your business environment that could tell you the fundamental forces are changing? Consider some lines of business that might be overdue for change.

For example, the fall of the Berlin wall certainly marked a point of inflection for firms involved in the defense industry. It became obvious very soon that the major world powers would be investing less in weapons development and scaling back on their standing forces. It also gradually became clearer that the huge investments in technologies used for warfare would be redirected to other purposes. Satellite technology, for example, stood to be refocused on communications, data transmission, and space research, and less on surveillance. Computer and telecommunications technology, as used in defense, has been refocused on "cyberterrorism," i.e., the use of information technology to attack national and military data systems.

Some experts contend that a point of inflection for the old-line investment brokerages, on Wall Street and elsewhere, was the arrival of online brokers on the Internet. A fundamental change in the technology and economics of buying and selling stocks could certainly present serious threats to the established structure of the securities industry. It could also radically change the role definition of the stockbroker. No one knows for sure how this development will unfold, but it certainly deserves careful study by those affected.

Was the arrival of the personal computer a point of inflection for public education in the U.S.? Or would it be the arrival of the Carnegie Foundation report in 1983 that pronounced American schools fundamentally unable to meet the needs of a modern information-based society? Or was it the development of the World Wide Web and its page-based structure for information? Which occurrence set loose the primal forces of change that will threaten the existence of the American educational structure? Perhaps all of them? Perhaps some other event that we haven't quite recognized?

Long Waves, Short Waves, and Choppy Seas

Futurists nominate a wide range of trends as important in shaping commerce over the next few decades. All of those trends deserve careful thought, even if not all of them materialize. These include trends in international politics, economic changes, ecological effects, changes in social values and structures, health trends, medical procedures, technology, and issues such as crime and terrorism, to name just a few.

To lend greater focus to this discussion, however, I would like to nominate three basic *macro-trends*, i.e., trends that incorporate other trends, for consideration in thinking about the environmental scan. These three macro-trends are powerful almost beyond belief, and they are intimately intertwined. They are:

Globalism. It has already become a cliché to say that all business is now global, capital moves around in the world in a global network, all stock markets interweave into a kind of global mega-market, and television news has made us all global citizens, or at least spectators in a nightly global drama. Cliché or not, it is true. This topic will receive much greater attention in later discussions. Business leaders need to reach beyond the easy terminology of the cliché and explore the actual "dominos," or linkage mechanisms that create cause-and-effect relationships between far-away events and their immediate businesses.

Cheap Information. Under all the hype and rhetoric surrounding the so-called "information age," digital technology, the Internet, and cybereverything, we can discern one simple and powerful macro-trend: the abundance of cheap information. The ubiquitous personal computer, combined with the declining cost of data transmission technologies and the explosive growth of online or Web-based information resources, means simply that information will become ever cheaper and hence ever more abundant. Don't be distracted by the preachings of the technopriests; the technological gadgets they worship are merely a means to an end. Cheap and abundant information is the state of affairs toward which we are all heading. And, by the way, it will be a very mixed blessing, as later discussions will argue in more detail.

Deconstruction. One of the many labels one can apply to the period beginning in the mid-1980s could well be the "age of paradox." Although one might expect a global environment of culture and business to tend toward a homogeneity of structure, views, and values, exactly the opposite is taking place. Particularly in the U.S., but increasingly in other countries, segmentation is becoming more pronounced. Social structures are disintegrating. Corporations are delayering, outsourcing, downsizing, and de-merging. Mass markets are disintegrating into segments and sub-segments. Demographic and psychographic differences are becoming ever more finely divided. Social, ethnic, political, and gender factionalism are all rising. Even countries are coming unglued. Attempts to create a "United States of Europe" are struggling with ever more intensified national and cultural differences. We will explore this paradox of structure in more detail later, but for this discussion it is important to point out that executives must be more and more the managers of complexity.

Notes

1. Albrecht, Steve. *Crisis Management for Corporate Self-Defense*. New York, AMACOM, 1996, p. 13.
2. For a thought-provoking view of global commerce, see Ohmae, Kenichi. *The Borderless World*. New York: HarperBusiness, 1990.

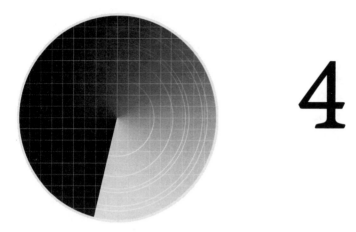

4

Surfing the Third Wave

Every few hundred years in Western history there occurs
a sharp transformation. We cross what I call a "divide."
Within a few short decades, society rearranges itself—
its worldview; its basic values; and its social and
political structure; its arts; its key institutions.
Fifty years later, there is a new world. And the people
born then cannot even imagine the world in which
their grandparents lived and into which their
own parents were born.[1]
—Peter F. Drucker
Post-Capitalist Society

A New Species of Human

Human beings have evolved into a new species. Meet *Homo iconis*—the symbol-using human. This creature represents a very new stage in human evolution. *Homo iconis* is both citizen and product of the modern age, the age of the Third Wave.

Previous human classifications, such as *Homo erectus* and *Homo sapiens*, have tagged our species in terms of our individual and local behavior. We were tool users, upright walkers, thinkers, and so on. This modern creature, *Homo iconis*, on the other hand, is defined by collective behavior, i.e., shaping and then being shaped by symbolic environments. This, more than any other characteristic, defines the phenomenon Alvin and Heidi Toffler have called the Third Wave.[2]

Anyone who hopes to succeed in marketing a product, an idea, a value system, a political view, or a course of action had better understand both *Homo iconis* and the unfolding environment that is shaping his or her consciousness, attitudes, wants, needs, feelings, and behavior.

A New Wave

The Toffler hypothesis of the Third Wave asserts that there have been three great waves, or shifts, in human existence, and that we are now well into the third one. The First Wave was the movement from the nomadic existence of hunters and gatherers to the development of agriculture. That took us about nine thousand years.

The Second Wave, arising sometime in the late sixteenth century, was the shift to industrialization. Building upon the success of agriculture, advanced societies developed the means to concentrate capital and organize labor into large enterprises. The industrial corporation, its machinery, efficient energy, and its counterpart institutions changed human existence forever.

Now comes the third of these great waves, which many futurists characterize as the wave of information. Beginning about the end of World War II, it has brought profound changes of its own, which we are just beginning to recognize.

This Third Wave is a wave of paradoxes. Its effects are simultaneously global and local, collective and individual, unifying and disintegrating. *Homo iconis* has both created and been created by the Third Wave. The worldwide environment of images, data, and information is now shaping us in ways we scarcely understand.

To risk oversimplification for the sake of simplicity: the First Wave was about cheap food; the Second Wave was about cheap energy; and the Third Wave is about cheap information.

How does a thoughtful person figure out this new world? How can business leaders decipher its threats and promises? How can political leaders and policy makers interpret its imperatives? The only ones who can possibly lead and guide others through this profound transition are those who comprehend its basic dynamics, perceive its likely effects, and understand the choices it poses.

Ironically, many of those who believe they understand the Third Wave are actually being seduced by its effects. They have cooked up a naive intellectual stew of hyperbole, gee-whiz possibilities, and wishful-shouldful thinking. Nowhere is this more evident, for example, than in the cult-like fanaticism surrounding the Internet. Although the Internet will certainly have far-reaching effects on our lives and cultures, its effects will probably be nothing like those predicted or wished for by the overexcited cybergeek cult.

The early advocates of commercializing the Internet's World Wide Web spoke glowingly of millions upon millions of eager Web-surfers, all presumed customers waiting to be captured by any business savvy enough to put up a Web page. Their naive misapprehension of the most basic logic of marketing led them to apply Second Wave thinking—mass marketing—to a Third Wave phenomenon, an atomized universe of special interests and disparate responses. The real promise of network technology is in *narrowcasting*, not broadcasting. Networks are very poor methods for people to find one another, but excellent tools for them to use when they have.

But more importantly, the Third Wave is ultimately not about computers or digital data or Internets. It's about a process of *atomization* that's going on at many levels. It's about the atomization of societies, institutions, social structures, nations, industries, markets, corporations, and enterprises of all types.

The Global-Tribal Paradox

Curiously, we Third Wave creatures are becoming simultaneously both global and tribal. This global-tribal paradox, the simultaneous unification and atomization of human experience, is one of the most important effects of the Third Wave.

Put in the simplest terms:

The more global we become in our awareness, the more tribal we become in our behavior.

Futurist John Naisbitt points to the recent deconstruction of nations into their original ethnic components.[3] Global trade has actually emphasized national differences, not minimized them. There are no mass markets any more. Businesses have to target their products and services ever more finely to reach their customers. The wishful myth of America as a cultural "melting pot" is contradicted every day by racial tension and the increasing definition of ethnic boundaries. Even male-female relations have become increasingly polarized.

At the social and political levels, our leaders are becoming more and more confused and frustrated as they fail to grasp the increasing plurality of our societies. Problems of crime, drug abuse, family disintegration, and many others all get the same "one size fits all" political solutions.

The Bell Curve

To say that we have become a new species is not to say that we are becoming all alike. In fact, just the opposite is happening. The Third Wave is actually stretching out the bell curve of human possibilities, revealing ever greater differences between the educated cognitive elite and those less educated. Humans differ greatly in their ability and preference for processing information. Highly educated people, technical people, conceptual people, and those who organize, plan, manage, design, write, and analyze tend to be skillful and proactive symbol-makers.

But people on the other side of a certain dividing line tend to be utterly uninterested in processing information in their heads. For various reasons unique to their development, they tend to view reading, writing, and calculating as necessary evils, not critical life skills. They function as reactive *symbol-users*, not *symbol-makers*. The symbol-makers will benefit handsomely from the fruits of the Third Wave information environment. They will have greater freedom and more choices of occupation, and they will be less confined to jobs that keep them in one place doing one thing. They will be the information elite.

Internet pundits have hailed it as "the great democratizer," meaning presumably that the possibility of universal access to cheap information will somehow lift the poor and the bewildered out of their disadvantaged state. In fact, it will have just the opposite effect. The information environment will be the great differentiator, if anything.

Notwithstanding IBM's politically correct television ads showing the six-year-old black girl somewhere in Africa logging on to the Internet, the bell curve is being stretched upward. The differences among people are becoming greater, not less. Most of the poor and the bewildered will remain that way, because of the impairment in cognitive ability, self-esteem, and social coping capacity that characterize their life positions. Most of them will not actively participate in the information revolution; they will, however, feel its effects.

One of the great ironies of the Third Wave is that the effects of the phenomenon itself tend to confound our very attempts to understand it. We are rather like fish trying to figure out what water is. But even at this early stage, we can detect some of the driving forces that are moving us in a new direction.

What's Driving the Third Wave?

At least five major primal forces seem to be driving the Third Wave. Understanding these key drivers can help us see, at least to an extent, where the Third Wave is taking us.

Productivity. The human impulse to do things quicker, better, easier, more cheaply, and more efficiently seems absolutely fundamental to our species. The agricultural First Wave produced phenomenal gains in food production, so that it no longer takes all of our efforts for us to feed ourselves. In the developed countries, a remarkably small percentage of the population can produce enough food for themselves, the rest of the people, and part of the rest of the world. In the United States, for example, the farm labor force is now only about three percent of the population. Second-Wave productivity has also increased at an astonishing rate, spurred by the release of labor from agriculture, the development of ever more efficient methods of manufacturing, and steady advances in education, research, and development. The rising standard of material comfort has freed more and more people for abstract kinds of labor such as education, entertainment, publishing, and worldwide communication.

Travel. Some would argue that the Third Wave came alive with the jet engine. Since the end of World War II, human beings have moved about the globe with ever-increasing frequency. The Second Wave enabled the development of cheap and convenient transportation, particularly jet air travel, with a wide range of supporting industries around it. This constant mobility, in the service of commerce as well as recreation, has put many disparate cultures in touch with one another. It has turned more and more people into global citizens with a borderless view of how things can be done.

Telecommunications. Even those members of *Homo iconis* who are unaware of the constant, frenzied transmission of billions of packets of digital information around the globe still benefit from it. We now have digital money, which flits about among satellites and earth stations as banks, brokerage houses, and governments move assets around the world. Stock exchanges all over the world link their activities through sophisticated telecommunications technology. Information flows much more quickly than ever before, which means commerce evolves faster, people interact faster, and events in one part of the world can have immediate effects in other parts. Many experts contend that the fall of communism resulted as much from radios, televisions, and fax machines as from guns and tanks. No national government has yet figured out how to build a wall high enough to keep satellite signals from reaching its people.

Images. The worldwide image environment has had some awesome effects on human consciousness. Hundreds of millions of people, all over the world, stopped what they were doing when the O.J. Simpson jury delivered its verdict to the television cameras. This was a unifying experience for a global "culture" of TV watchers. Yet in the United States, blacks and whites were bitterly divided by the verdict of acquittal. Americans were simultaneously global and tribal in their response to an event. The medium unifies and its content divides. At the same time, we've seen an ever-increasing pollution of the image environment. The popular media, such as television, radio, and the popular press, are now fully compromised, at least in the image-oriented cultures like America.

The amusement model has fully taken over as the paradigm of choice for commercial media. Thoughtful discourse and in-depth, linear analysis have been relegated to a few specialized media channels and publications. Indeed, the highly drama-tized, simplified, polarized, and flavored images can confuse and distract even clear-thinking people from making their own interpretations of Third Wave issues and events. A thoughtful person would be well advised to turn off the sound of a television broadcast and quietly study the flow of images to get clues to the shaping effect of electronic media on impor-tant information. Such a person needs less input, not more, and needs to subject that information to a much higher stan-dard of quality.

Ubiquitous computing. The real significance of the personal computer is in the way it has decentralized and secularized computing power. Less than half a generation ago we thought of a computer as a mysterious, imposing machine operated by a special sect of high priests. Only large organizations had them, and they used them to process only "important" infor-mation such as financial data or research data. Now virtually any small business can have the benefit of sophisticated com-puting. Managers no longer have to send their business infor-mation to a special place to have it processed. They enjoy the freedom and power that comes with the ability to mobilize knowledge in new ways. Children have access to astonishing resources for education and entertainment that were unimag-ined only five or ten years ago. The "online" phenomenon has put mind-boggling amounts of information at the fingertips of those who know how to get it. Much of it is useless, and much of the potential of ubiquitous computing and ubiquitous data is yet to be realized. But these technologies have brought irre-versible changes. For better or worse, there will be no turning back the clock.

Impacts of the Third Wave

Some people will find this new world picture depressing and discouraging, while others will find it exciting and challeng-ing. The case for optimism lies in understanding the likely impacts of the Third Wave and developing solutions to our issues and problems that take advantage of new truths. Some of the most significant impacts that we can capitalize on, or be victimized by, include:

Acceleration. Just about everything seems to be happening faster in this Third Wave. People move around the world within hours. Ideas move around the world in millionths of a second. Money flashes about at the same speeds. Newspapers are printed and published simultaneously in many parts of the world. The statements and actions of world leaders become part of our collective history in an instant. The antics of celebrities and misfits alike become part of the daily image-diet of people in all countries. In business, products are born and die in ever-diminishing life cycles. New industries reach saturation in one or two years instead of the ten years or more of past times. "Long-term planning" is a thing of the past. The emphasis in business now is on strategy formulation and adapting to a rapidly changing environment.

Atomization. In the Third Wave environment, big things break up into small things. Mass markets fracture into specialty segments. There are more competitors in most industries, and customers have more choices than ever before. The "big three" American television networks that seemed an eternal part of the entertainment industry have lost air-share to an increasing number of new special-focus networks and channels. Mass-circulation magazines have given way to an astonishing array of specialty publications. Corporations are downsizing, outsourcing, and disassembling themselves into more tactically viable structures. Social institutions are breaking up and dwindling. Traditional religious institutions are losing members as people have other options available to them. Technical and professional specialties are becoming ever more narrowly defined. The standard "community" that has been a basic construct of our notion of civilization for thousands of years is breaking up. Especially in America, the increasing mobility of the population, combined with high divorce rates and changing demographics mean that fewer people live in the traditional multi-generation family situation. More and more Americans don't even know the names or the faces of their neighbors. Twenty-five percent of American households have only one person. Whole countries are coming unglued, just as the USSR fell apart after the totalitarian grip of communist ideology weakened. Some of them are disintegrating with horrifying consequences, while a few have managed to do so peaceably. Megastates like China and India could well come apart as Third Wave influences deepen ethnic and social differences.

Accentuation. Paradoxically, the Third Wave environment tends to emphasize rather than minimize differences among people. Although many of us share the same superficial images and icons of our popular culture, we do not necessarily share attitudes, beliefs, opinions, or values. Two people in two different countries half a world apart can be eating Big Macs, drinking Cokes, and watching the same Hollywood-produced movie at the same instant, and still be worlds apart in their values and beliefs. Religious practices, political ideologies, attitudes about war, and attitudes about male-female relationships do not disappear just because two members of species *Homo iconis* use the same icons. As previously mentioned, the Third Wave will certainly widen the distance between haves and have-nots, not close it, whether the distance is measured in material standard of living, freedom of life choice, education, or access to information.

Agendas. Artist and counter-culture philosopher Andy Warhol's prediction twenty years ago that everyone would become famous for fifteen minutes has nearly come true. Anyone who can capture the attention of a journalist can get his or her particular agenda in front of the noses of millions of people. Terrorists become heroes, misfits become celebrities, and criminals become talk-show hosts. A strange characteristic of the continuous flow of sound and pictures in the Third Wave environment is that all stories, all messages, all issues, all points of view, all accusations, all arguments, and all agendas are raised—or lowered—to the same level of significance. Each bit of drama bursts into the collective attention at the same saturated level of significance as the one before it, only to be pushed off the stage seconds later by the next momentary celebrity. Political careers have been made and destroyed by telling images, crucial soundbites, and unguarded comments. Some analysts argue that the dramatic shift in power in the American Congress in 1994, from the Democrats to the Republicans, had more to do with political talk shows on radio than any basic change in voter sentiment. The Democrats didn't see the effects of this daily political assault until too late, and had no effective means to counter it. Beat poet and philosopher Allen Ginsberg commented in the late 1960s, "We're in science fiction now. Whoever controls the images—the media—controls the culture."

Using What We Know

There is much more we need to learn about the Third Wave and its effects on *Homo iconis*, but we can indeed make use of what we've figured out so far. Business executives, marketing people, legislators, policy makers, educators, and social activists can all do what they do better by understanding the dynamics of this exciting and challenging new environment. Whether our future as members of species *Homo iconis* turns out to be beautiful or ugly is largely a matter of the choices we make and our understanding of the context in which we think about those choices and the problems they solve.

Notes

1. Drucker, Peter. *Post-Capitalist Society*. New York: HarperCollins, 1993, page 1.
2. Toffler, Alvin. *The Third Wave*. New York: Morrow, 1980. Also see Toffler's famous book *Future Shock*, published by Random House in 1970.
3. See Naisbitt, John. *The Global Paradox*. New York: Morrow, 1994. Also see Naisbitt, John. *Megatrends*. New York: Warner Books 1982.

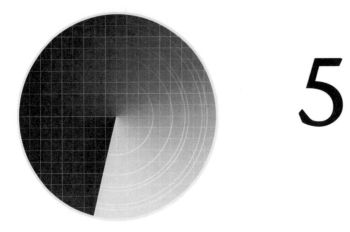

5

How to be Your Own Futurist— Without Getting Lost in the Ozone

What is is the was of what shall be.
— Lao Tzu
"The Way of Life"

The Future: Gee Whiz or Gee Won't?

The present always makes more sense than it did when it was the future.

Thinking about the future is one of the most peculiar mental activities a person can pursue. And trying to guess the impact of future developments on the success of one's business is even more peculiar. It seems to me that any business-like exploration of the future requires a certain level of discipline, a commitment to intellectual honesty, and a large measure of humility. Consequently, we should devote careful thought at the outset to the thinking process itself.

What does it mean to think futuristically? Does it mean you're more creative or imaginative than anyone else? Does it mean you can conjure up more fantastic possibilities than anyone else? That you're more optimistic? Or that you can extrapolate current trends further? How does a person think *usefully* about the future?

The first fact we have to face is that, not only can we not predict the future, we can't even come close. It's true that both Leonardo da Vinci and Jules Verne imagined airplanes and submarines, but aside from the inspired guesses of artists and writers, the track record of prognosticators is not very impressive. Having a wild idea is one thing, and discerning the means and the timetable by which it becomes a reality is quite another. Most of the significant technological, social, and political developments of our time have appeared with little fanfare and grew to become major factors in our lives. Most often, we have perceived them only when they have become obvious.

The second peculiar fact we have to face is that one can make equally good cases for an optimistic view of the future and a pessimistic view. Some futurists write articles about how we'll colonize the moon, conquer all known diseases, and fly around in our little air cars over cities that sparkle with unimaginable beauty. Others write about the depletion of oil reserves, the destruction of rain forests and wetlands, the falling of water tables and the coming of international water politics, and the decimation of populations by AIDS and other viruses yet to be discovered.

Presumably we'll all be driving economical, non-polluting electric vehicles someday soon. Meanwhile, 45,000 Americans die in traffic accidents each year. How do we get from here to there?

Presumably we'll eradicate poverty, illiteracy, violence against women, and abuse of children. Meanwhile, we have over one billion people on the planet who cannot read or sign their names. How do we get from the mundane present to the glorious future?

Presumably we'll all sit at computers and communicate all around the world via the Internet. Meanwhile, half the world's people have no access to electricity or running water. How do we get them online?

Expert estimates of the speed with which new technologies are put to practical use are almost uniformly optimistic. It took 1,500 years for the crossbow to move from China to Europe. The contact lens was invented in 1877 by a German glassmaker but didn't become generally accepted until the 1950s.

Estimates of the speed of social change are usually even more off base. The fall of communism in the USSR led to predictions of a new golden age of freedom and prosperity for all of the former client republics, and particularly for Russia. Yet ten years after the start of the much praised *perestroika*—reconstruction—Russia was mired in a worse state of economic ruin and social distress than ever before. Criminal factions, not the free enterprise system, took over the Russian economy, and it is commonly believed that Russia will struggle for at least another decade before climbing onto any kind of significant growth trajectory.

Fidel Castro's Cuba was supposed to become the next casualty of the worldwide decrepitude of communism, presumably embracing a capitalist theory right on the heels of Russian reconstruction. That did not happen.

The new brand of Chinese capitalism heralded by Deng Xiao Ping's rise to power was supposed to create mind-boggling opportunities for Western companies who had goods to sell there. The reality was a peculiar brand of "communistic capitalism" that dangled big promises in front of foreign marketing delegations while demanding control of the capital structures and even ownership of the imported technology. Many firms learned the hard way that Chinese capitalism was an economic model that served the aims of the Party.

In the world of digital technology, the stunning popularity of the Internet and particularly the World Wide Web led to breathless predictions of wonders to come "by the year 2000." Consumer marketing would be revolutionized, small firms would have the same competitive power as large firms, and every small business would prosper with the magical new strategic weapon called the Web site. As will be discussed in more detail in a later chapter, the reality was that the Internet quickly became a cesspool of polluted information, a sort of digital "citizen's band" radio, and a social Petri dish. Established firms that were already successful in conventional marketing began using online systems to strengthen their interfaces to their customers, but the expected consumer stampede to the Internet never happened.

If you're going to be your own futurist, you can choose from three main options. Option one is the "gee-whiz" futurist, the one who loves to sketch out the exciting view of wonderful things to come. The other extreme is the "gee-won't" futurist, or the gloomster who prefers the pessimistic scenario of ecological decline, overpopulation, famine, pestilence, social disintegration, and resource depletion.

The third option, which I prefer, is the issue futurist, who simply uses the discipline and methods of careful cause-and-effect thinking to try to answer relatively narrow questions.

Some time ago, I decided that studying "the future" is largely a waste of time. It's like studying life. The subject is simply too vast and too multifarious to be approached as a whole. You have to study the future of *something*. Organizations like the World Future Society[1] and others, while making important contributions, tend to struggle constantly for perspective. Not wanting to exclude anyone with any kind of interest or orientation at all, they are forced to advocate a loose and multifarious agenda. Organizations like the WorldWatch Institute[2] have adopted a tighter, more political focus but still suffer from marginalization in a society that perceives ecological specialists as one-note musicians.

The issue futurist makes no attempt to tackle the future in general. That is the occupation of gee-whiz futurists and gee-won't futurists. The issue futurist poses a question, such as "How will population demographics likely influence the costs of healthcare over the next decade?," and looks for the cause-and-effect chains of events and forces that can illuminate the inquiry.

The phrasing of the question is all-important, because it strongly influences the nature of the inquiry. It makes less sense to ask questions like "What will clothing fashions look like ten years from now?," and more sense to ask questions like "What segments of the population will be spending the most on clothing ten years from now?" and "Which fashion designers will probably have the longest-term effect on clothing styles?"

It makes less sense to ask questions like "How will the Internet affect public education over the next five years?," and more sense to ask questions like "Who will be the most influential stakeholders in the design of the education system?" and "What are the economic mechanisms that will drive the investment in digital technology for education?" We are much more likely to come up with a useful projection, however imperfect, by asking a set of issue-specific questions rather than one broad, general question.

Our approach in this book will not be to try to "gee-whiz" the future, or to project any kind of comprehensive view of the future. I've already declared that I believe that to be a useless, though noble and engrossing, endeavor. What we can do, however, is develop a method of posing intelligent questions about specific aspects of the future related to the success or failure of specific enterprises. By learning to formulate an inquiry concisely and meaningfully, we have a better chance of building workable scenarios than by asking global questions and trying to paint a picture with too big a brush.

A modest combination of common sense and analytical thinking can answer at least some of the more fundamental questions about future business prospects. How do the leaders of firms like Boeing and Airbus Industries estimate the potential world market for airplanes over the next ten years? To start with, they know how many airplanes of various types are currently in active service, and they can estimate the age and mileage of each. They know from experience how many years or miles of service each can provide before it is ready for retirement.

Simple arithmetic provides an estimate of the fraction of the worldwide fleet that will need to be replaced each year, from obsolescence alone. Further, they can talk to the major buyers of airplanes, such as military planners and airline purchasing people, and get an estimate of the additional seating capacity they plan to add. These two figures can provide a starting point for estimating the number of new planes that will be required in any given year.

Some of these interesting parameters can tell quite a story. I like to call them "bombshell facts." In the U.S., over three-fourths of the federal government's Medicare expenditures, providing medical care for the elderly, go for treatments provided in the last 12 months of patients' lives. As of about the end of 1998, the median age of the automobiles on America's roads was about eight years. The average number of telephones in the Philippines is about three per hundred people. From these disparate observations, what can we infer about business possibilities in the economic sectors involved?

Thinking Strategically and Futuristically

Having narrowed our approach to the future significantly, and presumably disappointing some readers while reassuring others, we can set a few key ground rules for futuristic thinking as it relates to the business environments we seek to understand.

1. *If a question is important, be willing to invest in answering it.* Are you betting your company on the assumption that a certain market will materialize, grow, or disappear? Do you have enough real evidence to support your conclusions? Or are you operating on intuition, hunches, and hearsay? There is a practical limit to the investment you can make in research, but it makes sense to isolate at least the key assumptions of your business strategy, or prospective strategy, and test them in some reasonably disciplined way.

2. *Distrust your own biases.* Wishful thinking can color your perspective on any investigation. If you're hoping your research will support a strategic decision you've already made, it's more likely you'll find the support you're looking for. If you have a strong need to believe something, you may unconsciously avoid studying it closely, for fear of getting an undesirable result.

3. *Second-guess all information sources.* As you read or hear any kind of business information, keep your "spin detector" turned on. Be especially aware—constantly—of the biases and personal agendas of journalists who shovel information into the business press. Sharpen your news-reading skills and train yourself to substitute your own interpretations and judgments for those of the writer. Most of us are continually assembling bits of information from all kinds of sources, and stirring it together into a stewpot of facts, projections, beliefs, assumptions, opinions, and conclusions. The best way to keep your stewpot of knowledge in good condition is to carefully censor the incoming bits of information at their source. Once they're in the stewpot, they can't be separated and evaluated on their own merits.

4. *Look beyond the generalizations and averages.* A stock market index conceals more information than it conveys. Look for segmentation, diversity, and variability, especially in evaluating information about people. When someone talks about "Internet users," recognize that the label they use can mask a wide range of differences and diversity. Which Internet users are we talking about: geeks, professional people, academics, children, or Internet moms? People who use the Internet for research, business, or just to kill time?

5. *Pose questions so they can be answered.* The structure and language of the question should imply the kind of information needed to answer it. Use focused, issue-specific questions that can deliver individual pieces of the answer to the problem you are trying to solve.

6. *Be willing to contradict all prevailing beliefs.* The majority is not always right, the conventional wisdom is not always wise, and the accepted doctrine could well be flawed. The more fashionable an idea, the more it is likely to be exempt from critical evaluation. Breakthrough thinking sometimes calls for contradicting the most widely held assumptions and beliefs.

7. *Get as many perspectives as possible.* If you're hearing the same prediction or conclusion from a number of sources, try to find a contrarian view. It could be that all the people who are touting the idea got it from the same source. Ideas with high drama potential are often picked up by journalists and passed around without real scrutiny. Someone with a radically different take on the idea can help you see it in better perspective, even if you eventually decide to accept it as valid.

8. *Learn to live with uncertainty and ambiguity.* Let's face it: we can't predict the future, so let's just get comfortable using the word *guess*. We're guessing the pattern of demand in a business sector. We're guessing what our competitors will do. We're guessing what a national government will do about a particular trade issue. We need to learn to evaluate our guesses, rate them in terms of the confidence we can place in them, and consider the level of uncertainty they introduce in our models of the world we're trying to cope with.

Liars Figure: Beware of Bogus Data

In one of the classic "Pink Panther" films, Inspector Clouseau, played by Peter Sellers, checked into a small hotel in the mythical kingdom of Lugash. In one corner of the small, cozy reception lobby, he spied a small dog. Thinking to make friends with the dog, he inquired of the elderly innkeeper, "Does your dog bite?," to which the innkeeper nonchalantly replied "No." When Clouseau reached down to pet the dog, it snapped at him and went into a ferocious barking frenzy. Indignant, Clouseau turned on the innkeeper and cried "You said your dog didn't bite!"

The innkeeper replied, just as nonchalantly as before, "That's not my dog."

Every prospective futurist must be keenly aware of the problem of defective data. What you ask, whom you ask, and how you ask can be critical in getting valid information. For example, anyone hoping to resolve key business issues must be very careful about reaching conclusions or basing actions solely on information found in the popular press. This includes news interviews with noted people, articles and editorials in business publications, and particularly the endless "surveys" that journalists love to report on.

There is no creature on Earth more dangerous than a journalist with a statistic.

It has become common practice in the Western press to publish curious little findings taken from vaguely identified surveys by vaguely identified investigators. *USA Today* in particular likes to publish "factoids" and cute one-question survey statistics, apparently intended for people with short attention spans and little ability to think comparatively. At best, these are amusing and harmless. At worst, they can create misleading impressions and launch durable myths into the culture.

Journalists who should know better often lower their intellectual standards just to fill in a few column inches. For example, an item in *USA Today* sported the headline "Heroin use rising among U.S. teens," and the lead sentence began "Heroin use has risen rapidly in recent years among U.S. teens, ..." The article went on to cite a survey published in the respected journal *Pediatrics*, which it said reported that "the proportion of American 12th-graders who had used heroin *doubled* between 1990 and 1996, *from 0.9% to 1.8%.*"

What's wrong with this statistic? Plenty. It's very unlikely that two surveys taken six years apart could produce matched sets of answers that are comparable to the extent that a difference of less than one percent of the respondents would be statistically significant. Typically, the range of uncertainty, or margin of error, for such self-reported surveys is in the range of three to five percentage points, which would mask any change of less than one percent. It is reasonably probable that heroin use could have actually declined, and that the 0.9% increase calculated was merely an artifact of the particular sample of students recruited.

But no matter. After all, we're reading "McNews." Why quibble over statistical niceties that few readers understand? And if it's good enough for *Pediatrics*, it should be good enough for the rest of us, right? Maybe, and maybe not. Possibly the study used a very large sample and various statistical techniques aimed at isolating heroin use. The article does not report the number of students surveyed, without which we can make no judgments about the conclusions. The result was reported to one-tenth of one percent, but that doesn't mean we can discern a difference in drug users of one person out of one thousand.

Another mysterious survey, widely quoted in 1997, concluded that nearly three-fourths of high school girls had been subjected to sexual assault. A bit of investigation disclosed that the survey had been conducted by a group of radical feminist academics, and that it defined sexual assault to include virtually any form of interaction from bottom-pinching, bra-snapping, and pony-tail pulling all the way to whistling and winking. It made no mention of the independent finding that high school boys reported roughly the same number of "sexual assaults" from girls. Many papers ran the story on its face value, however, and launched yet another agendite rocket into the public consciousness.

How many of these little "surveys" are pushed into the popular media and even the serious business press every day? How many people would read the report of the drug survey and file away the vague conclusion that "American kids are using heroin a lot more now. The drug problem is getting worse."

If we're going to make serious and consequential decisions about the future of a business enterprise, we can't afford to be taken in by bogus data, whether it's promoted by well-meaning but lazy journalists or by highly motivated special-interest groups with selfish political agendas.

By the way, to what extent do you rely on government statistics in making decisions about your business? Do you rely on other people who use such data? Have you ever wondered how reliable government economic information really is?

The U.S. government's Bureau of the Census estimates that it probably missed about five million people in the 1990 census count. That's about two percent—not actually surprising, when you consider the magnitude of the job. Bear in mind that about 4.1 million new Americans were born during the census year, and about 2.1 million others died. Further, estimates of the number of people in the country illegally, and therefore not counted, vary widely. Yet many people use government population statistics as if they were somehow beyond question.

My college physics teacher, Mr. Ofelt, annoyed all of us by insisting that we learn and apply a concept called "uncertainty." We were inclined to be a bit lazy, and tended to resent his demands, but we finally got in the habit of handing in our experimental calculations based on the *range of uncertainty* in the variables involved in the problem. This meant that we couldn't report the voltage in an electrical circuit as merely "10 volts," but instead we had to report it as "10 volts, plus or minus .05 volts," with the .05 volts being our estimate of how precisely, or imprecisely, we were able to read the needle on the voltmeter. If you didn't hold your head in the same position every time, relative to the needle on the meter, you might misread the numbers under the needle by as much as one-tenth of a volt. This uncertainty, when carried through the chain of calculations involved in reporting the results of the experiment, could produce a substantial variation in the outcome.

Mr. Ofelt was insisting that we not conceal the uncertainty and blissfully report out our results as if they were pure and perfect. He wanted us to be aware of the uncertainty in all of our measurements, and to deal with the effects of that uncertainty in a very conscious way.

A more concrete business example might help to reinforce this point, which I consider extremely important. In a strategy conference with the executives of one of the divisions of Australia's national telephone company, then known as Australia Telecom, the sales forecast for the upcoming year was being presented by a very bright and analytical chap who had done the analysis. He quickly and clearly laid out the revenue and earnings figures he'd come up with, which he expressed down to the level of the nearest thousand dollars. This seemed quite peculiar to me, in view of the fact that the total revenue figure totaled several billion dollars.

I couldn't help but inquire about the basis for his remarkably precise figures. He replied that he'd merely taken the previous year's sales figures, postulated a reasonable growth factor, and multiplied out the numbers to come up with the next year's figures. When I inquired about the rationale for the growth factor, he replied that he'd simply used the growth factor for the previous year, and bumped it up by a tenth of a percentage point. What started as a seemingly precise set of revenue and earnings figures suddenly degenerated into one guy's best guess. This is known as the *myth of false precision*, and it's all too common in business analysis.

Inasmuch as all of the other executives in the room would have to base their resource estimates on his forecasts, this was no small matter. This led to a discussion of the means for arriving at the earnings forecast, and particularly the way in which the executive team would use it. Still hearing Mr. Ofelt's voice in my ears, I strongly recommended that the group express the figures in terms of a *band of uncertainty*. This involved a nominal figure for the growth rate, as well as a more pessimistic figure and a more optimistic figure. By plotting all three variables on the chart of revenue growth, profitability, and cash flow, we saw a much different and more informative picture.

Each of the executives was then able to estimate his or her resource requirements based on a realistic range of uncertainty in the financial results. For some departments, the range of uncertainty dictated certain contingencies in their planning processes. For others, it made less of a difference.

Have you ever heard the newsreader glibly pronounce that "Retail sales rose three-tenths of a percent this Christmas season...," and wondered how the government can estimate such a gigantic economic variable to within one-tenth of a percent? When the newsreader reports that "Government figures show the economy grew at an annualized rate of 2.1 percent last quarter...," do you wonder how an economic process valued at hundreds of billions of dollars, or even trillions dollars in the case of the U.S. economy, can be measured down to one-tenth of a percent? If the one-tenth percent year-on-year change is valid, doesn't the range of uncertainty have to be much smaller, say one-hundredth of one percent? These are statistical estimates, after all, and there must certainly be a practical limit to the precision involved.

When Ronald Reagan was trying to unseat Jimmy Carter from the presidency of the U.S., he harped on what he called the "misery index," the arithmetic total of the unemployment rate, the inflation rate, and the home mortgage interest rate, all of which were uncomfortably high. However, when economists studied the inflation rate, they realized that it was heavily influenced by housing prices, which were climbing at historic rates during that period of intense real estate speculation.

The U.S. government's inflation index was based on a "basket" of expense items the typical citizen had to pay as part of his or her living costs. About forty percent of the expenses in the basket were attributed to housing, which was a fairly reasonable amount. However, with home prices rising at astonishing rates, the calculation reflected the assumption that every household moved to a new home every month and had to pay ever higher prices for the principal and interest. The obvious fact was that most people who owned their homes were making the same payments every month, with no inflation at all for them.

The Carter administration found a clever and easy solution to the problem: it simply redefined the formula used to calculate inflation, and inflation suddenly dropped. Reagan won the election anyway, but some people attributed that to the Iranian hostage situation, not the state of the economy.

I suggest that, any time someone presents a statistic, an estimate, and particularly a survey result, each of us should instinctively ask two questions:

1. How credible is the source of the data being presented?

2. What is the range of uncertainty in this result?

These two questions would go a long way toward flushing out fraud, deceit, misrepresentation, and just plain mental laziness.

Survey results in particular deserve a skeptical reaction until or unless we know, at a minimum, the answers to several key questions:

■ Who conducted the survey, and for what objective?

■ Who responded to the survey, how many respondents were there, and how were they selected?

■ What was the exact text of each question being reported, and for each multiple choice scale, what was the exact text of each option presented for selection, and how many people selected each of the options?

■ How did the demographic makeup of the respondents correspond to the population to which the survey presenter proposes to extrapolate the results?

If the survey reporter says "Sixty-three percent of the people polled expressed approval of the prime minister's performance," we know almost nothing. For example, "approval" might be defined as answering with only a score of five on a five-point multiple-choice scale, or it might include those people who answered with either four or five, or it might even be extended to include people who answered with three or higher. Some surveys use a forced-choice scale, such as four options, on which the respondent cannot register a neutral or "not certain" response. This can easily skew the results in one direction or another. And, of course, the exact phrasing of the options presented to the respondents can have a huge impact on their answers.

It should be our policy to *make no important conclusions* based on reported survey results, unless the report includes the answers to the key questions just cited. Statistics presented with no visible basis for validation are nothing more than hearsay.

Another significant source of misinformation, freely tossed about in the press, are growth estimates and projections for various markets. Few sources are so subject to biases and wishful thinking, especially estimates for the growth of anything connected with the Internet. Recognize that many journalists are virtually addicted to the Internet as a news topic, because it's so easy to dramatize the rapid growth story. And it's especially appealing to lazy journalists, because it's so easy to call a favorite geek-pundit for a prediction or find an entrepreneur who's come up with a new twist on Web site marketing.

In particular, a handful of market-research firms specializing in online commerce, or "E-commerce," have become the "go-to" sources of the dizzying predictions. An article in a popular newspaper quoted one such research firm as reporting that 1.2 million people had online stock trading accounts as of the end of 1997, and that the number "will reach 10 million by 2001." The prediction, however optimistic, might even turn out to be true, but does it make sense to bet your company on a one-line statistic reported in the popular press? Especially when everybody associated with the statistic—the research firm, the writer of the article, and the publisher of the newspaper—prefers to see the number as high as possible?

Russian novelist and social critic Alexander Solzhenitsyn said "It is a very dangerous thing to speak against the fashion of the times." This is equally true of speaking against the fashion of the Internet and the gee-whiz agenda that promotes it. Reputable studies suggest that the number of new Internet users is not growing as rapidly as it did within the first two years after the World Wide Web became known, and that users are spending less time on line, on average. Yet these results seldom find their way into the popular press. The "party line" for the gee-whiz agenda is that the Internet is, and always will be, growing exponentially in all of its measures—number of people, number of Web sites, amount of information, number of purchases, amount of money spent—on and on.

The principle of the "S-curve," discussed later, has no place in the gee-whiz agenda. So we have to live with the widespread belief that everything about the Internet will grow at a rate of 100 percent per year.

Of all predictions tossed about in the popular press and in business publications, we should question and scrutinize Internet predictions most carefully of all. There is no news topic in any of the developed economies that is so exempt from critical thinking and logical scrutiny as the Internet story. How can you evaluate an estimate of online sales volume and its expected growth without even knowing how the source is defining a term like "E-commerce"? Does it include only the sales registered by customers personally placing orders online? Or does it also include the transfer of goods between wholesalers and retailers, using the computer as a simple device for communicating the order? Does it include online bill-paying and banking transactions?

And, by the way, what's the level of uncertainty (remember my physics teacher's admonishment?) in the estimates of economic activity in such a chaotic environment? I often chuckle, and then sigh, when I read a journalist's glib pronouncement that "Online sales of tractor seats will rise from $65,000 this year to $37 million by 2005." One of the most often-quoted Internet research firms estimated Christmas holiday sales in 1998 as "$6 billion this year, and will leap to $40.6 billion in five years, a 577 percent advance." What remarkable precision! Sales of *$40.6* billion, not $40 billion or $45 billion, but calculated down to one-fourth of one percent. And an increase of *577 percent*, not 500 percent or 600 percent. Clearly, either the journalist or the firm providing the estimate indulges in a bit of intellectual chicanery to impart a false sense of precision to a figure that is little more than a wild guess.

Another published estimate put the value of software piracy, programs illegally copied and distributed without paying the publishers, at $13.1 billion worldwide. It's hard to imagine a more speculative estimate, and yet we have this very scientific-sounding figure, presumably accurate to less than one percent.

Another type of bogus information, which can affect the attitudes and views of business planners about the overall health of the economy, is the range of stock market indexes that are so popular in the news reports. For years the famed Dow Jones Average, and more recently the Standard & Poor 500 Index, have been offered as surrogates for the growth or decline of share prices for the biggest firms in the U.S. When the newsreader says "The stock market nose-dived today, on news that the Prime Minister of Malaysia had a heart murmur," he or she is usually referring to one of these two indexes. However, a close look at the changes in a large number of stocks traded on the major American exchanges usually shows that a few of them are moving strongly up or down and that a very large majority are changing very little.

For example, by early 1999, when both the Dow Jones Average and the S&P 500 had set new records, news reports hailed an increase of over twenty-five percent in the S&P 500. However, almost one-tenth of that gain was caused by one stock: Microsoft, which more than doubled during the year. Two hundred of the stocks making up the S&P 500 actually declined. Indeed, over three-quarters of the total gain in the S&P 500 came from just thirty companies.

So when the news report tells us the "stock market" posted remarkable gains, we're being handed a dangerous generalization. The fact is that a small number of large companies saw significant increases in their share prices. This is certainly not the same as a general increase in nearly all share prices. Statisticians refer to this as the *masking effect of averages*. In some cases an average conceals more than it reveals.

If we're going to be competent futurists, we must set for ourselves, and others, a very high standard of quality for the information we're willing to use in making our analysis and drawing our conclusions.

The S-Curve: Avoiding Premature Extrapolation

It's a basic law of nature, or at least an ordinance, that "nothing rises to the sky." Yet human beings insist on believing and acting as if just the opposite were true. *Trend hypnosis* is the tendency of humans to become transfixed by the momentum of events. Once a significant trend gets underway, such as a long rise in real estate prices, a run-up in stock market prices, a period of high or low inflation, high or low interest rates, or a popular fad such as the Internet, many people are quite willing to assume that it will continue indefinitely.

Stock market manias, real estate frenzies, and speculative investment bubbles of various kinds all demonstrate the remarkable power of trend hypnosis. More recently, the Internet craze has had millions of people enthralled. For a certain period, popular trends seem to feed on themselves, as more and more people join in because they see others joining in. Especially when people see the opportunity to make a quick and easy profit, and think they see others doing the same, many of them cannot resist jumping on the wagon.

In his charming book *A Short History of Financial Euphoria*, John Kenneth Galbraith describes, among others, the infamous "tulip bulb mania" that occurred in Holland in the 1630s. First imported to Holland from the Mediterranean in the 1560s, tulips grew in popularity. By some quirk of public perception, the possession of a tulip bulb, and particularly an unusual or exotic variety, conferred great social status on its owner. Demand for tulip bulbs grew, their prices rose, and at some strange point, people began to conceive of the things as having some intrinsic value beyond their utilitarian function of adorning flowerbeds and gardens. A strange euphoria seemed to set in, and by the mid-1630s people were buying and selling them at ever higher prices.

In an episode that was to become a prototype for various investment manias later in history, Dutch people of all stations in life were rushing to buy tulip bulbs before the prices rose higher.

According to Professor Galbraith:

> Speculation, it has been noted, comes when popular imagination settles on something seemingly new in the field of commerce or finance. The tulip, beautiful and varied in its colors, was one of the first things so to serve. To this day it remains one of the more unusual of such instruments. Nothing more improbable ever contributed so wonderfully to the mass delusion here examined.
>
> The rush to invest engulfed the whole of Holland. No person of minimal sensitivity or mind felt that he could be left behind. Prices were extravagant; by 1636 a bulb of no previously apparent worth might be exchanged for "a new carriage, two grey horses, and a complete harness."
>
> It was wonderful; never in their history had the Dutch seemed so favored. In keeping with the immutable rules governing such episodes, each upsurge in prices persuaded more speculators to participate. This justified the hopes of those already participating, paving the way for yet further action and increase, and so assuring yet more and ever-continued enrichment. Money was borrowed for purchase; the small bulbs leveraged large loans.
>
> In 1637 came the end. Again the controlling rules were in command. The wise and the nervous began to detach, no one knows for what reason; others saw them go; the rush to sell became a panic; the prices dropped as if over a precipice. Those who had purchased, many by pledging property for credit ... were suddenly bereft or bankrupt. "Substantial merchants were reduced almost to beggary, and many a representative of a noble line saw the fortunes of his house ruined beyond redemption," according to [Charles] Mackay.[3]

It is a rare individual who can study his or her current circumstances and conclude that they are out of the ordinary and ready to change. Escaping the tyranny of trend hypnosis is much like trying to build a box bigger than the one you're in.

Every would-be futurist should have, affixed to his or her wall within easy view, a simple diagram called the "S-curve." The S-curve portrays one of the primary dynamics of nature, on a par with the orbits of the planets and the path of the sun across the sky. It is almost mystical in its message:

Every trend eventually taps out the source of its energy.

Figure 5-1 portrays the S-curve in its awesome simplicity. A trend has a genesis, a beginning, shown by the "foot" of the curve, followed by a run-up, shown by the accelerating middle range of the curve, and a plateau, shown by the "shoulder" of the curve.

When people can only see the steady upward movement of a trend, they often get fixated on the upward movement itself, even coming to believe that it will somehow continue without end. Surely, most people will agree that no trend, boom, or streak can go on forever without limit. Anyone can grasp the idea that there are finite bounds on the number of buyers, the amount of money they can ultimately pay, and their willingness to buy. Yet it's very easy for many people to suspend their critical thinking processes—"for now," at least. The thought process seems to be: "I know it can't last forever, but I'm sure it will probably last a very long time, and that's good enough for me."

Economists describe the psychology of manias as based on the "greater fool theory," i.e., the belief by a rabid trend follower that there will always be a supply of new buyers, or at least one, coming along after he or she jumps in, willing to pay more than he or she paid. Unfortunately, when the last "fool" jumps in, a current population of fools pays the profit of those

Figure 5-1. The S-Curve.

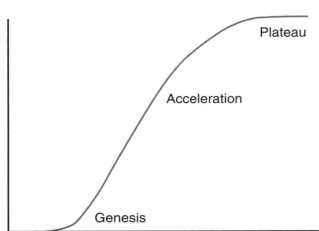

who were wise enough or lucky enough to jump out after the latecomers jumped in.

According to Professor Galbraith:

> Strongly reinforcing the vested interest in euphoria is the condemnation that the reputable public and financial opinion directs at those who express doubt or dissent. It is said that they are unable, because of defective imagination or other mental inadequacy, to grasp the new and rewarding circumstances that sustain and secure the increase in values. Or their motivation is deeply suspect.[4]

Trends, even manias, begin for good reasons and end for good reasons. Every major speculative boom in history has begun because something of value caught the attention of intelligent buyers. Trends only overshoot reality when others join in and buy because they've seen others buy, not because they recognize value when they see it. And an overextended trend dies when the intelligent buyers disassociate themselves from the asset because it no longer offers value.

When I say that I believe the S-curve is a fundamental dynamic of nature, I do not exaggerate. Take an example, offered by Theodore Modis, a management consultant formerly with Digital Equipment Corporation in Paris. According to Modis:

> Survival of the fittest dictates that the filling (or the emptying) of a niche in a competitive environment proceeds along the S-shaped pattern of natural growth. This means that the rate of growth—whether it is in world population, the spread of communism, or sales of the latest computer—is greatest in the middle of the life cycle, tapering off as growth reaches the saturation level.
>
> There are limits to natural growth, and the rate of growth slows down as the population of a product or a species nears its (ecological) limit. If you put two rabbits in a meadow, you can watch their population go through an exponential-growth pattern at first, but slow down later as it approaches a ceiling—the capacity of the ecological niche. Over time, the rabbit population traces a trajectory that is S-shaped. The rate of growth traces a curve that is bell-shaped and peaks when half the niche is filled.[5]

Much to the consternation of his colleagues at DEC's European marketing operation, Modis applied his S-curve thesis to the sales pattern of the company's successful VAX line of minicomputers on the continent and found the sales curve followed the familiar S-pattern quite closely. Even more startling, his S-curve graph predicted the next three years' sales closely as well.

Having read Modis' dissertation on the S-curve in *The Futurist* magazine, I began to reflect on the almost primal character of the mathematical form it expresses: a genesis, a rapid rise, and a plateau. Every trend eventually taps out the energy that fuels it. I began seeing it in other trend-type variables. As an amateur photographer, I was struck by the odd realization that even the light-response of black and white photographic film follows an S-curve. An underexposed image will produce only a slight darkening of the silver emulsion on the film. Adding just a bit more light will cause a much bigger change, the sudden rise of the S-curve, and adding more light than that will cause the film to darken completely. The ideal exposure is in a narrow range of light intensity in the middle range of the S-curve of its response. Above a certain exposure, the silver emulsion darkens completely and no matter how much more light falls on it, it cannot darken further because all of the silver in the film is fully converted.

I have come to believe that the S-curve is one of the most sanity-preserving tools for the would-be futurist's toolkit. It helps one to see beyond fashionable fads and manias, and to consider the source of the energy that is driving them. A legitimate trend in a real business phenomenon will tap out the energy that is driving it on a schedule that is determined by the demand that is causing it. And even a mania will tap out the manic energy that is driving it, whether it is euphoria, hysteria, greed, fear, or simply the need to be included in something.

The S-curve can be remarkably useful in building models of various growth processes. It's a good starting point for guessing about future demand for various goods and services, growth in any economic sector, and the rate at which a new technology will grow and diffuse. And it also provides a reference point for sanely observing manias, euphorias, panics, and other stampedes that can distort the reality of doing business in the New Economy.

Drivers, Dominos, and Wildcards

The next step in organizing our attack on the future is to find a way to assemble and reduce the "radar data," i.e., the results of the environmental scan, into a coherent story. We need a common language, or model, for expressing the picture that emerges on each of the radar "screens." We will explore integration methods such as storyboarding and cartooning in more detail in the last chapter. For the moment, however, we can identify a few useful models for organizing the findings from each of the radars.

One simple and useful tool for extracting meaning from a particular environmental sector is the idea of a key "driver." An environmental driver is any trend, event, force, or state of affairs that will have a primary influence on your options. These environmental drivers will be very specific to your business. A factor that is a powerful driver for your particular business might have little relevance to some other kind of business.

If you're in the business of selling cellular telephones worldwide, a key customer driver could be the rate of privatization of telecom industries in the developing countries, where demand could grow dramatically. Customer drivers include not only the attitudes and desires of your customers, but also the factors that create or reinforce those intentions.

If you're in the healthcare business in the U.S., and particularly in the managed care sector, one of your key economic drivers will probably be the federal government's system of rules for paying the costs of treatment for the elderly. Another might be the age demographics of the population you serve, because healthcare needs tend to become more costly with advancing age.

If you're in the stock brokerage business, one of your economic drivers will probably be the rate of inflow of funds into the stock market, which tends to be linked to the increasing or decreasing attractiveness of other competing forms of investment. The more assets your clients have in their portfolios, the more fees you will typically earn from transactions and asset management accounts. Wall Street veterans are fond of warning "Don't confuse genius with a bull market," meaning that profits may be rising more because of capital inflows than the marketing skills of the firm.

It's important to identify the drivers that will influence your business opportunities, and equally important to be able to focus on the critical few that have the primary effect. You'll need to condense the results of the environmental scan to manageable proportions in order to put them to use effectively in your strategic planning process.

In addition to identifying the primary environmental drivers for your business, it may be appropriate to consider the "drivers behind the drivers," i.e., the forces that are influencing the forces that influence your business. We can think of this in terms of a "domino chain" metaphor, i.e., a series of factors that cascade through one or more sectors of the environment and that can produce significant effects at a distance.

Case in point: the public seminar and conference business is highly sensitive to the overall economic conditions in the country in which a particular organizer operates. Because a certain amount of my lecturing activity is arranged by trade associations and commercial organizers, I often see the effects of economic changes in their environments. An organizer in Chile, for example, found it necessary to postpone a conference due to the effects of economic conditions in Asia, caused by the recession that began in 1997 and continued through 1998 and beyond.

How does a recession in Asia cause problems for a seminar organizer in Chile? Because many firms in Chile export a significant portion of their goods to Asian countries, particularly China. With falling demand for their exports, their revenues and profit margins begin to shrink, and they turn to cost-cutting procedures to defend their shareholders' assets. One of the first casualties of any economic downturn is usually the budget for training programs and conferences. And so the conference organizer finds himself at the end of a domino chain.

Case in point: when Philippine Airlines ran into financial difficulties in mid-1998, and temporarily went out of business, it canceled orders to Boeing Aircraft Corporation for new jumbo jets. Boeing scaled back its production schedule as a result of that and other cancellations and postponed orders. Hundreds of smaller firms supplying various parts, materials, and assemblies to Boeing experienced a drop in orders from the company and saw increasing pressure on their profit margins. A domino chain beginning in Manila had an effect as far away as Seattle, southern California, and dozens of other parts of the U.S.

This domino chain effect comes into play in many industries, particularly those in which businesses buy and sell from one another. As part of your environmental scan, it's important to trace out the possible domino chains that could be affecting your opportunities. Your dominos may not all be strictly economic. For example, a change in a law, or a change in international trade policies or tariffs could affect the behavior of your customers or their customers. Government policies can cause domino effects throughout various business sectors, which can cascade through a series of impacts.

It's important to review the known drivers and dominos, but what about the unforeseen event, the "wildcard" factor that comes as a surprise? What about the potentially significant change that might or might not happen? Your opportunities might be significantly different if a certain law takes effect than if it doesn't. A significant merger of the two biggest firms in your industry could change all the rules of the game if you're not one of them. Normalizing relations between two political factions, such as Israel and the Palestinian groups, or between countries such as the U.S. and Cuba, could create significant business opportunities.

Some wildcards seem to come from nowhere, catching everyone by surprise. For example, many foreign banks and investors were stunned in mid-1998, when the Russian government did the unthinkable: it reneged on billions of dollars of foreign debt. It suspended payments on foreign loans and froze assets in securities markets that might have been withdrawn from the country. Malaysia's prime minister, Mohammed Mahathir, took a similarly provocative step when he froze foreign capital flows out of the country to put the brakes on currency speculation against the ringgit.

Although it's obviously not possible to think of all the surprises that might happen, even in your particular industry, it may still be worthwhile to speculate on some of the imaginable possibilities. For example, what about the death or downfall of the head of state of a country where you're planning to do business? How would the death or incapacitation of a high-profile corporate leader like Microsoft's Bill Gates, Disney's Michael Eisner, or GE's Jack Welch affect the individual business and the futures of various enterprises linked to it? How might a major ecological disaster affect the fortunes of a particular industry or company? How might a major medical breakthrough affect the market for an existing pharmaceutical product?

Think of an environmental wildcard as a recognizable possibility that is sufficiently significant in its potential impact that it deserves to be studied and planned for.

We can put together the results of the environmental scan in terms of the drivers, dominos, and wildcards we've been discussing in a simple diagram such as Figure 5-2.

By categorizing the drivers in terms of the degree of their influence, i.e., the primary drivers and the dominos, on the horizontal dimension, and arranging them by likelihood, i.e., known drivers and wildcards, on the vertical dimension, we can build comparable pictures for each of the eight key radar screens.

The lower-left quadrant of the diagram tells the basic story. For a particular radar dimension, such as the technological radar, it lists those few primary events, trends, forces, or conditions you have identified that you believe will have the strongest influence on the growth possibilities of your business. The lower-right quadrant lists any secondary drivers or dominos, i.e., cause-and-effect sequences that you consider important to your success. On the upper level, the upper-left quadrant lists the primary speculative events, i.e., wildcards, that you consider sufficiently influential that you choose to track them on your radar. And the upper-right quadrant lists the wildcard dominos that could materialize under certain circumstances.

Now that we've warmed up our minds and armed ourselves with the proper tools and cautions, we can proceed to study

Figure 5-2. Drivers, Dominos, and Wildcards.

Wildcard Factors	**Wildcard Drivers**	**Wildcard Dominos**
Predictable Factors	**Primary Drivers**	**Primary Dominos**
	Direct Influences	Indirect Influences

each of the eight strategic radar screens to see what we can
learn that may be useful in growing a business enterprise.

Notes

1. The World Future Society has a publishing program, sells books and
   reports related to futures issues, and holds an annual conference. Its
   monthly magazine, *The Futurist*, carries articles on a wide range of specific topics of interest to futurists. You can contact them through their
   Web site at wfs.org.
2. The Worldwatch Institute conducts studies, sponsors conferences, and
   publishes articles and a monthly bulletin dealing with specific issues
   related to sustainable development. You can contact them through their
   Web site at worldwatch.org.
3. Galbraith, John Kenneth. *A Short History of Financial Euphoria*. New
   York: Penguin Books, 1993, page 28. The lines attributed to Charles
   Mackay by Galbraith are from his celebrated book *Extraordinary
   Popular Delusions and the Madness of Crowds*, published in London in
   1841.
4. Ibid., page 6. The lines attributed to Charles Mackay by Galbraith are
   from his celebrated book *Extraordinary Popular Delusions and the
   Madness of Crowds*, published in London in 1841.
5. Modis, Theodore. "Life Cycles: Forecasting the Rise and Fall of Almost
   Anything." *The Futurist*, Sept-Oct 1994, p.20.
6. An indispensable reference for information about the United States is
   the U.S. Department of Commerce's *Statistical Abstract of the United
   States*, published annually. Readers unfamiliar with it may be aston-
   ished at the range and depth of information about almost every conceiv-
   able aspect of America and its people. It also contains a useful list of
   key U.S. government agencies, with their contact details and Web site
   addresses, as well as a list of statistical abstracts published by other
   major nations, and where to get them. You can start at the
   Department's top-level Web site, doc.gov, and go from there to a wide
   range of other useful sources of information.
7. A useful reference for firms wanting to do business in various major
   countries is *Dun & Bradstreet's Guide to Doing Business Around the
   World* by Terry Morrison, Wayne Conaway, and Joseph Douress
   (Englewood Cliffs, NJ: Prentice Hall, 1997). You can contact the authors
   through their Web site at getcustoms.com.

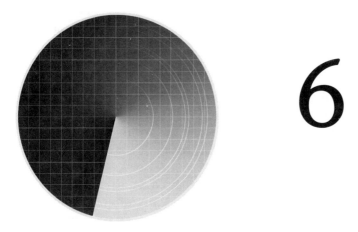

Your Customer Radar

If the people don't want to come out
to the ballpark, how ya gonna stop 'em?
—*"Yogi" Berra*
American baseball star

The purpose of the customer radar is to understand the behavior and intentions of your customers, and the forces shaping them. This definition provides a focus for our exploration, so we aren't tempted to wander in all directions studying interesting facts and figures that have no bearing on the decisions we have to make about the strategy of the business.

Markets or Customers?

For this discussion, I propose to replace the comfortable but vague term "market" for the more specific term "customers." This may seem like a fine distinction to some, but I believe it makes a difference in our thinking process, and in the frame of reference we use for the environmental scan.

Many executives make a habit of speaking of markets as if they were battlefields or playing fields for sport. We can talk about a market in terms of numbers, statistics, and revenue volume, but it's easy to lose contact with the idea of *a group of customers* who are making choices. Airline executives speak of the "Paris-Frankfurt" market, meaning the people who fly between those two cities. Broadcast executives speak of "the rural Illinois market" or "the Dallas market," referring to the people in those geographic areas who watch or listen to their shows.

I believe this habit of dehumanizing the discussion of customers, and reducing it to the impersonal language of numbers, tends to handicap the thinking process. It is a typically masculine line of thinking, much like the mechanical vocabulary of warfare. Another tendency of "market" thinking is to define market segments that match the company's products, i.e., the buyers of product A are one market and the buyers of product B are another market. Presumably, wine drinkers are a market, beer drinkers are another market, and drinkers of liqueurs, cordials, and other fancy products are another market. But any one person might use each of those products on various occasions, for various purposes. I'm not claiming that market thinking is fundamentally wrong in any way, only that customer thinking can often bring marketing issues into clearer focus.

My favorite definition of marketing is:

the process of matching the resources of the organization with the aspirations of its customers.

Marketing is not the same thing as selling. It means finding a match between something we can do well and the needs, problems, or desires of people who are willing to pay us for doing it. Disciplines such as product design, brand management, advertising and promotion, distribution management, and pricing all flow from a consensus about the customer buying dynamic. Marketing is more than pushing your existing products to a new set of customers. It also includes evolving your total value package to bring it into sync with the wants of existing customers as well as potential new ones.

The "Molecular Customer"

In our discussion of the customer radar, as well as most of the other radars, we may have to take different views and use different methods depending on what the customer looks like. In particular, we have to consider whether the customer is the consumer, i.e., the direct buyer and end-user of our value package, or a more complex buying entity. In some cases, the customer may be a "molecule," i.e., a special combination that may include people and organizations, or even political or other entities.

For example, if we are an insurance firm trying to sell a special plan to the members of an association, we will probably have to make one kind of sale to the elected leaders of the association, another kind of sale to the appointed executive director, and another kind of sale to the individual members who may or may not want to buy it. To make the sale and continue doing business with this "customer," we have to think in molecular terms. We have to understand how the various participants in the customer molecule relate to one another, what their respective desires and motivations are, and what kind of offering we must create to have a successful relationship with them.

If we are publishing a newspaper or a magazine, we typically receive most of our revenue from the businesses whose advertisements we transmit, so obviously we must offer them an appealing value package. But we must also have an appealing information product that will bring enough people into contact with their messages. In this case, who is the customer, the advertiser or the audience? The answer is: both. Our value package must serve the needs of a molecular relationship. Actually, in the case of an information product, journalists might argue that the publishing firm itself becomes part of the molecular relationship by delivering a socially valuable product which must meet some ethical standard of quality irrespective of the commercial considerations.

As another example, suppose we sell paints and other coating materials used by companies that manufacture various commercial products. The primary focus in this case will be on the company that buys our products, and we can rely on them to specify the requirements for the coatings that will satisfy the quality requirements of their end-users. However, our company customer is not a single entity, but actually a molecule in its own way.

For example, we may be dealing with the purchasing manager who tries to get the best price by playing us against our competitors. We may also have relationships with the company's manufacturing experts and design engineers, in which we can show them better ways to build their products using our materials. We may become a preferred supplier, and advance to the level where we link our ordering and accounting systems with theirs, strengthening our relationship so that we can maintain an edge over many competitors, if not all. In using our customer radar, we have to focus on each of the key participants in the customer molecule. We have to understand not only what each of them values, but how they interact with one another, and how those interactions affect our opportunities.

As we will see, most of the methods we can use to understand the individual consumer customer will apply, with appropriate variations, to the process of understanding the molecular customer relationship. One is necessarily more complex than the other, but they are conceptually very similar.

Demographics: The Great Engine of Marketing

If your customers are businesses and not consumers, don't be in a hurry to turn the page. If your customer's business is demographically driven, then yours is too.

One of the most important starting points for building a radar picture of your customers, or any particular group of customers, is the demographic profile. A thorough discussion of demographic techniques is well beyond the scope of this book, but we can review the basic thinking process that can help you discover interesting possibilities about your customers. I will apologize in advance to readers well-schooled in demographic analysis, who may find this discussion a bit elementary for their needs. However, those who are not may benefit from an explanation of the basic logic of demographics.

The compelling feature of demographic information is a certain sense of predictability, almost bordering on inevitability, due to the fact that human populations change in fairly predictable ways. The current number of people in a certain demographic category, plus the number of people moving into it for various reasons (birth, coming of age, making certain life changes, etc.), minus the number of people moving out of it for other reasons, will equal a fairly good estimate of their number in the future. Twenty years from now, the number of people on the planet in the age range of 40–50 can be no larger than the number who are in the range of 20–30 today and will certainly be less.

We cannot predict the exact number of people who will be living in Canada one year from today, but we can guess what it will be fairly confidently, using the information we have at hand today. Barring significant wildcards such as a natural disaster of epic proportions, an unprecedented rise in birth rate, or unheard-of levels of immigration or emigration, we know the number of people there will probably not exceed a certain level. That knowledge, applied to doing business in Canada or any other country, or in fact, any economic sector, can establish certain boundaries for our estimates of what is possible.

One of the most common and useful tools for demographic analysis is the *population pyramid*, a chart that shows the number of people in various age ranges, usually divided into males and females. A population pyramid can tell a compelling story about the people of a whole country, or those in a certain economic sector we're interested in exploring.

For comparison, look at the population pyramid shown in Figure 6-1, which shows a typical age distribution for a fast-growing, underdeveloped country. Note the simple shape of the pyramid, with relatively large numbers of infants and young people due to the high birth rates, and rapidly declining numbers of people in the higher age ranges due to high death rates from disease (and, in some cases, warfare).

Now contrast the third-world country's pyramid with that of a highly-developed nation, in this case the United States, as shown in Figure 6-2. Note the radical difference in the pattern of ages. In fact, the American pattern could hardly be called a pyramid; it resembles a "Coke bottle" pattern, to use a symbol from the American popular culture. A number of other highly-developed countries, such as Japan and others, tend to follow this same general pattern, with individual variations.

The peculiar bulge in population about halfway up the American pyramid is a result of a decline in birth rates during the Depression years of the 1930s, followed by an explosive

Figure 6-1. Population Pyramid: Developing Country.

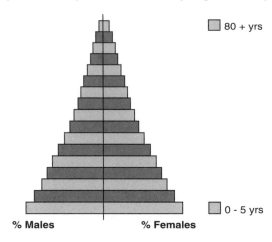

Figure 6-2. Population Pyramid: U.S.

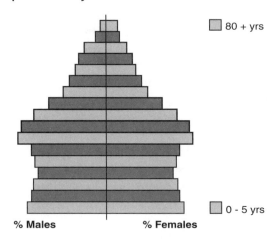

increase in births after World War II—the infamous "baby boom"—followed by a decline in birth rates to more typical levels. As the women of this *age cohort*, as demographers call it, moved into their child-bearing years, they produced a secondary boom, but one proportionally smaller than their own.

Although age is only one of a number of important demographic drivers of customer behavior and intention, it is one of the most powerful of all variables in predicting changes over specific periods of time. Many patterns of buying, saving, investing, consumption, and leisure activities show strong age correlations. Home buying, for example, is clearly age-related. It takes most young families some period of time to achieve sufficient financial stability and confidence to undertake the purchase of a new home. As they accumulate wealth over a number of years, they may trade up to more expensive homes. Past a certain age, they tend to remain in the homes they have, or in some cases to relocate and trade downward to more modest homes.

Most people who invest seriously begin doing so only after reaching a certain point of income stability. In their early adult years, many people tend to favor greater spending on their material possessions and tend to invest more extensively as they grow older, earn better incomes, and have accumulated many of the material possessions they wanted.

Marketers of lifestyle products and discretionary items such as music, fashion clothing, and movies know that age is a primary driver of customer preference. As people age, their preferences for sporting activities and other forms of recreation tend to shift. Tennis is a more highly favored sport for people below the age of forty, while golf becomes progressively more popular with people over forty.

Healthcare is clearly age-related in its demand patterns and its costs. Serious illnesses such as cancer, heart disease, and stroke tend to afflict those over fifty years old much more extensively than those under fifty. A large fraction of medical costs involves treating people over the age of sixty, who tend to have more acute health problems, and who are very costly to treat when they have terminal conditions.

Retirement is becoming a serious demographic issue for most of the developed countries because of the shifting age structure of their populations. The median age for the American population shifted from about twenty-six in 1950 to about thirty-five in the late 1990s. Japan has seen an even more significant shift. As the members of the post-war baby boom move into the age range typically thought of as the retirement years, they will nearly outnumber the wage-earning portion of the population who must pay taxes to subsidize their retirement.

As conditions change in the developing countries, their population structures will shift toward the pattern of the developed countries for a number of reasons. For one, it has become clear that as economic conditions improve, women tend to have far better opportunities for education. As they become more educated, they tend to have fewer babies. Huge families give way to smaller, planned families. In addition, infant mortality rates drop, fewer women die in childbirth, and people tend to live longer as a result of better nutrition, better healthcare, and the reduction of disease. Overall population growth rates decline, and the population pyramid tends to become taller and less sharply diminished at the upper levels.

Many other demographic variables come into play in estimating the behavior and intentions of your customers, of course. Educational level is very often a strong predictor of customer preference. And, certainly, income level or general financial status strongly influences patterns of buying and investment. Other factors such as ethnic origin, occupation, religious preference, and health status also come into play.

Differences in geographic location can be correlated with customer preference, in the sense that they relate to community attitudes and values, or to the extent that they are associated with other significant demographic variables such as age. The median age in the city of Miami, Florida, is over fifty, compared to about thirty-five for the U.S. in general, because of its high concentration of retired people.

Geographic differences can cause consumer demand to rise much more rapidly in some regions than others. Asia, for example, has further to go than the wealthy Western economies, and so the proportional rise in demand there will be dramatically higher. Economists predict that, shortly into the 2000s, China alone will have over 200 million middle-class households, with the usual middle-class aspirations and consumption patterns. The number of Asian households classified as affluent, i.e., incomes equivalent to U.S. $30,000, will double to over 50 million. Asia will have over 250 million TV households, with all of the associated socioeconomic side effects.

Identifying the demographic drivers for your business might be fairly simple, or it might require careful thought and investigation. If you're in the business of selling funeral services, you're in an age-related business, but other demographic factors will come into play as well. If you're in the business of selling sporting goods, age will be a factor, as well as gender. If you sell computer software, educational level may play a significant part in your customers' choices.

One obvious way to understand your customer demographics is to measure, or estimate, the demographic characteristics of your current customers. What are the age patterns? The proportion of males and females? What seems to be the typical level of education? What are the most likely levels of income, based on various cues that signal their lifestyle choices? Many firms neglect to capture even the most elementary demographic information about their customers. Except for intuition and general hunches, many strategic planners can only guess the demographic profile of their customers and may have little insight into the major variations within their customer populations.

As mentioned previously, if your customer is a business, then you may need to understand the demographic patterns of your customer's customers. For example, if you sell custom-molded plastic parts to manufacturing firms, and your largest single customer makes sporting goods, then the rise and fall of that firm's customer demand flows through to affect the demand for your products. If age demographics favor an increase in your customer's business, then you can be thankful, but if demographics favor a steady decline in demand for the customer's products, you'd better be planning for the effects on your business.

Whatever Happened to Customer Service?

For a stretch of about ten years, from 1985 through about 1995, American business flirted with the idea of "customer service" as a possible competitive weapon. The service revolution spread from the U.S. to many other countries through books, conferences, consultants, and seminars. Some firms became permanent advocates of the concept of *strategic customer focus*, others tried to implement it with disappointing results, and still others never understood it at all.

I hope I may be permitted the privilege of a short dissertation on this topic, inasmuch as it was my book *Service America!: Doing Business in the New Economy*,[1] co-authored with Ron Zemke, that largely triggered the so-called service revolution. In 1983 I had discovered the germ of an emerging

concept in Scandinavia that advocates there were calling
service management. It invited a complete rethinking of the
paradigm of western management, with the customer's experience as the starting point, rather than the organization and
its processes. I brought the concept to the U.S., created an
implementing model called the "service triangle," and began to
write, speak, and consult on applying the methods of service
management.

Service America! sold over a half-million copies and spawned
a whole sub-industry in the consulting and management education sector. International congresses devoted to "service
excellence" sprouted all over the world. Seminar organizers,
training firms, and corporate training departments dutifully
included programs on various aspects of winning customers
in their catalogs. Consulting firms of all sizes went to work
helping their clients implement "customer focus" programs.
Companies of all stripes, and government agencies as well,
tried their hand at becoming "customer-driven." Outstanding
service companies such as Disney, Federal Express, and Ritz-
Carlton Hotels became role models for the study of "best
practices."

As we predicted in *Service America!*, the attempts to apply
customer focus principles brought mixed results. Some companies approached it thoughtfully and with great determination, and many of them repositioned their companies in their
competitive environments. A larger number flirted with the
customer focus concept, either because it was fashionable and
they had nothing else to do, or because they thought it would
be easier than we had warned it would be. And probably half
of American firms either did nothing or simply adopted the
slogans of customer service as a minimal gesture to the trend.

The focus on service did achieve excellent results for many
firms, giving them a clearer sense of focus and purpose, and
improving their relations with their customers. Many of those
firms continue to maintain and build their commitment to the
strategic service model. However, many who tried it failed and
their programs withered to nothing. The third category of
firms mentioned, those who merely flirted with the concept,
simply went on with life. Some of them also flirted with
control-based methods like Total Quality Management, or
TQM, also with little permanent effect.

Most of the very large firms ultimately showed little or no lasting effect from their dabbling with customer focus programs. The airlines, the mega-banks, the giant retailers, the dominant brokerage firms and insurance firms, almost all survived and grew by capitalizing on their sheer size and market dominance, not by any special magic called "customer service." Of course, it was *de rigeur* to declare in the corporate annual report that "We are customer-driven," "We listen to our customers," and the like. However, most of their senior management teams never lost sight of size and market power as their real competitive advantages.

So, in the post-customer revolution period, many firms continue to maintain a strong competitive focus on customer value, but many more rely on asset-based competition. Indeed, there is notable evidence that more and more of the mega-firms have virtually abandoned customer value as a primary competitive factor. Virtually all of the American airlines, for example, operate as if they see themselves as basically in the freight business. The operational model is essentially that of transporting livestock. The progressive reduction of personal attention, the impoverishment of the on-board experience, exploitive pricing, punitive fees and charges, restrictive policies governing refunds and changes, and overselling and bumping of full-fare customers have all diminished customer approval and driven brand preference to a minimum.

Case in point: America West Airlines recalled one of its planes, en route from Phoenix to Dallas-Fort Worth, ordering it to return to Phoenix and land. Gate agents off-loaded fifty-three ticketed passengers to make room for a sports team, the California Angels, who had just finished playing a game. It had contracted with the team to transport its players to California, but the plane assigned to their flight had developed mechanical problems. To comply with the provisions of its contract, airline management decided to sacrifice the commercial customers, some of whom were stranded for the night in Phoenix. The incident triggered angry letters, government inquiries, and negative press reports across the country. The company tried to telephone all of the alienated passengers with an apology and an attempt at atonement, but the damage was permanent.

In early 1998, the U.S. Senate took up a bill that would hold airlines more accountable for the abuse of their customers, including the introduction of a "passenger's bill of rights." A much-publicized incident in which Northwest Airlines detained several hundred passengers against their will in airplanes parked for hours on a snowed-in runway, fueled the anger many travelers felt toward all airlines.

Case in point: In a personal experience, I lost my ATM card to a rogue cash dispenser operated by a large California-based bank in a shopping mall near my office. The machine seemed to lose electrical power a few seconds after I inserted the card. When the screen came up again, it had no recollection that it had taken the card. I went to a pay telephone and dialed the bank's toll-free number, given on the ATM for help. After a fifteen-minute wait on hold, I asked the bank representative to arrange to have my card retrieved and returned to me. She told me that the bank did not return kept cards; they destroyed them. I would have to go to my own bank, which issued the card, and have a new card issued.

Case in point: When we set up the first Web site for our firm, we ordered the hosting service from one of the eager Internet service providers that contacted us immediately after we registered the domain name. Their sales people assured us that it was easy to get started, and that they provided plenty of help and supporting materials. Once we signed up, we discovered that the assistance in setting up the site consisted of nothing more than a long, rambling email. Heavily laced with geek language, it didn't even answer the three or four most basic questions about setting up the site. After a long series of email requests for help, interspersed with telegraphic answers in geekspeak, we finally discovered the proper procedure by trial and error. Of course, the firm was kind enough to send us frequent offers to upgrade to other services, and helpfully provided our address to other firms that wanted to sell us additional services.

Some experts and commentators on the state of management thinking contend that the service revolution is over, and that this or that concept is the new theory of choice. That may be true or it may be overstated. In any case, I still believe that, for some firms, creating customer preference by means of a differentiated customer experience still makes a lot of sense. Before we give up on customer focus, or declare it a fad that's had its day, we should think carefully about what it takes to win and keep the customer's business.

Working hard and having a pure heart are no longer enough to succeed in today's environment of hypercompetition. If size is all that matters, then you'd better be the biggest and strongest player in your sector, or at least one of biggest few. But if you don't have the advantages of size and brute strength, then you'd better find a recipe that works for you. Customer focus could still be a valuable asset for firms in that situation.

The Myth of Customer Loyalty

More than ten years ago, whenever I asserted that the term customer satisfaction encoded a flawed concept, I would get almost one hundred percent blank looks from the executives I talked to, what one of my associates calls a "staring ovation." The statement was often perceived as a word game, an attempt to obfuscate the obvious. "Everybody knows what customer satisfaction is—it's when you deliver exactly what the customer expects." This was one piece of evidence, among many, that proved the manufacturing quality mindset had automatically become the default mindset for thinking about the management of service.

But the realization gradually set in that customer approval is not simply a binary proposition. You succeed or fail in the customer's eyes to a greater or lesser degree, rather than by simply hitting a mark or missing it. Then the much-revered Dr. Edwards Deming offered the proposition that the objective of every business was to "delight the customer." As other thinkers and writers promoted the same view, the term customer satisfaction tended to become a source of confusion. What did it really mean?

Shortly into the customer revolution, a number of thinkers and writers began to promote the idea of customer loyalty, on the premise that it was more appropriate to focus on *lifetime customer value* than simply on the management of customer-contact episodes. That further complicated the debate about the choice of labels.

The problem with this debate about customer satisfaction versus customer loyalty is not in our intentions, but in our vocabulary. I have long believed that subtle differences in our choice of the labels we apply to problems do as much to promote

or subvert helpful analysis as the thought processes themselves. Wendell Willkie, an early political figure in America,
observed, "a good catchword can obscure analysis for fifty
years." Mark Twain said "the difference between the right word
and almost the right word is the difference between lightning
and the lightning bug."

Let's delve into the ideas behind the slogans, and look for
the operational truth about how to win and keep the business
of our customers.

The answer to the satisfaction-loyalty debate can be both
disheartening and challenging, depending on how you choose
to view it. There are two basic, "awful truths" we must face in
order to develop a strategic customer focus strategy that has
any chance of succeeding.

*Awful Truth #1: aiming for customer satisfaction is a pre-
scription for mediocrity*. If satisfying the customer means per-
forming at the level of his or her expectations, you've sworn a
solemn vow to be perceived as no better or worse than your
competitors. Parity with your rivals gives you no competitive
advantage at all. The customer might just as well choose a
supplier at random, and indeed many do.

There can be a big difference between meeting customer
expectations and creating the perception of value. If the customer is accustomed to being abused, neglected, cheated, lied
to, and pushed around, you can probably meet his or her
expectations fairly easily. However, the latent desire for value
goes unanswered. This was one of the founding principles of
the Saturn car company, with its "one price, no hassle" selling
philosophy. This is why SuperQuinn food markets in Dublin
enjoys higher sales volume, higher margins, and greater customer return rates than its price-obsessed competitors.

Worse yet, expectations and desires usually vary significantly from one customer to another. Age, gender, income,
lifestyle, education, social values, and experience with a particular product or service all influence a person's desires, expectations, and standards. If you don't know what the expectations
are, how can you meet them? As the Third Wave progresses,
mass markets disintegrate and new microsegments of customer interest emerge.

And, of course, we know that in many types of businesses
the customers themselves often don't know what to expect.

Being hospitalized may be a once in a lifetime experience, so the person who goes into the hospital may have very little idea of what's in store. This often presents the opportunity to *manage customer expectations*, i.e., to help the customer form a clear concept of the desirable outcome, and then to do the right things to improve upon it.

The basic "Theory of Service Relativity" says:

$$V = R - E,$$

which means that *Customer Perceived Value* equals Results minus Expectations. In other words, your customer's perception of the benefit of any experience with your business is relative to his or her expectations going into the experience and the results he or she actually experiences coming out of it.

If the results fall short of the expectations, however vaguely stated they may be, then customer perceived value is negative. The surprising implication of this basic quality equation is that, when results are about equal to expectations, customer perceived value is zero. Customer preference results from the accumulation of many such episodes, or, for some businesses, a critical few episodes. This means the battle for future business has to be fought at every transaction, at every "moment of truth."

Awful Truth #2: there is no such thing as customer loyalty. The term customer loyalty also encodes a flawed concept, just as customer satisfaction does. Both concepts are equally dangerous, because they can lead us to dangerous assumptions about customer behavior.

Customer *loyalty*, as most of us like to think of it, usually exists only at the level of one-person microbusinesses, like hairdressers, stockbrokers, travel agents, and therapists. The term loyalty implies a personal bond, rather than merely a continuing relationship of convenience. How can a person be loyal to an airline or a hotel chain? You may do business regularly with a bank, but you'll take your business elsewhere if the bank fails to perform to your minimum standards. The larger the business, the less sense it makes to speak in terms of loyalty on the part of the customer.

The operative term is not customer loyalty, but *customer preference*, which is the customer's predisposition to do business with one supplier over others. It's highly perishable, and it's the best you can hope for. But customer preference is something we can measure and strive to build. There are several options, or levels of technique used by businesses in trying to build customer preference. Some are more effective than others, and some are more noble than others.

Customer inertia—it costs you money, time, and inconvenience to move your checking account from one bank to another, so you generally put up with a certain amount of abuse before you change banks. A bank in South Australia discovered that virtually no new customers signed up because of its advertising campaign or giveaway promotions. A review of the data showed that almost all of them came because they were fed up with the abuse they received from its competitors. However, it was passing on its own frustrated customers to other banks at the same rate it was receiving them. Information technology is gradually destroying the inertial advantage for many businesses. For example, the brokerage industry now has a system that allows a stock market investor to move all of his or her holdings from one brokerage to another with a simple telephone call.

Brand preference—strike the words "brand loyalty" from your vocabulary. Is anybody really loyal to a soft drink or a particular running shoe? It's marketing investment, not customer value, that creates powerful brand images that become cultural icons. A few companies with great determination and huge levels of free cash flow have succeeded in creating worldwide awareness and preference for their brands. In the battle to sell flavored water, is Coca-Cola really better than Pepsi or some other brand you've never heard of? Yet investment guru Warren Buffet commented that "if someone gave me 500 million dollars and asked me to overturn Coca-Cola as the most-preferred brand of soft drink, I'd give it back and say it can't be done."

Customer handcuffs—frequent-flier programs seem to be the only hope most American airline companies have of maintaining any kind of customer preference, and those apply to a fairly small number of customers. Once a super-flier reaches a certain number of miles, he or she gets additional incentives to keep using the same airline. However, people like me, who fly in many directions, tend to spread the miles among several airlines, once the total goes over the required threshold for any one carrier. In the software market, Microsoft is working feverishly to handcuff as many customers as it can to its Windows operating system, but few could argue that its products offer impressive customer value. Intel has enjoyed the same kind of handcuffed relationship with users of its computer chips, even while rival firms have produced better and cheaper processor chips.

A superior customer experience—a few firms actually consistently outperform their rivals and deliver a *total value package,* which is attractive enough to warrant repurchase and word-of-mouth promotion. Firms like Disney, Daimler Benz, and Waterford Crystal have created legends for themselves by their unswerving commitment to the value package itself, combined with down-to-earth business practices.

Customer intimacy—achievable by some kinds of businesses more than others, customer intimacy means nurturing an enduring relationship with the customer that naturally creates more selling opportunities. One reason Volvo Svenska Bil sells insurance to its Swedish customers is to stay in contact with them. If a car buyer disappears into customer land after leaving the dealership, the company has to wait (or pay) for the customer to show up again. With a *continuity product* such as insurance, the continuing contact provides opportunities to build preference and strengthen the buyer-seller relationship.[2]

Understanding Customer Value: The "Need Context"

We've emphasized heavily the need to understand your customers in demographic and behavioral terms. But you need to go even further if you want to be able to create new possibilities for doing business with them. You have to understand the *source* of their behavior and intentions, the *psychographic* factors that drive them. You have to figure out what's making them behave as customers, and what might make them behave in ways that benefit your business. In psychological terms, you have to identify the *need context* that forms the intention to buy what you have to sell, as illustrated in Figure 6-3.

The need context of your customer is simply the set of circumstances in which he or she (or it) operates, insofar as those

Figure 6-3. The Customer's Need Context.

circumstances influence the customer to perceive what you offer as meeting a need, solving a problem, or adding value.

For example, suppose your firm provides services for importing and exporting goods between two countries. Suppose a prospective customer is a firm that seeks to gain access to the business environment you're operating in.

The first thing to do is try to live a day in the life of your customer. How does the firm operate now? What are its most pressing problems? What are its business circumstances that have led its principals to pursue an exporting strategy? What are its strengths and weaknesses? Do the firm's executives have a high degree of knowledge and familiarity with importing and exporting, or are they just beginning? Do they have a clear concept of what they want to accomplish, or are they guessing? Are they realistic about what can be accomplished, and the amount of money and time required? These questions express the old adage of the service firm: make the customer's problems your problems.

As a consumer example, suppose you're selling investment services such as retirement planning, asset management, and financial advice. Are your clients simply a group of statistical accounts, or does each one present unique revenue opportunities based on his or her particular circumstances?

Many financial services firms have remarkably little useful information about the need context of their customers, so they tend to think in terms of their own financial "products" rather than in terms of individual opportunities. They may have large numbers of "inactive" clients, many of whom have actually defected to their competitors as a result of neglect. Who knows how many of these inactive clients have experienced significant changes in their circumstances, such as retirements or inheritances, which might make them candidates for new business? The customer radar should identify these kinds of opportunities.

Part of understanding your customer is knowing what goes on in his or her life. If your customer is a business, you need to know something about the industry in which it operates. Who are its customers and who are its competitors? How do firms in that sector do business? Learn the customer's vocabulary, which can give you great insight into the thinking processes that shape their competitive choices. The core vocabulary, the slang, the metaphors, and the figures of speech in an industry can telegraph the dominant paradigms, the mindsets, and the ideologies that make the industry what it is. Healthcare has its unique lingo. Publishing, insurance, broadcasting, construction, food service—all lines of business have their unique semantic reference systems.

Of all the possible avenues to customer preference just discussed, the strategy of customer intimacy offers a special kind of appeal. It is, of course, more feasible in some lines of business than others. However, it is worth exploring ways in which any firm can begin to progress up the hierarchy, or spectrum, of strategic customer value, pictured in Figure 6-4.

Each of the five levels of the spectrum has its own unique characteristics:

1. *Products*—tangible items the customer takes custody of. This includes the car, the food purchased in the market, the software product, or the rented tuxedo. In many cases the appeal of the tangible product accounts for almost all of the customer's perception of value received. There is usually some kind of transaction associated with the delivery of the product, but it may be only a matter of necessity.

Figure 6-4. The Strategic Value Hierarchy.

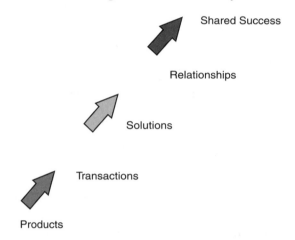

2. *Transactions*—the simplest and least enriched level of involvement with the customer. It may include the handover of a product or other tangible goods to the customer, or it might involve a pure experience such as a hotel stay or getting a tooth filled. The customer shows up (or we show up), a one-time transaction takes place, such as in a bank or a post office, and it's over with. In its simplest form it has no past and no future; it exists only in the present.

3. *Solutions*—unique sets of ideas, information, designs, products, and transactions that meet an individual need. The firm must understand the customer's particular problems, needs, preferences, and constraints, in order to sell a designed package of value that answers a particular set of needs. This is the wedding, the vacation package, the planned medical treatment, or the rehabilitation of a home damaged by a hurricane.

4. *Relationships*—the ongoing interactions, exchange of ideas, sense of empathy, responsiveness to changing needs, mutual definition of value to be delivered, and joint participation in the creation of the value. This is the value package offered by the consultant, financial advisor, trading partner, or the mall operator who promotes the success of the tenant businesses.

5. *Shared Success*—the state of affairs in which both customer and provider recognize and value their interdependence.

It can be the franchiser and franchisee, the automobile maker and the dealers, and the consultant or financial adviser who has a long-term relationship with the client.

Not all businesses are equally suited to climb this hierarchy toward customer intimacy and shared fate. Some are very well suited to do so. In general, however, the search for customer preference has to move more and more toward creating the perception of significant value. We have to do everything possible to differentiate our offering from those of our competitors, and one place to start looking is in the very nature of our relationship with the customer.

At the end of World War II, General Douglas MacArthur commented, "There is no security in this life; only opportunity." We have no God-given right to our customers' business. As the level of hypercompetition moves ever higher in this increasingly chaotic business environment, ideas like customer satisfaction and customer loyalty give way to ideas like delivering customer value, earning customer preference, and building customer intimacy.

We can put the strategic value hierarchy to use at these various levels of intimacy by finding out what the customer is really trying to buy when he or she confronts the business. People don't buy "products" or "services;" they buy *value*. They buy solutions to their problems, answers to their needs, and improvements in their lives. The first critical skill in using your customer radar is learning to think in customer-value terms. This is what the *customer value model* enables you to do.

A customer value model is simply a set of critical attributes of the customer experience that the customers themselves tell us are the most important factors in forming their perception of value received. Whether it's having surgery, flying from one city to another, opening a bank account, buying or selling shares of stock, or buying a new outfit of clothes, every customer experience has a basic value model embedded in it.

Discovering and defining the customer's value model is the first step in learning how to deliver it. How can we win the customer's business if we don't know what he or she really wants and doesn't want? What is the most basic and critical appeal of the service experience to the customer? Once we clearly understand this *value proposition*, we can engage in a dialogue with the customer that will help us discover the critical

elements of the service experience that make it real. Figure
6-5 shows a typical customer value model, for a hospital stay.

The process of building customer value models for various
customer segments or lines of business, known as *customer
value modeling*, is becoming more widely used in a number of
business sectors. Modern customer research methods focus on
helping the customer tell us, in his or her own language and
perspective, what the real value proposition is. Using sophisticated computer technology known as *electronic polling*,
researchers invite customers into focus group workshops and
pose key questions which they answer by pressing numbered
keys on wireless keypads. A computer collects the responses
and instantly displays the group consensus. Using these and
other techniques, researchers can produce much more reliable
models of customer value and preference than were possible
with conventional techniques, which depend heavily on expert
interpretations of the discussions.[3]

One of the pioneers of this method of instrumented focus
group research, Dr. Kevin Austin of Australia, believes that all
firms can benefit by forming and using specific customer value
models to describe and understand what their customers are
actually trying to buy. According to Austin:

Figure 6-5. A Typical Customer Value Model.

Customer Value Model: Hospital Patient

- Feeling Empowered as a Customer
- Trust in Systems, Continuity, & Teamwork
- Quality of Clinical Results
- Physical & Emotional Comfort
- Respect for Family & Friends
- Information & Education
- Coordination With Other Caregivers
- Costs of Treatment

If you're going to get everyone in the organization to concentrate on delivering customer value, you've got to give them a concrete model of what that value is, as defined by the customers themselves. It's not enough to ask employees to smile and be nice. You need to give them a workable definition of the value they're expected to deliver, and then help them learn and use the critical work practices that deliver that value.

The key idea of the customer radar is to help you understand customer value: what it is, how the customer defines it, and what you have to do to provide it in a more appealing way than your competitors.

Notes

1. Albrecht, Karl and Ron Zemke. *Service America!: Doing Business in the New Economy.* Homewood IL: Dow-Jones Irwin, 1985. See also Albrecht, Karl. *The Only Thing That Matters: Bringing the Power of the Customer Into the Center of Your Business.* New York: HarperBusiness, 1992.
2. The discussion of customer loyalty is adapted from an article originally published in *Quality Digest*, April 1998. Copyright Karl Albrecht, all rights reserved. Used with permission.
3. For a copy of a bulletin describing value modeling in detail, contact the author's Web site at albrechtintl.com.
4. For a collection of useful articles on service and customer focus, see Ken Shelton's *Best of Class* (Provo, Utah: Executive Excellence Publishing). You can contact the publisher through their Web site at eep.com.

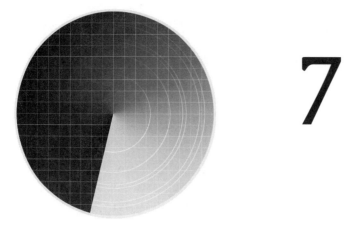

7

Your Competitor Radar

Chance favors the prepared mind.
— Louis Pasteur

The purpose of the competitive radar is to understand the intentions of your competitors and the forces shaping them.

Who Is Your Competition?

This might seem like a strange question. How can anybody be in business and not know who the competitors are? Actually, it is a trick question. Of course, we know who our competitors are, in the sense of the other businesses who contend with us for the customer's trade. But consider carefully that there may be other options open to your prospective customers for satisfying their requirements by means other than buying what you and your rivals sell. Those avenues are also your competition.

Case in point: some years ago, executives of a cruise line operating in the Caribbean began exploring the issues related to growth of the business. The available customer data at that time showed that only four percent of the American public had ever taken a cruise of any kind. Everybody knew about cruises from the romantic literature, movies, and especially the popular television series *Love Boat*. But in fact, very few people had actually participated in the experience behind the fantasy. It was also well known that most non-cruisers held various apprehensions about the experience—seasickness, boredom, formality and ceremony, and, of course, prices. However, almost all of the company's advertising and promotion was oriented toward the pleasures of cruising that would only be known to experienced customers.

It became clear during the review of the data and the marketing strategy that the real competition was not the rival cruise lines. The real competition was the set of other options available to the customers for spending their vacation funds. Rather than fighting the other companies for market share when the entire market represented only a four percent share of the total vacation market, it made more sense to fight for a much larger slice of a much larger pie. The strategy shifted to promoting cruises as attractive alternatives to other vacation options.

Case in point: with the remarkable popularity of the Internet and Web-based stock trading, the old established brokers—the "wirehouses" as veteran brokers call them—came under threat from discount brokerages. Of course, it's correct to say that the online brokers are the new competitors to the full-service brokers. But in the larger view, it also makes sense to say that the customers themselves have become competitors to the wirehouses. Once a person figures out how to execute a trade by going to a Web site, and decides that the personal advice and support he or she had been getting from a broker did not justify the fees being charged, this person becomes a new kind of customer.

Case in point: in the world of digital technology, many firms worry less about being knocked off by other firms that offer products similar to theirs, and more about alternative ways to create the value they offer. In recent years, the search for an alternative to the Windows operating system has intensified as Microsoft has increasingly used its technical monopoly and brand power to squelch competitors. The Java programming language, combined with the Web page structure for managing information, is part of a combination that could represent a technological alternative to the Windows style of doing things.

Case in point: traditional music publishers see serious competition from Internet pirates, i.e., those who digitize commercial music and install it on Web sites for free access by anybody who wants it. This has raised some extremely difficult issues regarding intellectual property and the legality of much of what goes on in the Internet "culture." In this sense, the competitors are not other music companies, but people who can use low-cost digital technology to destroy part of the demand for the products.

The point of this discussion is that, before you get to the sophisticated techniques of competitor intelligence, market share analysis, and competitive comparisons, it makes sense to identify clearly the competitive forces you are actually facing. In this respect,

> **a competitor is any entity that offers options to your customers which can diminish the appeal of the options you offer.**

This may involve some very creative thinking and far-reaching associations, but it can be very important to establishing a clear understanding of your strategic prospects.

The Enemy of Your Enemy Might or Might Not Be Your Friend

In today's increasingly chaotic and fluid competitive environment, it's becoming more and more difficult to tell the difference between enemies and allies. In one situation, a particular firm might be your ally or competitive partner. In another it might be your customer. In another it might be your supplier. And in still another it might be your competitor.

Travel agencies in recent years, particularly in America, have discovered that the airlines they thought were their business partners have become their determined enemies. In 1995 Delta Airlines, followed within days by United Airlines and American Airlines, announced caps, or ceiling amounts, on commissions paid to agencies for selling their tickets. Whereas airlines had for many years paid commissions to agencies of about ten percent of the ticket price, they announced that no domestic commission would exceed twenty-five dollars for a one-way ticket or fifty dollars for a round-trip ticket, no matter what the price. Since studies showed that the typical agency incurred costs of about twenty-one dollars per ticket issued, this move virtually crippled an already profitless industry.

With the introduction of so-called "ticketless travel," i.e., simple confirmations without any ticket documents, airlines saw the prospect of further reducing their selling costs and attracting the customers directly to them. A series of further reductions in commissions and restrictions on the most profitable tickets put thousands of agencies out of business. However, many agencies were still bound to multi-year contracts for the use of the electronic reservation systems, such as United's Apollo and American's Sabre, which were owned by the same airline companies supplying the tickets.

Some of the largest companies that sell branded consumer products such as clothing, perfume, cosmetics, and sporting gear have been experimenting with direct sales to consumers over the Internet. This may turn out to be a ticket to disaster, especially for firms that have no experience or infrastructure for direct selling. Levi Strauss, for example, began offering its full line of jeans and related clothing items over its Web site, to the dismay of retailers who carried its products. Some retailers worried that the company might offer better prices over the Internet than customers could get in their stores, especially since the Internet has become fiercely price competitive, in many cases amounting to a digital going-out-of-business sale.

Apple Computer began promoting its new iMac product over the Internet, making many loyal retailers very uncomfortable. It and many other firms have tried hard to put a positive face on the moves, assuring retailers that they are not really competitors. Increasingly, however, this will be a difficult sell, and many suppliers may find that the additional costs associated with selling direct to the public, combined with less than spectacular sales and animosity from retailers, will cause them to rethink the policy.

Just as it's important to understand your competition, it's also important to understand the circumstances that may be driving competition in your line of business. Before we apply the fancy techniques of competitive analysis, we have to be sure we know who the players are and how the game is really being played.

Which Companies Will Dominate? Ask Your Broker

One person who may be able to help you make sense of the picture on your competitor radar is one you might never think to ask: your stockbroker. What does a stockbroker know about business fundamentals? Plenty, if he or she is highly trained in valuing firms listed on the major exchanges.

Robert Frazier, an economic consultant and registered professional financial adviser, says:

> Expert brokers and analysts have to make dispassionate judgments about the business prospects of industrial firms every day, in every industry. We do it by looking at the firm's position in its competitive arena and then evaluating its earnings prospects based on what's likely to happen over the next six months, twelve months, and out three to five years.

According to Frazier, a few key parameters can tell most of the story about each of the competing firms in a particular sector. Management's know-how, by the way, is not at the top of his list, although it does appear. Frazier's comparative model for business success includes the following variables:

1. *Working capital and free cash flow.* Generally speaking, the firm with the deepest pockets will win most of its battles. It can outspend its competitors on R&D, brand building, advertising and promotion, capacity growth, and acquisition of other firms. It can also usually drive prices, at least temporarily, by underpricing its rivals and sustaining lower profit margins for longer periods. A crowded market may be a good opportunity for a well-capitalized firm to enter if it contains many small to mid-sized competitors. This has been well demonstrated by firms such as Wal-Mart, which has soaked up demand in almost all rural and suburban areas it has entered, putting many smaller retailers out of business.

2. *Low operating costs.* Low levels of debt and consequently low costs of capital, streamlined operations, minimum organizational waste, low labor costs and high productivity, good deals with suppliers, and efficient use of information technology give a firm greater freedom to deploy resources. A cost-efficient firm can withstand price wars more effectively than others, and it can use its working capital and free cash flow better to sponsor growth. Microsoft, for example, sells products composed of almost pure information. The costs of software packaging and associated materials are almost negligible. With little capital tied up in plant or equipment, high free cash flow, and few competitive pressures, it enjoys virtual immunity to price competition.

3. *Brand power.* For the top few players in each sector, brand power is almost the whole game. If you're not one of the few brand leaders, you must adopt a whole different set of competitive priorities because you can't bark as loud as the biggest dogs in the neighborhood. The Coca-Cola Company spends over $800 million per year on advertising to keep its position as the world's most widely recognized brand. Procter & Gamble invests heavily in maintaining its army of consumer brands. Nestlé Incorporated has managed to keep its Nescafé brand in strong position for many years, in second place behind Coke as the most widely recognized beverage.

4. *Market growth potential.* The best-managed firm can't magically create demand in a situation where the causes of that demand are disappearing. There's no substitute for a strong product in a growing market. Intel has ridden a steady wave of demand for its microchips for several decades. Cisco profits from the powerful growth of Internet traffic, creating demand for its servers and data networking equipment. Nokia, the fast-growing Finnish maker of cellular phones, benefits from worldwide demand for mobile communications.

5. *Customer access.* Contact with the customers, or those who sell to the customers, is crucial to growth in revenue and earnings. If you can't get your products onto the shelves or otherwise in front of the customers, you can't sell them. The dominant players who have the biggest presence in the distribution channel, or who can afford to get their message to the customers, will tend to edge out their competitors. Customers can't buy what they don't know about. Procter & Gamble enjoys almost unchallenged elbow room on supermarket shelves for its range of consumer products. Frito-Lay Incorporated dominates the packaged snack foods industry, with ready access to store shelves. Consulting giant Andersen Consulting, with its thousands of consultants in constant daily contact with client companies, has almost unlimited opportunities to grow its base of business, while small consulting companies have to fight for every possible client opportunity.

6. *Competitive density and capacity.* The sheer number of suppliers and the capacity they bring to the marketplace will affect the profit opportunities for all players, and particularly the weaker firms. In a fast-growing marketplace where capacity hasn't caught up with demand, opportunities and options are more wide open. In a crowded marketplace with too many suppliers or too much capacity, the competitors fall into destructive price wars that decimate the weakest players and erode the profits of the stronger ones. The world car market, for example, has become grotesquely overcrowded in recent years, with Asian conglomerates building more factories and launching ever more unsuccessful models. The semiconductor business also suffers from boom-bust cycles, superimposed on a generally rising curve of world demand. DeBeers, the South African diamond marketing giant, has single-handedly controlled the world diamond market for years by *limiting* the flow of diamonds to the retail channel, thereby keeping diamonds unnaturally scarce and prices high.

7. *Unique competitive advantage.* Any special situation, such as a unique geographic location, ownership of a patent, ownership of critical information, dominance of a very specialized niche, control of a wildly popular consumer product, or any similar factor that only your firm has, can give you a special form of leverage over your competitors. This may also include a product or service with unique appeal. A fad toy, when it's hot, is a remarkable thing to see. A best-selling book or a wildly popular movie gives its owner a big dividend on the investment. A brand that stands alone, such as Rolex, Waterford Crystal, Mercedes-Benz, or Disney, creates a special advantage that competitors or imitators cannot copy.

8. *One-time opportunities or circumstantial wildcards.* The break-up of the former Soviet Union, the fall of the Berlin Wall, the handover of Hong Kong to mainland China, the release of a blockbuster product such as the impotence pill Viagra, the Y2K software bug, or any other significant and singular event can present special opportunities to firms that might be in a position to capitalize on them. This may also include a major scandal that wrecks the public image of one of the competitors in a sector, the loss of a significant lawsuit, the death of a CEO, the fall from grace of a celebrity who has endorsed a certain firm's products, or any of a countless number of unpredictable events that could drastically change the economic prospects of one or more competitors.

9. *Executive leadership.* A strong CEO, supported by a talented and well-integrated leadership team, and armed with a sound strategic plan, can make the most of all other advantages that might be presented by the business environment. Legendary leaders such as General Electric's Jack Welch, Asea Brown Boveri's Percy Barnevik, Microsoft's Bill Gates, and Intel's Andy Grove have become almost synonymous with their firms in the minds of their customers, competitors, and investors.

10. *Organizational culture and structure.* In some cases, the firm's culture and values are uniquely appropriate to the mission it has undertaken. Or its particular organizational structure might support the mission much better than the types of structures being used by competitors. Morale, teamwork, and a sense of destiny can play a big part in accomplishing the mission and staying true to the strategic direction. Competitors who are malorganized or afflicted with stressed cultures will make less effective use of the knowledge and talent of their people. Apple Computer started with a frenetic, "we can do anything" blue-jeans culture, but gradually lost its spirit and its best people as it drifted deeper and deeper into its strategic dilemma. IBM's corporate culture has, at times, served as a major asset and, at other times, a handicap. Some analysts credit 3M Corporation's flexible, product-driven structure with the firm's capacity to bring a mind-boggling flow of new products to market.

A basic part of your competitor radar picture should be an objective comparison of your firm with the primary and secondary competitors in your sector against these critical predictive parameters. How would your stockbroker evaluate your firm and its competitors? Which would he or she recommend most enthusiastically as a sound investment?

Consolidation: The David and Goliath Scenario

In 1910, 300 automobile firms were operating in the U.S. Today, there are three successful ones.

One of the more unnerving trends in many industries, intensifying from the 1980s onward, is the ever-increasing consolidation caused by mergers and acquisitions. Although companies have been buying and selling one another for many years, the increasingly competitive environment in almost all sectors has led to a condition of too many firms chasing too few customers. By Darwinian selection, a few grow to dominance and the rest tend to die off or get eaten up.

Economists point to the phenomenon of *increasing returns*, or the principle of *self-reinforcing advantage,* among the dominant players in any sector. When one or more firms manage to gain a competitive edge early in the development of an industry, they tend to be able to increase that advantage little by little over time, until they are significantly stronger than the rest. At some point, the competitive advantage begins to accelerate, and the dominant firms become stronger and stronger at the expense of those who do not enjoy the advantages of size and capital strength.

For example, the mega-store can usually offer the customers better overall value than the smaller store, in terms of a wider range of merchandise, discount prices, and frequent sales or promotions. In recent years, the so-called "category-killer" stores in America such as Blockbuster Video, Bookstar, and Circuit City, as well as mass discounters such as Price-Costco, have won customers away from smaller competitors with the ability to stock in depth and offer deep discounts. The traditional "personal service" appeal is difficult to sell in the face of more products and lower prices. Increasingly, consumers face the choice of "all service" or "no service," and when the price is lower, most of them vote with their wallets. Small is no longer beautiful, at least to the typical consumer.

This size dominance is analogous to the "alpha male" in a troop of monkeys or a band of gorillas, who manages to maintain and reinforce his dominance over the other males and his privileges with the females for a very long time. Often the only change in the alpha male position comes when the current leader dies or grows so old that a younger male can successfully challenge him.

The "alpha competitor" may gain that status in any number of ways, such as being first in the marketplace, having a far superior product, having more money to spend, or perhaps just by benefiting from a major blunder on the part of a key competitor. Whatever the initial reason, as the alpha leader typically becomes more and more successful, it gains a self-reinforcing advantage. If the lead firm doesn't stumble or run into unforeseen problems, it can ultimately outspend its competitors and buy market share, customer access, and production capacity. It can advertise more heavily to build and reinforce its brand power, which in turn adds to its increasing advantage. Some analysts contend that Apple Computer lost its position as the potential alpha firm in the PC business when Steve Jobs took his eye off the ball by picking a fight with IBM and missing the real threat from Microsoft's Windows until too late.

Coca-Cola has been the alpha company in its sector for many years. Kodak enjoyed a similar position in its category. IBM certainly did so for many years. In recent times, Intel has dominated the computer chip business, with ever-increasing technological advantages, brand power, and market share. Microsoft has similarly dominated the market for PC operating systems for over five years. The fact that the shares of both Coca-Cola and Microsoft have long traded well above the nominal prices justified by their profits shows that investors have decided that they have virtually no competition, for all practical purposes.

This "David and Goliath" scenario—the steady consolidation and aggregation of competitors and the movement toward the existence of a few giants surrounded by a number of smaller and weaker firms—seems to be an almost inexorable trend in a wide range of industries. As the larger firms have continued to consolidate over the past ten years or so, most of them seem to have lost interest in the customer experience and concentrated almost solely on issues of structure and capital strength. The result seems to be an increasing perception on the part of many customers that the larger the firm, the more it takes its customers for granted, and the less it is inclined to pay attention to delivering superior customer value. This may work to the advantage of smaller or mid-sized firms, if they can move to capitalize on it.

When it comes to evaluating the picture on your competitor radar screen, it makes a big difference whether your firm is the alpha male of the business or not. If you are one of the handful of firms large enough and blessed with sufficient capital to win most of the customers, your competitor radar should be focused on identifying possible threats to that dominance, including fundamental shifts or changes in the structure of the market, which might nullify all or part of your advantage.

If you're one of the "others" in the sector, your competitor radar should be focused on exploiting any weaknesses or gaps in the value offered the customers by the alpha firms, and finding ways to distinguish your firm in the minds of the customers. If you can't compete on the basis of raw economic power, then you'll have to do it by making yourself more attractive to certain specific customers in specific ways.

Is There a Merger in Your Future?

Worldwide merger activity in 1997, measured in the value of corporate assets acquired, set a new record of over one trillion dollars. By the end of 1998, it had topped $2.2 trillion. The worldwide stock of available capital, together with astronomical share prices on U.S. exchanges, led to unprecedented levels of asset concentration.

Not all mergers make sense, either strategically or economically, and not all of them produce positive results. Some firms get caught up in the "growth psychosis," seeking sheer asset growth at the expense of market logic. On average, less than half of corporate mergers ultimately increase the value of the assets of the shareholders of the acquiring firm. Growth for the sake of growth is the ideology of the cancer cell, not the successful enterprise.

On the other hand, some mergers are important enough to cause fundamental changes in the way an industry operates. Others make sense but do not reshape the landscape in any permanent way. Each combination needs to be understood in its own context.

If you operate in a business sector in which mergers and acquisitions are increasing, or likely to increase, it's important to understand how consolidation can affect your possibilities, and indeed whether acquiring other firms or being acquired makes sense for your business. To understand how mergers can influence your business, it is important to understand why they happen.

A person has to read news reports in the popular press and business magazines with a degree of skepticism when it comes to the announcement of corporate mergers. It seems to be the style for newsmakers to report each new mega-merger with all the drama of a moon landing, and to hint at great new powers for the merging companies while hinting at grave consequences for all other competitors who will presumably be "left behind" in the new order of business.

Most merger stories suffer from an excess of drama and a shortage of information about exactly why the merger is such a good idea and exactly how it will benefit the shareholders of the combined firms. Indeed, it often seems that newswriters all have the same standard merger-story template stored in their word processors, and they simply have to insert the names of the merging companies, their share values and market capitalization, and a few references to the business sector involved. After that, it's basically a matter of admiring the merging companies and scaring the hell out of the others.

When AT&T and Telecommunications Incorporated (TCI), the cable-TV company, decided to merge, various news reports heralded the plan as a brilliant strategic move that would "send competitors scrambling to find partners, or risk being left out." Presumably the merger would put AT&T into the cable-TV business, or put TCI into the local telephone business, or put both companies into the Internet business. The prize was supposed to be the Internet cable-access market, in which consumers could connect to the Internet through TCI's local cable systems, and AT&T would carry their messages over its existing long-lines structure. However, little was said about the need to sell special equipment (cable modems) to subscribers, and massively upgrade the cable infrastructure for two-way transmission. Without the questionable Internet rationale, the merger would be a simple combination of balance sheets.

When Citibank and Travelers Group announced plans to merge, many news reports immediately predicted the inevitable demise of most of the smaller and mid-sized banks in the U.S., presumably because of some obvious advantage created by the sheer combination of capital assets. In particular, it was presumed that the two companies could easily cross-sell their financial products to each others' customers. That may turn out to be true, but simply bolting together two financial firms does not automatically confer the divine right of greater market dominance. It has to be earned. In Europe, for instance, a new wave of consumer privacy laws may very well put fences around the various business units within financial firms, preventing them from sharing customer data across market areas without customer permission. Although privacy issues tend to get lip service in the U.S., European governments take them much more seriously.

Ironically, RJR Nabisco, the food conglomerate, has been under increasing pressure from influential shareholders to *demerge*, separating its tobacco operations from its consumer foods businesses. Many analysts believe the total market value of the separate businesses would rise to exceed that of the original firm.

If you want to understand how a merger in a particular industry might affect the future of your firm, you'll need a more precise thinking process than that offered by the Goliath-watching journalists. If you understand the basic logic of mergers, you can substitute your own judgment for the vagueness and drama of the news reports and decide for yourself what the merger's effects will likely be and how soon, if at all, your business might experience them.

Let's review the major kinds of mergers in terms of their reasons, or the logic behind them. Here is a quick catalog of the most common merger motives, ranging from the questionable to the defensible:

1. *Vanity mergers.* Two CEOs get together and play "big business." There may be little or no market synergy, brand logic, economic leverage, or added value for the shareholders. A number of big corporate mergers in the 1970s and 1980s were more about vanity than value. AT&T in particular gobbled up a computer company and a cellular telephone company, announcing that it had become the "global solutions company." It later split up again, spinning off its R&D arm, Lucent, as well, and went back to concentrating on the long-distance telephone business that built it. A variation on the vanity merger is the copycat merger, put together to answer a presumed threat from other companies that have merged, whether it makes good strategic sense or not.

2. *Balance sheet mergers.* Some mergers, and many acquisitions, are simply combinations of resources with little or no added value or synergy. Depending on the prices paid and the market values of the stock involved, shareholders may experience them as ranging from value-losing to value-added. But after the commotion, many consolidated balance sheets show just about the same asset picture as the simple sum of the two parts. Reporters sometimes tout these mergers as clever moves or inevitable consolidations, and knowingly explain how the merger gives the acquiring firm new product lines, access to new markets, and greater competitive power. In many cases, the simple sum of the parts is still the sum of the parts. One part of the operation may include a business sector the parent was not previously engaged in, but market share, revenue, and earnings from that sector have not changed just because the two balance sheets were bolted together. Ford Motor Company's purchase of the Jaguar operation did not put Ford in the luxury car market, except by name association. Its later bid for Volvo's car operation showed the same "one plus one equals two" arithmetic.

3. *Fire sale mergers.* When adverse economic conditions drive the stock price of an otherwise successful company to unreasonably low levels, the firm may become a target for a takeover. In a hostile move, another company may simply acquire the stock by tender offer on the sharemarkets. In a friendly takeover, or at least one not completely hostile, the troubled firm may agree to an acquisition for the benefit of its shareholders. Its executives will try to negotiate a takeover price that values the shares higher than they are currently fetching on the market. If the buying firm's shares happen to be highly valued on the sharemarkets, it may be able to acquire the other firm without having to borrow funds for the purchase, or even putting up any cash all, by trading its own shares for the shares of the firm to be acquired. Fire sale mergers that have no other accompanying advantages can sometimes turn into long-term disappointments once the price distortions work themselves out.

4. *"Crown jewel" mergers.* Sometimes a desirable product, technology, or brand is embedded in a company that otherwise would not interest the acquiring firm. The purpose of the merger is to acquire the prize asset, and once the deal is made, the buyer simply disassembles the acquired firm and sells off or closes those operations it doesn't want. Several of the most venerable of the old book publishing firms in New York were torn apart in this process of asset stripping, as mega-firms like Viacom bought them and resold their "imprints," i.e., publishing programs with well-known brand names and established customer bases.

5. *Extermination mergers.* These are also called "clean-up" mergers or "pest-control" mergers. Sometimes a dominant firm buys off a budding competitor in order to keep the competitive picture clean and simple. A large player may acquire a number of smaller players in its market in order to clean up the marketplace and reduce the noise caused by too many competing brands. With the competing brands out of the way, it becomes easier and more economical to build customer acceptance of the surviving brand. Some analysts contend that a number of Microsoft's acquisitions of start-up software companies and Internet operators have the effect of stalling the development of alternative technologies that might gain wider support and eventually threaten the dominance of its Windows operating system.

6. *Capacity mergers.* When a company is well-positioned for growth, such as a firm like Home Depot, which sells tools, supplies, and materials for do-it-yourself homeowners and small construction firms, it needs to move into new geographic areas and add capacity in an orderly way. In that scenario, it often makes sense to buy up existing firms that would otherwise be competitors. Instead of adding more local capacity and facing competition, it simply acquires the needed new resources. This approach tends to work well only when the existing resources fit the business model, or can be transformed to align with it.

7. *Synergy mergers.* More mergers have been justified on the basis of presumed strategic or economic synergy than any other reason, but few measure up to the claims. News reporters tend to take it for granted that important synergies are part of every merger, and many of them can find synergies that require especially good eyesight to perceive. A synergy merger is one in which the capabilities of the two firms combine in such a way as to create advantages such as increasing revenue opportunities for one or both, leveraging assets belonging to one on behalf of the other, increasing customer access for one or both, building brand power, or creating customer value not offered by either alone. For example, two computer retailers with regional market dominance might merge to create a single mega-brand, with the possibility of national reach and national brand power. Truly synergistic mergers tend to offer the greatest threat to competitors because they can change the rules for competition, or at least change the competitive priorities. Compaq Computer Corporation's acquisition of Digital Equipment Corporation (DEC) promised significant synergy, because it brought together DEC's highly successful computer services capability with Compaq's strong product line.

8. *Efficiency mergers.* The most obviously justifiable mergers are those that reduce overcapacity in a crowded marketplace and create a single firm with the same total revenues and lower costs. This is often the case when competing banks with similar service areas merge. Instead of fighting tooth and nail for the same customers, with two sets of branch banks facing one another across every street corner, the result is one set of branches serving the same number of customers at vastly lower costs. In addition, the combined operation can make use of one infrastructure, one marketing process, one advertising message, and one brand image. When oil giants Exxon and Mobil announced plans to merge, at a time of historically low oil prices, their immediate focus was to reduce overall costs at the same level of combined revenues. Mergers that reduce capacity do not necessarily threaten other competitors in and of themselves. However, when merged firms enjoy unusual cost advantages, or become economically huge in terms of working capital and free cash flow, they can usually outspend their competitors on R&D, advertising, brand positioning, and expansion of product lines. In that case, the merger is not only beneficial for the shareholders of the firms involved, but a definite threat to their competitors.

Space does not permit a discussion of other significant aspects of merger impacts such as government regulatory actions, stock market valuations, and financing methods. However, from the standpoint of simple competitive effects, it is advisable to study the prospects for consolidation in your business sector very carefully. Merging could make sense for your firm under certain circumstances. And whether it does or not, the potential for mergers and acquisitions among your competitors can have a significant effect on your growth options. There is no need to panic every time a merger is announced, but it makes good sense to understand the effects of consolidation on the competitive dynamics of your particular business environment.

Branding: The Endless Battle for Mindshare

Few companies devote enough attention, energy, and resources to building and maintaining their brands, i.e., the psychological identity of their product in the mind of the customers. Aside from the super-brand companies that have achieved worldwide "top of mind" recognition, many others seem to think of brands as basic necessities of business but not as powerful competitive weapons.

Yet it is abundantly clear, everywhere you look, that brand recognition, once achieved, brings with it a host of advantages large and small. Brand awareness causes biases, both unconscious and overt, in customer buying habits. It makes selling easier. The existence of a few powerful brands in a particular sector usually forms a *de facto* barrier to entry for new competitors. In retailing, where shelf space is constantly allocated according to earning potential, branded products that create their own natural "demand pull" will always have the advantage over lesser-known products. In services, where perceived competence, trust, and reliability are often crucial, buyers tend to gravitate to known and trusted names.

As discussed in Chapter 6, "Your Customer Radar," it is important not to fall into thinking in terms of "customer loyalty," which I have argued doesn't exist. Brand preference is not a matter of loyalty; it is a matter of perceptual advantage.

According to the principle of self-reinforcing advantage, brand power is a major engine of profit, either because the brand leader can outprice its lesser-known competitors and thereby grow by volume, or because it can charge higher prices—sometimes known as the "brand tax"—and enjoy a better cost structure. At wholesale levels, the brand leader can usually demand better deals, or at least grant fewer concessions, to those who profit by moving its products.

Although the topic of branding deserves more attention than we can five it here, we must at least consider the role of brands and brand strategies in evaluating the competitive arena in any business sector. And it is worthwhile to rekindle a proper sense of awe and respect for the power of brand psychology.

If your firm enjoys the position of one of the brand leaders in a certain industry or category, you have a certain set of priorities and imperatives with regard to deploying the power of the brand for competitive advantage. If you are a lesser-known player, or a new entrant to the field, you have an entirely different set of priorities. However, being small or unknown does not mean that you cannot use brand-building principles and techniques to your advantage. Every firm, in every sector of business, should devote strenuous efforts to achieving whatever measure of brand power is feasible in its circumstances.

Building brand power, or coping with competitors who have it, requires a clear understanding of what a brand is and what it is not. According to marketing consultant Al Ries, many brand-conscious companies proceed from faulty theories about how branding actually works. According to his book, *The 22 Immutable Laws of Branding*, co-authored with Laura Ries:

> In the long run, a brand is nothing more than a name. Don't confuse what makes a brand successful in the short term with what makes a brand successful in the long term.
>
> In the short term, a brand needs a unique idea or concept to survive. It needs to be first in a new category. It needs to own a word in the mind. But in the long term, the unique idea or concept disappears. All that is left is the difference between your brand name and the brand names of your competitors.
>
> Xerox was the first plain-paper copier. This unique idea built the powerful Xerox brand in the mind. But today all copiers are plain-paper copiers. The difference between brands is not in the product, but in the *product names*. Or rather the perception of the names.[1]

This concept of a brand as a word seems so simple that it repels the mind. We are tempted to think of a brand as a complex idea, or a set of feelings on the part of the customer, or an overarching corporate identity behind it. But the process of *brand-building* is really the process of teaching customers to associate a word or phrase with some new or unique value proposition; the process of *brand-exploitation* is the process of using the brand name as a shorthand message to break through the noise and clutter of a crowded marketplace.

Many executives tend to confuse their brand identities with their company identities. A brand, and the concept behind it, should be narrow rather than broad. In fact, according to Ries, the narrower the focus of the brand's meaning in the mind of the customer, the stronger the brand becomes. Conversely, the broader the message the brand is expected to carry, the weaker it becomes. To cite another example:

> Think Chevrolet. What immediately comes to mind? Having trouble? It's understandable.
>
> Chevrolet is a large, small, cheap, expensive car...or truck. When you put your brand name on everything, that name loses its power.
>
> Chevrolet used to be the largest-selling automobile in America. In 1986, for example, the Chevrolet division of General Motors sold 1,718,839 cars. But trying to be all things to everyone undermined the power of the brand. Today Chevrolet sells less than a million cars per year and has fallen to second place in the market behind Ford.[2]

Ries also attacks the tendency of marketers to squander brand power with approaches such as *line extensions* and *mega-branding*. A line extension is a variation of the brand, aimed at a portion of the market not included in the original brand's definition in the mind of the buyer. For example, Mercedes-Benz has recently moved down-market with a relatively low-priced model, which risks contradicting the original idea of the marque as representing expensive engineering and quality. Volvo has introduced a sporty variation, a positioning that is unrelated to the powerful brand image of safety and durability it has always enjoyed.

AT&T has struggled for years to persuade Americans that it's something more interesting than a long-distance telephone company; it's in the peculiar position of trying to shake off a powerful brand identity, conferred on it by generations of customers. American Express has introduced a bewildering variety of credit cards with names that take off from the original. Levi Strauss, the firm that made "Levi's" synonymous with "blue jeans" has recently flirted with a wide range of fashions and styles that fuzz up the perception of a once-powerful brand name. The effect of line extensions, according to Ries, is to weaken the brand's selling power in the long term, for the sake of stealing sales from other sectors in the short term.

Mega-branding usually involves promoting a popular brand to the status of an umbrella symbol, with component brands tucked under it like satellites under a mother ship. In many cases, the customer can no longer associate the brand name with the original *value proposition*, e.g., a specific car, beverage, or telephone service. The marketer then faces the awesome task of trying to re-educate a large number of consumers to accept a diverse set of associations with the recognized brand name. This is what General Motors tried to do with the Chevrolet brand, what American Express tried with the concept of the "American Express Card," and what Disney has tried in recent years with its forays into broadcasting and even the Internet.

An important thing to remember in brand-building and brand-exploitation is the concept of *singularity*. There is a powerful tendency of the human mind to simplify and iconize complex ideas into simple symbols. A brand name is a *word* (or at most a simple phrase), one which evokes a specific, localized, self-centered idea of value in the mind of a prospective customer. Xerox means copier. Coca-Cola means soft drink. Volvo means a safe, durable, and dependable car. Waterford means fine crystal. Harley-Davidson means motorcycles. Winchester means guns.

Logos and other visual symbols may help to signal the value proposition in the mind of the customer, but "in the end is the word." For example, when you see the highly recognized black-and-yellow "K" symbol used by Kodak, you probably recognize it immediately, but a split second later, you probably hear your mind's voice saying "Kodak."

A second important thing to remember is that it's the customer who actually defines the brand, not the marketer. The brand perception is the association formed in the mind of the customer between a value proposition, such as discounted stock brokerage services, and a particular product entity, such as Charles Schwab. Brand psychology argues that Charles Schwab & Company is not the important entity in the mind of the value-conscious investor. To several million investors, "Schwab" means a particular experience of making investments and receiving information, not a company. Kodak is not a company—it's a film. Coke is not a company—it's a soft drink. McDonald's is not a company—it's a place to feed and amuse your kids cheaply. Confusing the brand perception with the identity of the company usually leads to mistakes in brand-exploitation.

The entertainment industry has had remarkable success with branding in movies. Disney, in particular, has perfected the art of branding a movie concept and marketing it as a total package. Popular children's movies such as *The Lion King* serve as models for the process of extending the brand identity to collateral products such as videos, T-shirts, toys, posters, lunchboxes, and almost every kind of impulse purchase imaginable. Its marketing alliances with McDonald's have given it enormous market reach at virtually no cost, as children encounter buying opportunities in each of the more than 10,000 burger shops.

The phenomenal commercial success of the movie *Titanic* made the ship's name an icon and an instant brand. The film generated well over $3 billion in revenue. The video version sold over sixty million copies, setting a new record. All over the English-speaking world, advertisers were trying to link their products to the *Titanic* brand; magazines turned out a tide of stories about the legendary young actor Leonardo DiCaprio; and TV producers found a hungry audience for a host of shows based on shipboard romances and sea tragedies. Cruise lines saw demand for cruise vacations skyrocket. Even *Moby Dick* enjoyed TV reruns.

A person can become a brand. This is particularly true of entertainers. Madonna is as much an economic entity as she is a person. The instant recognition of her name and the association of a set of social and cultural values to her role as a performer is the core concept of a "Madonna industry." Elvis Presley was, and still is, a legendary commercial brand. Mystery-horror writer Stephen King has become a brand. Evidence for this is the fact that his name usually appears on the book cover in letters larger than those used for the title. Publishers fight for the privilege of paying millions of dollars to publish stories he hasn't even invented. The remarkable success of young golf star Tiger Woods made him an instant brand, with the commercial power to sell all sorts of products. His name itself is a perfect brand name.

A memorable name can be a natural asset. No U.S. president has ever had an unpronounceable name. Would you go to see a movie starring an actor whose name is Marion Morrison? You have if you've ever seen a John Wayne film. Which is the more memorable name, Leonard Slye or Roy Rogers? You may not recognize Nathan Birnbaum as a famous comedian, but you probably know him by his stage name: George Burns. You may not recognize a comedian named Allen Konigsberg, but you may know him as Woody Allen. Your brand name is the stage name of your product.

One the biggest and most successful human brands of all time is the American basketball star Michael Jordan. His performances for the Chicago Bulls team increased attendance well above the levels enjoyed by competing teams, brought tourist revenue to Chicago, and increased the economic value of the team franchise to astronomical levels. The saddest people on the day he announced his retirement from the game, at the peak of his career at age 34, were the team owners and the army of business operators who had marketed Jordan merchandise. By some estimates Jordan, as a one-man brand, represented a $10 billion industry over the span of his career.

Curiously, however, Jordan's short stint as a professional baseball player was a commercial flop by any measure. His status as a legendary basketball player had virtually no carryover value in the minds of baseball fans. Few sport fans in America can even remember the name of the team he briefly joined, or what position he played.

A third key truth of branding, just illustrated, is that every brand has a certain range of meaning in the mind of the customer. Trying to stretch the marketing message beyond the limits of this *brand envelope* is to risk confusing the customer and undermining confidence in the brand.

Many entertainment celebrities have learned the hard way that celebrity status is very specific, and often not portable. A number of Hollywood figures have dabbled in businesses unrelated to their commercial identities, only to find themselves no more blessed than any other competitors in their chosen industries. Actors Bruce Willis, Demi Moore, Arnold Schwarzenegger, and others backed the extravagant Planet Hollywood restaurants, most of which lost money. Actor Tom Selleck and partners closed their Black Orchid restaurant in Honolulu when it could not compete for the limited "carriage trade" clientele in the islands. Famed producer Steven Spielberg even tried his hand with a deep-sea-themed restaurant in Los Angeles named Dive!, which sank without a ripple.

Even within an industry such as entertainment, a brand envelope can be very narrowly defined. Mega-stars such as Sylvester Stallone and Arnold Shwarzenegger, and other type-cast adventure actors have failed spectacularly when they have tried to reach into other genres within the movie industry, especially comedy. Once moviegoing customers develop an iconic recognition of Sylvester Stallone or Steven Segal as a muscular, monosyllabic, one-man killing machine, they don't seem willing to think of him as funny.

Consumer research techniques can help you define the envelopes of various brands and compare customer perceptions of your brand with perceptions of those of your competitors. These techniques can apply just as well to a service firm as to the more conventional packaged goods products.

The technique of *semantic profiling*, for example, involves presenting a group of customers with a set of adjectives that could plausibly describe various aspects of the brand or brands under investigation. The customers participating in the research simply select the adjectives they think best apply to each of the competing brands or companies, for example "refreshing," "convenient," "friendly," "efficient," "economical," "trusted," or "exciting." By graphing the frequency scores of the various adjectives, one can draw a visual profile that uniquely describes the psychological envelope of the brand. By overlaying the profiles of competing brands, one can quickly discover gaps, disparities, inconsistencies, or key differences that can help to clarify, redefine, or reposition a brand against its competition.

The point of this discussion of brand psychology is simply that all business leaders, and particularly those who are not fortunate to enjoy the status of mega-brand owners, need to understand the dynamics of branding in their competitive environments, and to incorporate brand thinking into their competitive strategies.

A smaller player can work to create a new category or subcategory in which to plant a flag. By spotting the progressive weakening of a dominant brand, the smaller firm may be able to take action to strengthen its own. And, in any case, the firm's leaders can map a competitive strategy that has a realistic chance of succeeding, based on a clear understanding of the marketing power structure in its industry.

The Struggle for Differentiation

If the David and Goliath scenario continues to become the model for competition in most industries, then the competitive strategies and priorities will be radically different for the two kinds of players. Goliaths have one set of strengths, weapons, and tactics, while Davids have a different set. In the simplest terms, your competitive radar screen will tend to show Goliaths as becoming ever more capital-oriented, cost-focused, and inclined toward standardizing the customer experience, with the Davids becoming ever more value-oriented and focused on creating a different and preferable customer experience.

Review the recent developments in industries such as banking, insurance, brokerages, air travel, and telecommunications and you'll see a steady trend toward an emphasis on asset structure as the primary competitive weapon among the larger firms. The era of "customer service," at least for the larger dominant firms, seems to have faded. It may be fertile ground for the smaller and mid-sized firms, but they will have to do such a good job at it that they can offset some of the advantages of size and deep pockets.

Over the long run, notwithstanding the biblical story that favored David, the Goliaths tend to win. This is largely because they are financially able to offer the customers a bigger and better package of choices at lower prices, or at least at lower costs, which gives them the self-reinforcing advantage previously discussed. When the Davids win, or at least survive and thrive by staying out from under the feet of the Goliaths, it is usually because they have created some kind of differentiation they can use to create sufficient customer preference to allow them to profit and grow.

Building and defending a niche can be a ticket to long-term success. Sotheby's, the famous 200-year-old auction house, is virtually without peer when it comes to moving the assets and artifacts of the rich and famous. Harrods, the quintessentially English department store, has used its commission as provider to the royal family as its badge of aristocracy for many years.

But the famous and legendary firms aren't the only ones who can take advantage of niche thinking. A surprising number of clever or unusual value concepts demonstrate that it's possible for the Davids to stay out from under the feet of the Goliaths.

Case in point: A small British firm, AirFoyle, acquired an unusual airplane from the Ukrainian military forces, who could no longer make good use of it after the Cold War thawed. The craft, an Antonov 124, was an ultra-heavy lift cargo plane, one of a few created by the famous Antonov Design Bureau in its heyday. This flying monster has a hinged nose and tail section, both of which swing up to reveal a giant tunnel-like cargo bay complete with overhead cranes. It can carry up to 150 tons of people, equipment, or machinery. For transporting certain kinds of objects, such as huge statues, monuments, rocket bodies, and things of awkward size and shape, it has no equal. The firm makes its plane available to clients all over the world who need to move difficult things, and who gladly pay its asking price for a service they can get nowhere else.

Case in point: Shouldice Hospital in Toronto has established a worldwide reputation since 1945 as the best place to go for one particular kind of surgery: inguinal hernia repair, the only kind it offers. How can a hospital survive and thrive on a single surgical procedure? Its founder, Dr. Edward Earle Shouldice, distinguished himself by repairing hernias for young men who would otherwise be disqualified for military service in World War II. By the end of the war, his reputation was already well established. He and those who came after him concentrated on becoming the world's best practitioners of that one procedure. Shouldice is recognized throughout the world at the place to go for hernia repair.

Case in point: How about a firm like 1-800-AUTOPSY? The steadily declining use of autopsies in America, and in most developed countries, has caused medical associations and other advocates to call for an increase in the practice. Autopsies, from the medical point of view, are useful in gathering medical statistics, discovering unknown disorders, evaluating the accuracy of medical diagnoses and treatments, training medical students, and detecting medical malpractice. Medical plans and managed care companies have steadily cut back on autopsies, so much so that in some cities the percentage of autopsies has fallen to one-fifth their number in 1960.

In response to the American Medical Association's appeal for more autopsies, Mr. Vidal Herrera founded Autopsy/Post Services. Equipped with vans and mobile autopsy gear, he performs over 800 autopsies per year and plans to franchise his service in 72 American cities and 16 foreign countries.[3]

Of course, large firms can also benefit by concentrating intensely on differentiation. Companies such as Disney have created one-of-a-kind customer experiences that set them apart from their competitors, and indeed even put them into a category all their own. Nordstrom Corporation has given its department stores a special "signature" style of service and merchandising, which they have used to great competitive advantage.

The lesson in a nutshell is: if you're big and dominant in your sector, you can compete on the basis of asset strength, but if you're small, you must be agile, well-focused, and differentiated in a way that creates customer preference and offsets the limitations of size. Some firms have been able to do both. Few can survive by doing neither.

Notes

1. Ries, Al and Laura Ries. *The 22 Immutable Laws of Branding*. New York: HarperBusiness, 1998, page 74. Contact the authors through their Web site at ries.com.
2. Ibid., page 9.
3. "1-800-Autopsy," *The Economist*, January 2, 1999, page 29.

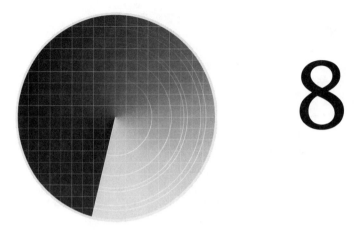

8

Your Economic Radar

Business is what, if you don't have, you go out of.
— Jewish merchant's proverb

The purpose of the economic radar is to understand the economic factors that can create or destroy opportunities to grow your business.

The economic radar, in particular, is one whose signals cross over the imaginary boundaries of the other radars. Many issues are not solely economic, solely political, or solely legal, for example. As with each of the radars, we must be careful to avoid getting caught up in categorical thinking, and to trace the issues freely across all boundaries.

The Big Shift: Intangible Economies

Virtually all of the major economies of the world have been undergoing a profound shift since the 1950s and 1960s, and, in fact, as far back as the 1900s. This has been most noticeable in the US economy, but the others are all moving in the same direction. The sustained growth in consumer economies, despite occasional recessions, has made possible a standard of living in which people can enjoy a range of services not previously available, or even possible.

As economies pass through their "agricultural period" into their "industrial period," they become more and more efficient at producing "things," i.e., durable goods and various tangible products. This increases overall productivity and liberates human energy and talent (formerly called "labor") for the creation of additional value. This additional value often takes the form of personal and professional services, as well as public services. Education gets better, more widely available, and more cost-effective. Sectors like healthcare, publishing, entertainment, education, travel and hospitality, financial services, insurance, law enforcement, and many others can grow and flourish as the "Thing Economy" delivers its value at ever-lower costs.

This "productivity engine" is really quite astonishing in its effect. Consider that, in 1900, about seventy percent of the U.S. workforce engaged in farming. By the early 1990s, fewer than three percent of the workforce was producing enough to feed a population that had grown to more than three times its size in 1900, as well as exporting food to much of the rest of the world. This has led to a profound shift in the American economy, and a similar trend in all of the other developed economies of the world, as shown in Figure 8-1.

For example, although many people like to think of the American economy as an industrial economy, and many Americans take pride in their country's historical leadership in manufacturing, as of the mid-1990s fewer than fifteen percent of the jobs in the U.S. workforce directly involved manufacturing.

The profound structural shift in the American and other developed economies toward a service structure, i.e., a "nonthing economy," has presented economists and government statisticians with a difficult problem: how to measure and classify economic activity that has no physical output? Increasingly, the old boundary lines that have separated economic sectors seem to be dissolving, or making less sense, especially the stereotypical categories of "manufacturing" and "service."

For example, economists can't decide whether to classify the printing business as a manufacturing industry or a service industry. On one hand, it involves machinery, raw material, and finished products. On the other, it involves an added value

Figure 8-1. The Big Shift.

US Economy 1900-2000

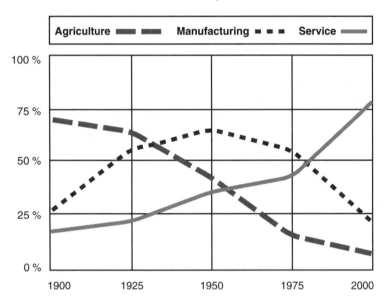

operation defined by applying information to the raw material. A catalog marketing firm may never see the raw materials involved in its operation. It provides the computer files that define the graphic layout of the catalog, and the mailing firm handles the setup and prepress operation, prints the catalogs, applies mailing labels created by its computer equipment, and delivers the catalogs to the government postal center.

Traditional measures of output seem to make little sense for many business operations. For example, economists can estimate the value of inventories held by manufacturing firms, but what is the "inventory" of a hospital? A bank? An airline? How should we measure the productivity of a university? A police force? An online news service? Does the concept of return on capital make sense when the primary asset is merely information?

Another peculiar aspect of the shift toward intangible economies is the difficulty in measuring imports and exports, and indeed even defining them. Can a service be exported? If it is consumed in one country by people visiting temporarily from another country, does it count as domestic commerce or an exported service?

For example, suppose a business person in Canada subscribes to a magazine such as *The Economist*, which is published in England. Should the statisticians count the value of the copies mailed to Canada under exports, deducting it from the figures for the domestic market? Suppose the same customer downloads information, for a fee, from the publisher's Web site. Should the publisher report the revenue from foreign customers as exports? With a larger and larger fraction of commerce involving the movement of information, government measures of economic activity become progressively less precise.

As another example, consider that the U.S. has over 1,000,000 foreign students residing there at any given time. Each one spends thousands of dollars for lodging, food, clothing, books, entertainment, and all the other expenses of studenthood. Although the products and services each student buys are consumed locally, they are sold to a foreign person. What defines a transaction as an export, the place where it is consumed or the person who consumes it? Do government economists count the university tuition fees paid by foreign students as exports or as domestic purchases? The same question obviously applies to purchases made by tourists in any particular country which amount to many billions of dollars annually.

More and more, business people have to think beyond the old artificial boundaries—boundaries between "industries," commercial sectors, governments, nations, and economic regions. Commerce always outruns the ability of governments to describe, measure, influence, and regulate it.

As the developed economies become increasingly knowledge-based, the educational status of their workforces becomes ever more critical. As information technology develops, it works both for and against the economic opportunity of workers. On the one hand, it enables lower-skilled workers to fill jobs they could not otherwise handle by down-skilling the required knowledge and cognitive skills involved.

For example, a person with limited schooling, or indeed even a mildly retarded person, can learn to operate a cash register in a fast-food restaurant just by pushing the keys that have pictures or symbols representing the various products. If the job required them to add up prices and total the customer's order with a pen and paper, as was the case a few decades ago, many of them would not qualify. This opens opportunities to those with minimal education and cognitive skills.

On the other hand, the information technology that drives the down-skilling of labor demands a higher level of skill on the part of other workers, the ones who develop it. People who write software, set up accounting systems, maintain and repair computers, operate corporate networks, and interpret data are more and more in demand. Technology will create opportunities for both high-skilled and low-skilled workers, but the gap between the two will become ever wider. This means that those at the upper end of the bell curve of information skills will benefit proportionately more than those at the lower end. Economic growth in all of the developed countries will be increasingly paced by the capacity of their educational systems to produce people with strong information skills.

Economics as a Behavioral Science

It has always seemed to me that economics, as a science or an attempt at science, has been put together all wrong. This may be one reason why so few people feel they understand it, and why so many economic pronouncements create confusion rather than relieve it.

Economics should be a behavioral science, not a mathematical science. It should deal directly with the attitudes, feelings, and actions of people, not the indirect consequences of their actions. Probably because most university professors and academic researchers prefer to express theories in abstract, mechanistic terms, with support from statistics and calculations whenever possible, the study of economics has been constructed as if people and their behavior were not part of the discussion.

This mechanistic tradition has completely infected the business press as well as the popular press. It appears most clearly and tellingly in the vocabulary newswriters and newsreaders use to explain things. There is a nearly universal tendency to describe economic activity using a vocabulary normally used for objects, machines, or figurative creatures.

For example, a news report may describe a nation's economy as "overheating," its currency as being "battered by international turmoil," and its stock market as "needing a breather." One description evokes an image of something like a steam boiler, another the idea of a bruised prizefighter. The last metaphor evokes the image of a stock market as an animal, perhaps a racehorse.

American newswriters are fond of referring to "Wall Street" in terms that might suggest an emotionally unstable human being, or at least a creature with humanoid tendencies. They may say "Wall Street turned gloomy today...," or "Wall Street was bursting with confidence...," meaning presumably that the people buying and selling stocks on Wall Street felt that way. They describe "the market"—whatever that is—as being "nervous," or "gripped with fear," or "in a wait-and-see mode," or "searching for direction," as if referring to some excitable creature.

This tendency to objectify complex forms of human behavior, and to displace the discussion of them to the vocabulary of things, is not wrong in the purely semantic sense. However, it does tend to discourage a more precise manner of describing and explaining what people do, which could help us make more sense out of what's happening.

For example, the phrase "Wall Street staged a rally today..." completely obscures the otherwise obvious fact that people were *selling* stocks as well as buying them. Why were the sellers parting with shares at exactly the same prices buyers were willing to pay to acquire them? Presumably the expression means that the buyers paid the sellers higher prices on average than other buyers paid other sellers the day before.

Using a machine or a metaphorical creature as a surrogate for people's actions leads to another important type of fuzzy thinking. It blurs an important distinction between two different kinds of people who are doing the buying and selling. News reports often refer to "investors" as if they were all basically the same. In truth, all stock market activity involves two very different kinds of actors: investors and traders. Investors are individuals who occasionally buy and sell securities as investments, using their own money and taking their own risks. Traders are paid professionals who use large amounts of other people's money to buy and sell securities on a daily basis.

Sudden, large swings in share prices are almost always caused by traders, not individual investors. These are mutual fund managers and managers of other large portfolios who trade billions of dollars worth of stock each day. They respond to hourly news events, earnings reports, government announcements, and momentary price changes.

Yet many newswriters imply with their vocabulary that "mom and pop" are the ones who are causing the instability, because of their supposed naiveté and emotional reactiveness. In truth, mom and pop don't sit at a computer screen watching financial news reports all day and reacting to the latest release of government unemployment figures. Most of them are busy making a living, and they may check the prices of their holdings every few days, not every few minutes. They are much less likely to sell on bad news or buy on rumor than the so-called professional managers are. In most cases, the swings are over before they discover they've happened.

Financial newswriters also tend to refer to currencies with mechanical metaphors, for example, "the Thai baht fell sharply against the dollar today...," which actually means that many more people placed orders to convert baht to dollars than orders to convert dollars to baht. Or it could mean that currency speculators, a peculiar breed of investors, sold large quantities of baht in anticipation of actions by other actors that would lead to unbalances in supply and demand.

They may further confuse themselves and their readers when they speak of the risk that "the Hong Kong dollar could pull other Asian currencies down with it." Can you picture these currencies as nasty little creatures like crabs in a barrel, clawing at one another and pulling one another down? What does a currency look like when it's been "battered"? Is it ready to be deep-fried?

Even expert economists who should know better can fall into this sloppy and potentially misleading style of description. In a recent issue of a well-known investment newsletter published in America, a columnist chided the Federal Reserve's chairman, Alan Greenspan, for taking certain actions that he felt resulted in a too-rapid growth in the U.S. money supply. The writer noted that Greenspan had gone on a binge of "printing money." In another part of the article he reported that "the Fed has been running the printing presses night and day." An intelligent reader, unfamiliar with the Fed's activities, could easily get the impression that the organization was literally printing paper money and sending it out into the world. The Fed does no such thing.

The Federal Reserve, and typically most other central banks, have only two ways to increase the supply of money. One way is to cut the interest rate it charges to member banks (and the rates banks charge one another) for the money they borrow from it, enabling them to borrow more money and lend it out. This puts more money in circulation. The other way it can increase the money supply is to buy government bonds on the open market, thereby putting some of the money it holds into circulation.

To reduce the money supply, or slow its growth, it can increase those same interest rates or sell some of the government bonds it holds, thereby taking money out of circulation. Aside from certain other methods too technical to explain here, these are the primary ways a central bank can affect the money supply of its parent country. It does not literally print money, and the economist who wrote the article in question is guilty of incompetent use of metaphors.

If you'd like to try a curious exercise, read a typical article from the business news and underline every word or expression that uses a mechanical or animistic metaphor to describe some economic activity. For each one, try to restate the underlying information in terms of human behavior. What did certain people do to cause the result? If a stock "rose" or "fell," try to explain who did what. If a currency "showed strength" or "lost ground," try to explain the actual behavior that led to the price changes. In some cases, you might find that the clever metaphorical description fails the test of common sense. Something that seems to make sense in metaphorical language may make less sense when translated into the simple language of behavior and cause and effect.

I'm not suggesting that we outlaw all mechanical figures of speech from economic discussion. However, I do assert that the careless use of metaphor and slang instead of more specific descriptions of human economic behavior leads to a sense of fuzziness and imprecision in explaining cause and effect. And when we are tempted to use one set of metaphors as logical inputs to a thinking process that is expressed in other metaphors, we run the risk of being not only inaccurate but, in some cases, actually wrong.

You may find it worthwhile to train yourself to use operational and behavioral language more carefully and consciously in describing the economic factors that affect your business. It might very well keep the discussion focused more clearly on the primary drivers you need to track and understand.

Domino Economics: The Knee Bone's Connected to...

The more you study the business environment, the more it becomes obvious and intuitively plausible that "everything affects everything else." Everybody does business with somebody, and whatever affects anybody will have a domino effect on somebody else. Having a clear sense of this interconnectedness can help you interpret the picture on your economic radar screen and trace the chains of cause-and-effect that eventually reach your enterprise.

For example, how do falling oil prices increase the profits of United Parcel Service (UPS)? Well, when you consider that UPS is actually one of the largest airlines in the world, i.e., it operates a fleet of more than 250 planes, and that aviation fuel is one of its biggest operating costs, the domino connection becomes obvious.

A drop in customer orders and revenues experienced by a major manufacturer, such as Boeing Aircraft Corporation, affects not only the firm itself, but virtually all of the suppliers who do business with the firm. When customers buy fewer airplanes, the firm buys less paint, fewer tires, less electrical wire, fewer radars, less fabric for seats, fewer communication systems, less plastic, fewer autopilots, less aluminum, fewer windshields, and on *ad infinitum*. Firms like Boeing, General Motors, and 3M Corporation have tens of thousands of suppliers of various sizes. All of them feel the effects of any major change in the sales of these mega-customers.

The world's second biggest exporter of poultry, the Asian conglomerate C.P. Pokphand, experienced a sudden drop in sales because Brazil's government allowed the price of its currency, the *real*, to decline in value against other currencies. That action gave Brazil's poultry industry, the world's largest, an advantage by repricing its products lower, as measured in other currencies, than before.

A major strike by the employees of one firm can create immediate undeserved benefits for its competitors. When UPS had its first strike in many years, early in 1998, one of the biggest beneficiaries was the U.S. Postal Service (USPS). In recent years, the USPS has been actively competing with private-sector firms for rapid-mail and parcel services. It went from a stodgy, unresponsive model for poor public service to a quasi-commercial operation that even advertises on TV. When news of the impending UPS strike first began to circulate, thousands of firms of various sizes whose businesses depended on shipping packages to their customers began to turn to the USPS, Federal Express, DHL, Rodeway Express, and others.

Even more important, some of those customers who abandoned UPS during the strike never came back. A major dislocation such as a strike or a materials shortage can sometimes cause a permanent or long-lasting shift in market share or market structure.

Of course, changes in society can cause domino effects that create new industries or business opportunities. The increasing atomization of society, coupled with public fear about crime, is driving unprecedented growth in lines of business such as home security. Industrial theft, sabotage, and espionage are driving demand for plant security, asset safeguarding, executive protection, and data security. Workplace violence drives increasing demand for assistance in dealing with employee problems. Increasing concern about ecological issues drives growth in waste disposal services and special methods for handling toxic waste.

If your firm is one of the major players in its sector, it is wise to keep your radar tuned for special opportunities that might arise as a result of your competitors' misjudgments or misfortunes. Conversely, it makes sense to pay close attention to the kinds of events that might befall your organization and create undeserved advantages for your competitors. A labor strike is not just a conflict between your firm and a union; it also involves your competitors, as UPS learned the hard way.

If you are one of the smaller or mid-sized firms in a particular sector, your competitor radar should be tuned for events or trends that could change the competitive dynamics of the major players. In some cases, a shift in the power structure among the alpha players might threaten your firm's opportunities; in other cases, it might work to your advantage.

Death-Row Economics: Industries Slated for Destruction

The demand for typewriters just isn't what it used to be. Vinyl LP records only sell well in antique shops and collectors' stores. The encyclopedia salesman was put out of business by the CD-ROM. The Boy Scouts, Girl Scouts, and a wide range of service clubs have experienced steadily declining membership; some have gone extinct. Church attendance in the U.S. and many other industrialized countries has been declining for many years. Over time, structural changes in societies, economies, and industries cause the basic appeal of certain value propositions to go into permanent and irreversible decline.

If your firm operates in such a business sector, you are probably well aware of it. However, what about the possibility that changes that are now barely visible may eventually cause such a decline in a business sector that seems healthy, or at least not in jeopardy? Suppose your line of business, or your most important customers' line of business, is headed for decline? How do you detect the early warning signals at the point of inflection, as Intel's chairman Andy Grove calls it, and how do you interpret them?

A whole industry, or a category, goes into decline either because the value proposition on which it operates loses its appeal or because the value can be delivered by other means in a way that is more attractive to the majority of customers. The macro-trends described in Chapter 3, "The New Realities of Business," i.e., globalism, cheap information, and deconstruction, can all create impacts that can destroy businesses and whole industries.

Cheap information is the business killer most often mentioned in the press recently, and possibly one of the most devastating. As will be discussed further in Chapter 9, "Your Technological Radar," the availability of cheap and abundant information will destroy some businesses and create others. Although many observers dwell on the marvels of "digital technology," the technology itself is relatively unimportant. Cheaper, faster, and ubiquitous computers are simply the means for making information cheap and abundant. The Internet and the Web page concept for structuring information, although fascinating developments in their own right, are simply schemes for deploying information more cheaply and abundantly. It is the cheap and abundant information that is destroying and creating opportunities, not the digital technology that manipulates it.

Any business sector or category that has traditionally depended for revenue on the control of information is probably in serious jeopardy. Whenever the relationship between customer and provider is based on privileged access to information on the part of the supplier and a dependent need for that information on the part of the customer, the tendency for information costs to fall steadily can radically change the customer's options.

Specifically, almost any business or person operating under the label of "agent" or "broker" has serious cause for concern. The traditional full-service stock brokerage, for example, has always charged substantial fees for executing stock transactions but has represented them as an inseparable part of a presumed added-value relationship between the investor-customer and the professional broker. Supposedly, the customer or client received advice, assistance, and valuable information not otherwise available as part of the relationship.

However, with the advent of discount trading offered by firms such as Charles Schwab and various Internet brokers, clients have been "unbundling" the service product and buying it in separate pieces. By calling a discount brokerage, an investor can place a trade for a fraction of the cost previously charged by the so-called full-service brokerage. The client gets no advice or special information as part of the transaction, but many clients say they got little support of that type from the broker in the past.

Further, by signing on to a Web site, the client can not only place trades at ever-lower discount prices but can also pull down huge amounts of useful financial information for free. The sharp rise in online investing, and investing activity in general among computer-using adults, has been triggered largely by the ready availability of free stock market information.

Instead of having to wade through pages of microscopic newsprint to pull out daily stock prices of the firms they are following, investors can now get a complete list of prices and associated performance factors quickly and at no cost. An investor can now easily follow stock market performance, literally on an hourly basis.

Stockbrokers now have to face the daunting prospect of persuading clients that they do indeed add value by what they do, and that paying them high fees for something—whether it's executing trades, giving advice, or providing special information—is in the best interests of the clients. It has become a tough sell, and it's getting tougher all the time.

Unfortunately, many online investors will only succeed in shrinking their assets faster and more cheaply by trying to outguess the markets with their newfound trading power. The value issue is not how cheaply one can trade securities but how effectively one can choose what to buy and when, and what to sell and when. Many online investors will learn the hard way that low trading costs are an invitation to destroy capital. Those who do may well turn back to consultative relationships with financial advisors who can support their self-reliant style of investing with valuable advice, education, and counseling.

Travel agents are another endangered species. As information technology has enabled airlines to reduce their "distribution" costs, i.e., the costs associated with taking reservations, collecting the customers' money, and issuing tickets, they have less and less use for travel agents. With the trend toward electronic tickets, they hope to eliminate completely the costs associated with printing tickets and physically distributing them to the customers. They have also been promoting online sales of tickets, i.e., direct sales through the Internet, although these sales represent a very small fraction of total revenues so far.

With each new application of information technology, the potential economic added value supplied by travel agents diminishes. It seems clear that all major airlines intend to bypass or eliminate travel agencies from the distribution system eventually, as soon as they can reduce their costs to a level lower than the costs of using the agencies to sell and distribute tickets.

But perhaps the greatest appeal to the airline companies of bypassing travel agencies is in changing the triangular relationship between the airline, the customer, and the agency, and making it a simple two-party direct relationship. The greatest impediment to airline pricing freedom has always been the huge number of agencies—30,000 in the U.S. alone—who are constantly shopping all airlines for the lowest possible fares for their clients, the people who want to fly. Travel agencies use sophisticated "fare shopper" software programs and little-known scheduling tricks that allow them to keep working the fares down, even after the ticket is sold. Without this constant pressure on prices, airlines are likely to gain much greater pricing power, because relatively few customers will be tenacious enough to call many carriers for price quotes or visit a great number of Web sites looking for the best fares.

Another distinctly American sector at risk for demolition by information technology is the real estate finance industry. This is a cartel of service businesses that has long antagonized its customers with high fees and miscellaneous charges, as well as mountains of red tape and condescending treatment of both buyer and seller. In order for a residence to change hands in America, the buyer and seller will typically spend a total of $7,000 to $10,000 in loan fees and "closing costs." A typical uncomplicated deal will involve as many as one hundred pages or more of documents and various fees with mysterious names such as "loan origination fee," "administrative fee," "documentation fee," "recording fee," "appraisal fee," "title search fee," and "escrow fee." Frequently, the bank making the loan receives a commission on these fees from the specialty firms it chooses to do the work.

Further, most banks play psychological games with prospective borrowers, dragging them through detailed and time-consuming documentation and credit investigation processes. Inasmuch as most buy-sell transactions take place against a deadline—at the instigation of helpful real estate brokers who want to push the sale through as quickly as possible—the prospective borrower usually receives the terms offered by the bank so late in the process that he or she has no time to seek competing offers. It simply isn't feasible for the customer to go through the application process with more than one lender. Very few buyers or sellers get through a real estate deal without feeling exploited and resentful. Most of the firms in the real estate cartel fully deserve the collective image they have as manipulators and exploiters.

With the popularity of the Internet, lenders are now being forced to compete against one another more transparently by disclosing rates and terms on the Web sites where they advertise. The first casualty of online lending will probably be the mortgage brokers who collect thousands of dollars in commissions, paid by the borrower, and do little more than make a few telephone calls and help with the documentation.

The second casualty of online lending will probably be the administrative service firms who run the red-tape mill. Banks will be forced by competition to disclose itemized estimates of all closing costs. It will probably only be a matter of time before they find themselves offering packages with guaranteed or fixed closing costs and using suppliers who can provide the services for less.

And, of course, the venerable real estate agent may become an endangered species. It is highly likely that bulletin-board-type real estate listings will proliferate within cities or communities, in which buyers and sellers can find one another without paying big commissions to brokers. The new term of art in real estate may well be "FISBO," which is agent slang for "For Sale By Owner." To the extent that the firms in the real estate business fail to offer a significant economic added value in return for the fees they charge, newly liberated customers will feel free to seek value and reduce their costs by making their own connections.

Information technology is not the only macro-trend that will destroy or eclipse whole industries or lines of business. And, of course, it will create new ones as well. Actually, the world of cheap information will require more middlemen, not fewer. With an unmanageable glut of information and no easy way to separate it by usefulness or validity, we will probably see a new generation of information organizers and advisers.

Librarians may enjoy a newfound role as information consultants, leaving behind their traditional image as custodians of books. Stockbrokers, travel agents, and real estate brokers who can show their customers real value as a result of their superior knowledge, judgment, and ability to marshal information may be able to reinvent their businesses and possibly succeed even better than before. For those who can't, however, the business prospects seem ever more uncertain.

Economic "Weather" Factors: How They Affect Your Business

As you review the macro-economic environment to see how it affects your business, you typically have to consider at least five overall "weather" factors, i.e., the vital signs of overall economic strength of the national economy in which your business makes its home. To the extent that you do business in a number of economies, you of course have to make the same analysis for each of them. And to the extent that your major customers are businesses, you also need to understand how the economic weather factors are affecting their operations.

As with certain other topics, I will apologize in advance to expert readers who are intimately familiar with economic analysis, who may find this discussion a bit elementary for their needs. However, it seems fair to provide a brief summary for those who are not.

Five key economic weather variables you have to consider are:

GDP, or gross domestic product, growth. The overall rate of growth, or contraction, of the host economy signals the general level of economic energy, buying power, and typically consumer activity. As the proverb has it, a rising tide lifts all boats. And conversely, a falling tide typically makes it more difficult to sail any one boat. Clearly, a growing GDP tends to favor starting a new business, growing an existing one, or doing business with other firms in the same environment. A declining GDP not only tends to dry up demand for most firms' offerings but often a kind of recession mentality can depress demand, especially for highly discretionary purchases.

Employment levels. At or near the so-called level of full employment, i.e., the level at which almost all qualified and motivated people have jobs, barring a statistical number who are in transition, most firms do not experience intolerable economic effects. However, when employment is very high and economic growth continues to create additional jobs, some firms may have more and more difficulty filling their best jobs. In the late stages of an economic expansion, the last-hired workers tend to be the marginal ones, lacking in education, skills, and work attitudes. In the past few decades, labor shortages tend to be most acute among the higher-skilled jobs, including professionals. Healthcare and information technology are two areas in which firms find it increasingly difficult to find qualified people. A number of firms have had to curtail growth plans or revise their competitive strategies to some extent because they haven't been able to locate the needed talent. In recent years, the U.S. Congress has increased quotas for immigrant workers who have special qualifications such as computer and software design. Conversely, as unemployment levels increase, firms tend to worry because fewer gainfully employed people means fewer customers for the goods and services being produced. This is why many economists make a strong case for a full-employment policy.

Interest rates. Here, too, we have a double-edged sword. High interest rates make it difficult for consumers to finance major purchases such as houses and the things that go into them, making it difficult for firms selling these kinds of goods—and the firms that do business with them—to grow through demand. Higher rates also make it more costly for companies to find capital for investment or expansion. And, of course, some firms benefit or suffer directly from changes in interest rates because of the very nature of their business activity; this includes banks, insurance companies, and various kinds of financial service firms. Conversely, lower interest rates free up capital for investment and growth.

Inflation. Inflation is a widely misunderstood concept, and many newswriters contribute to the misunderstanding. Broad-scale inflation, i.e., a generalized rise in prices throughout a country, is caused by money corruption. As governments and central banks send money into circulation, banks create even more money by recirculating it. More money offered for the available goods and services causes prices to rise. Because a price is basically a signal in a complex communication system, rising prices confuse the signal system and cause confusion and distortions. Businesses that are not free to increase their prices and people whose compensation is not price-flexible are the ones who suffer. Those who have fixed-income securities such as bonds, annuities, retirement payments, bank deposits, and the like see the buying power of their assets decline as other prices rise. Another myth is that full employment causes inflation. Without an increase in the money supply, as just explained, inflation can only be local and selective. That is, if unions can force higher labor costs on the host companies, these increased costs will be paid at the expense of other purchases or investments that will not be made. It is not possible, as many journalists believe or imply, for rising labor costs to trigger generalized inflation. Nor does a rising stock market cause inflation; it simply attracts capital from other sectors of the economy. Some sectors, such as information technology and, more recently, oil, have experienced deflation, allowing capital to move to other sectors. As with many environmental drivers, inflation tends to be selective in its effects.

Currency exchange rates. Imbalances in trade amongst various countries contribute to variations in the exchange rates between their respective currencies. These variations can significantly influence prices and costs of doing business. This particular topic deserves a special mini-lesson, which is provided in the next section.

There are, of course, many other economic parameters that influence the growth prospects of a particular firm, such as tax laws, costs of patent rights, licensing costs, franchising costs, regulatory costs, and the like. Some of them are generalized and others are quite specific to the type of business. In addition to the five key factors described here, the executive team has to consider the full range of variables that can drive its own environment. Taking all of these together, they can then develop a profit model that can help them think about strategic options and priorities.

How Currency Exchange Rates Affect Business Performance

Many business people are baffled by the effects of currency exchange rates and have difficulty understanding the connections between exchange rates, international trade, and profits. They hear the newsreader report that the Italian lira "strengthened" against the German mark, or that the Japanese yen "lost ground" to the U.S. dollar. They hear that a country's "weaker" currency favors its exports to other countries, but many don't clearly grasp what's being said. Very few news reports or articles in business magazines explain the logic of exchange rates, possibly because the writers assume everyone understands the subject, or maybe they feel it's just too hard to explain. Possibly, some of them don't understand it themselves.

Actually, it's fairly simple. Here again, I appeal to the expert reader for patience if he or she finds the following discussion a bit elementary. However, I believe it is appropriate for many business people who don't have that level of expertise.

If you want to buy a product from a producer in a foreign country, you first have to buy the currency of that country, and then use the foreign currency to buy the product. Conversely, if a business in another country wants to buy your product, you want to receive payment in your home currency. The simple reason is that native businesses operating within any particular country buy and sell in their own national currency. This obvious reality may be obscured in the chain of events that's visible to you, but it can have a big impact on the economics of your business.

For example, suppose you operate a luxury hotel in Tokyo, and you want to provide your guests with a special wine made only in South Africa. If you didn't have access to wine brokers and importers who could take care of the logistical arrangements for you, then you might travel to Cape Town, exchange your Japanese yen for South African *rand*, pay the wine producer for the wine, and bring it or have it shipped home with you. This seems obvious once you study it in its simplest form; the company producing the wine must pay its expenses in rand. Its employees don't want to receive Japanese yen, Mexican pesos, U.S. dollars, or Korean won in their pay envelopes. They can only pay their rent and buy food with rand.

The simple procedure just described is basically what happens when you order the South African wine through your local wine broker, although various intermediary firms handle the arrangements. The broker places an order with a foreign distributor, or directly with the foreign producer, and instructs its Japanese bank to wire funds to pay for the order. The broker's bank deducts enough yen from the broker's account to buy the rand at the exchange rate that prevails at the instant of the electronic transfer, buys the rand, and wires it to the foreign distributor's bank. Either of the two banks, or intermediate banks in between, might have an inventory of rand to make the exchange. The bank making the exchange charges a fee for the service of converting the currencies. The distributor in South Africa receives the rand and uses it to pay the producer, while the Japanese broker bills your company in yen.

Every purchase transaction between people or businesses in two different countries involves purchase of currency, except for unusual cases where both parties agree to use one country's currency. Even as a tourist, you typically have to buy the currency of the country you are visiting before you can pay for food, hotel rooms, or transportation. In some countries, shopkeepers will accept strong currencies such as the U.S. dollar, but they are still basically acting as currency exchangers, and they typically charge you more than the bank's exchange rate for accepting your currency. Then they deposit your currency in their bank accounts, at the exchange rate charged by their banks. When you use a credit card to buy something in a foreign country, the merchant charges you the price in the local currency, and your bank sells you the foreign funds when it converts the charge to your home currency and calculates your monthly bill.

The obvious question arises: why do the exchange rates fluctuate, and why are governments always so concerned about them? The answers to those question are also fairly simple.

The buying and selling of currencies, i.e., exchanging one for another, exactly mirrors the buying and selling of goods and services between countries. The same principles of supply and demand apply to currency as to all other products. If beef is scarce, the price goes up. If oil is plentiful, the price goes down. If German marks are scarce, the price, expressed in units of some other currency, goes up.

For example, if a huge imbalance in trading activity causes more dollars to be exchanged for yen than yen for dollars, then dollars become more plentiful in the banks' treasuries and yen become more scarce. The banks have to buy more yen from other banks to keep their supplies up. If more people need to buy yen than dollars, the sellers of yen can raise their prices. This is what economists mean when they say "the yen gained strength against the dollar."

Economists sometimes confuse people when they say things like "the British pound *rose* against the dollar," when they actually mean that a dollar will now buy *fewer* pounds than before. An easy way to eliminate this confusion factor and quickly understand which currency is being more heavily bought is to visualize a pattern of the foreign currency as *increasing* its exchange rate as it *weakens*, or "falls" down the chart, compared to the primary currency, as shown in this hypothetical example:

U.S. Dollar	Japanese Yen
$1.00	110
$1.00	111
$1.00	112
$1.00	113
$1.00	114
$1.00	115
$1.00	116
$1.00	...

When the report says "the Japanese yen *fell* (or weakened) against the dollar," you just have to visualize it falling down the list of increasing exchange rates, as shown above. At a rate of 115 yen to the dollar, the yen is weaker against the dollar than at a rate of 110. In other words, if the yen is stronger, i.e., rising up the list as shown above, then a person buying yen with dollars will receive fewer yen than before. If it is weaker, i.e., falling down the list, a person buying yen with dollars will receive more yen.

You can apply this same simple chart to all exchanges between currencies. Put the primary currency in one column, and put the various levels of the other currency in the other column, ranging from smaller values to larger values on the way down.

The next question you are likely to ask is "So what?" "How do these exchange rates affect my business?" Returning to the example of your hotel in Tokyo, you will find that your local wine broker charges you more or less for the South African wine you want, depending on whether international buying and selling of all goods and services has strengthened the rand against the yen or vice versa. The winery's price for the wine in rand might not have changed at all, but if your yen buy fewer rand, then you'll have to give your broker more yen for the same amount of wine.

Clearly, a weaker currency favors the foreign buyer who gets more goods for the foreign money spent. The seller is not directly affected, unless the buyer finds the price in the original currency too high and decides not to buy, or buys less of the product. Or the buyer may begin to look for cheaper substitutes for the product in other countries with more favorable exchange rates. This is one of the causes of trade politics among nations.

For example, Japan has long enjoyed a trade surplus with most of the other developed countries, especially America. Because more and more American importers have to buy yen in order to pay for the Japanese products, the demand for yen increases and the demand for dollars falls. Dollars become more plentiful in the international banking system and yen become more scarce. This allows the exchange banks to raise the price of yen, as measured in dollars. This trade imbalance, and the higher exchange rate it has caused, has allowed Japanese companies to buy imported raw materials and various other ingredients more cheaply than their competitors, and to minimize their manufacturing costs.

However, if a country's currency continues to appreciate against most others, then the prices foreign buyers have to pay for its products, as measured in their own currencies, continue to rise. At some point, the country's products become too pricey for foreign consumers and more difficult to sell. This has the effect of weakening demand for its currency and slowing the rise in its exchange rate.

Conversely, if a country's currency is weak against most others, particularly those of countries to which it can export its goods, then foreign buyers pay lower prices for its products, as measured in their own currencies. This increases demand for its products and can have a powerful effect on the growth of its economy, provided its currency does not become too expensive as a result of the increased trade.

Obviously, some businesses are much more affected by currency exchange rates than others. Companies that routinely do business across national borders may have to do business in several currencies at once. Airlines, for example, pay for landing fees, on-board supplies, certain maintenance procedures, and sometimes crew salaries in the currency of the country they visit, while their revenues usually come in the currency of the country whose people they transport. Oil companies may buy oil in various countries and import it to their home countries where they refine it and sell it in their home currencies.

If the government of a country, such as Japan, sees its currency as becoming too expensive, its central bank may start selling some of its currency reserves to make it more plentiful and reduce the exchange rate. This is generally a limited strategy which few banks can maintain for more than a short period of time. Conversely, a government such as that of Brazil, seeing its currency becoming too cheap, gets concerned that foreign investors may sell it for more desirable currencies, so it may buy its currency on the markets to reduce the supply and drive up the exchange rate.

Governments can also adjust interest rates to create favorable conditions for their own companies. And, of course, tariffs and trade regulations are part of the political interactions that make international trade more complex than simply selling goods and services.

Exchange rates can also affect profits coming back from foreign operations. If a firm has a division operating in a foreign country, and it transfers the profits back to its home country, then the actual profit, as measured in its home currency, will depend on the exchange rate. A weakening foreign currency means the foreign profits will buy less of the home currency and consequently decrease the final profit figure. A strengthening foreign currency will buy more of the home currency, increasing the final profit figure.

Some large firms use *hedging* techniques to reduce the effects of currency fluctuations on their profits. Although these techniques are too technical for our purposes here, they involve buying and selling the foreign currency, or trading in financial instruments called options. If the foreign currency gets weaker, the currency trading can produce profits that offset some of the conversion losses. If it becomes stronger, then the returning profits are higher and the cost of the trading activity is treated as an "insurance" cost.

To understand how currency exchange rates can affect your business, you have to sketch out the picture of your customers' business activities and your own, and identify the points at which currencies change form. This picture can help you make decisions about whether to make certain products yourself or purchase them from others, how to finance your operations in other countries, and whether to operate your own business activities abroad or simply work through agents and foreign partners. The more susceptible your revenues, costs, and profit margins are to currency influences, the more carefully you must plan for growth and the more flexibility you need in arranging the financial structure of your business.

The Euro: The Great Equalizer?

A key part of the economic struggle for modernization that's going on in Europe is the concept of a transnational monetary unit, the *euro*. To some, it promises nothing short of a profound transformation of the European economic system. Others prefer to view it as merely one of a number of tools for enhancing trade and promoting economic efficiency across national boundaries. Surely, the euro will play a key role in reshaping commerce on the continent, but much needs to be done to truly rationalize and coordinate the disparate commercial systems among the eleven primary countries that are leading the modernization.

A key argument in favor of a universal currency, at least in Europe, is that it will promote the freer movement of goods and services throughout the continent by eliminating economic frictions involved in cross-border financial transactions. Eliminating the huge costs of currency exchange operations would be just a start. Price disparities among countries for the same goods and services would become obvious, and this would give rise to competitive forces that would presumably reallocate demand and drive down prices overall. A single currency would, of course, encourage suppliers of goods and services to market more widely outside their own countries and would simplify the financing and payment for imports and exports. Coupled with reduced administrative procedures and controls on the transfer of goods across borders, it could reduce the overall costs of trade significantly.

The agenda for a single monetary unit goes almost as far back as the origin of the European Union itself. But just as the EU has faced a turbulent history, so will the euro face difficulty in becoming the standard European currency.

The plan for the Economic and Monetary Union, as the currency project was called, began with eleven of the fifteen EU member countries participating. Notably, England did not choose to join the euro project in its first phase. According to the plan that emerged from the 1991 Treaty of Maastricht, the euro was to be phased in over a period of three years, beginning on January 4, 1999. The treaty also created a European Central Bank, whose powers would ultimately supersede those of the member countries' central banks.

The architects of the new "United States of Europe," as some called it, realized that formidable political barriers stood in the way of full acceptance of a superordinate monetary system, not the least of which was public attitude in the various member countries. Thus, they decided to phase in the new currency over a three-year period. In January, 1999, the euro became, symbolically at least, the official currency of Europe with each member country's currency pegged to it at a predefined exchange rate. All prices on the European stock and bond markets were to be quoted in euros. However, the individual national currencies remained in full force.

The euro plan called for the progressive introduction of the new currency in various stages. The objective was for all of the national currencies of the member states to disappear from circulation by about the end of 2001 and for the euro to be the single, universal unit of money.

Clearly, the success—or failure—of the euro poses huge potential impacts politically and socially, as well as economically. The transition to a single super-currency places severe restrictions on the governments and central banks of the member states, and the Maastricht treaty dictates stringent standards for government budget deficits, interest rates, and expansion of the money supply. Trade politics remain difficult and complex across the continent. Popular support for the euro, and for its implications for national identity, have been relatively thin from the start. Government actions to combat recessions in individual countries could severely strain the fabric of the economic union and could test the willingness of member states to subordinate the selfish interests of their citizens to the presumed common good of the economic fraternity.

Non-European firms doing business on the continent will probably find the single monetary system helpful to their operations, as will European firms. However, the euro will probably be a decidedly mixed blessing for some time to come. For example, some analysts predict that the euro will threaten the U.S. dollar for its role as the world's primary reserve currency and standard of commerce. Oil prices, now typically quoted in dollars, might shift to euros. Depending on the euro-dollar exchange rate, this could help or handicap American firms. It could be like lining up all of the individual European currencies against the dollar, and trading at the level of the strongest one.

If the unprecedented conversion to the euro succeeds, it could lead to other regional attempts at currency consolidation. Some Asian and South American countries have already "dollarized" their economies to some extent by maintaining a fixed exchange rate to the U.S. dollar.

Actually, the much-publicized economic integration of Europe has stolen the spotlight from an equally impressive integration of the "Americas," i.e., the range of trading partners all the way from Canada and the U.S., through Mexico and the Central American countries, to South America. The North American Free Trade Agreement (NAFTA) and a variety of other trade treaties have radically reduced the barriers among those countries. By the time Europe reaches a significant level of integration, the "United States of America" might refer to the whole of the Western hemisphere as a kind of mega-free trade zone.

The Organization of American States, or at least individual countries, might even adopt the U.S. dollar as a common currency for their own individual motives. The idea of a world currency, however appealing in its abstract form, is probably many decades away, however.

Of course, international trade agreements, as well as existing tariffs and import policies, all affect the picture on your economic radar screen. They may also create various issues or opportunities that show up on your political radar as well.

As you study your economic radar screen, it makes sense to learn as much as possible about the economic integration taking place in Europe, whether your home market is there or elsewhere. Depending on your type of business, an integrated Europe could be easier or harder for your firm to cope with. The commercial benefits of the euro and the other aspects of European integration will be mixed, slow in coming to pass in some cases, and selective in their effects. For most firms, it will take some careful thinking and planning to make the most of them.

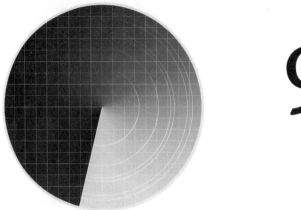

9

Your Technological Radar

The concern for man and his destiny must always be the chief aim of all scientific endeavor. Never forget it amidst your diagrams and equations.
— Albert Einstein

The purpose of the technological radar is to understand the effects of technological developments that can create or destroy opportunities for growing your business.

Spotting Winners: Corporate Binoculars or Blindfolds?

The history of technological forecasting is not very impressive overall. Many sophisticated attempts since World War II to anticipate major technological developments have been wide of the mark. While some highly optimistic predictions have failed to materialize, other significant developments have surfaced without warning.

Further, few large organizations can mobilize the energy and commitment needed to turn new developments into applications. Having a new idea and not acting upon it can be as bad as not having it. With a few notable exceptions, such as 3M Corporation, large companies tend to drift into a kind of intellectual menopause that limits their capacity to innovate.

For example, the history of Xerox Corporation is one of technological opportunities lost and found. When Chester Carlson, an obscure inventor and entrepreneur, succeeded in building a gadget in his kitchen that would transfer an image onto a piece of glass, he knew he had the basic idea for a photocopier, but he was still light years away from having a viable commercial product. He knew he would need the resources of a large firm to make his concept a reality. He approached dozens of major corporations, among them the household names of American industry. RCA, General Electric, Westinghouse—every one turned him down.

Carlson finally found a partner in Battelle Memorial Institute, a research foundation in Columbus, Ohio. Battelle's scientists provided funds and advice, and arranged a joint venture with Haloid Corporation, a small firm that made photographic products. They named Carlson's process *xerography*, from a Greek term meaning "dry writing." Haloid, renamed Xerox Corporation, introduced the Xerox 914 copier in 1959, and launched the hugely profitable photocopying industry. Carlson lived to see his invention become spectacularly successful and died a wealthy man. Battelle Memorial Institute got a huge block of Xerox stock, worth a sizable fortune.

In the late 1960s, researchers at RCA's Sarnoff Research Center began playing with a peculiar electrical effect in transparent plastic films. When they treated certain types of films with certain chemical processes, the films became *photoreactive*, i.e., they suddenly became opaque when a tiny electrical current passed through them. The researchers realized that, by building the films in various patterns, they could make them display information—alphanumeric characters—in response to electrical signals.

Until that time, so-called digital information displays used large glass-bodied vacuum tubes, one per digit, which needed substantial amounts of electricity. Suddenly it became possible to create digital display units that used very little energy and could fit into very small displays, such as digital watches. They knew that with additional research they could develop ways to manufacture these "liquid crystal" displays cheaply.

Remarkably, when the researchers went to RCA's management and proposed commercializing the liquid crystal technology, they got blank stares. They knew they were looking at a technology that would ultimately be worth billions of dollars, but they never succeeded in making a business case for the development. As word of the discovery began to circulate in the research community, Japanese firms, particularly Sharp Electronics, became keenly interested. They signed agreements for the rights to the technology, which RCA did manage to patent, and a key part of the digital electronic revolution got under way. RCA made huge profits on licensing fees, but never brought a profitable product to the market itself.

The liquid crystal display, or LCD, played a key part in the design of digital watches as well as many other consumer electronic products. Early on, Japanese firms such as Casio and Seiko took the lead in designing and marketing low-cost digital watches. Despite the fact that the technology originated in the U.S., American firms were slow to exploit it, and quickly lost the battle to the Japanese.

Hewlett Packard pioneered the handheld electronic calculator, and marketed a series of quality products that set a high standard for features and functions. Yet the firm never achieved the dominance many people expected when the calculator went mainstream and became a hugely popular consumer product.

This pattern of "invented here, appreciated elsewhere" happens often in the history of major technological developments. The company presumably best positioned to carry a new technological concept forward is often not the one that takes the lead.

For example, although Swiss firms had virtually dominated the watchmaking industry for decades, they were very slow to move to electronic technology. Indeed, it appears that Swiss designers had design concepts for digital watches on their drawing boards well before the Japanese got interested, but never put them into serious production. Only with the low-cost fashion watch, the Swatch, did Swiss designers regain significant influence in watch design. After a number of years, the fashion pendulum swung back toward expensive-looking, two-handed watches, and the traditional Swiss strengths in design and aesthetics became an advantage again.

Another peculiar story of missed opportunity lies buried in the early history of the personal computer. Although many people have the impression that Microsoft Corporation appropriated the visual "look and feel" of the Windows operating system from Apple Computer Company's Macintosh, few seem to know that Apple itself did not create that design concept. The "iconic" style of presenting information, i.e., using visual symbols, cartoon-like graphics, and the mouse as an intuitive means of instructing the computer what to do, was born in a quiet research lab in northern California, operated by Xerox Corporation.

At Xerox's Palo Alto Research Laboratories (PARC), engineers had thoroughly developed the icon-based user interface in the form of an early prototype computer code-named Star. For a variety of reasons, mostly organizational, the company never moved the product from the laboratory to the marketplace. However, Steven Jobs, one of the cofounders of Apple, happened to visit PARC one day, saw the Star concept, and immediately decided to "borrow" it for his company's new product, which became the Macintosh.

IBM also displayed a curious "ho-hum" attitude toward the new personal computer. In some ways, the "IBM PC," introduced in 1980, gave legitimacy to this new gadget. People began to feel that, if IBM endorsed it, then it was probably no longer a toy and might be worth trying. Yet IBM never moved with the speed or energy of which it was clearly capable and failed to gain a lock on the PC market as many people had expected.

For at least the first five years, IBM's management gave only lip service to the new product. The path to career success in the company continued to be the "big iron," i.e., the mainframe computer products and the corporate market. A number of the original advocates and architects of the company's PC product line became frustrated with the firm's lack of enthusiasm for the product and left.

Of course, IBM was not the only large firm to miscall the future of the PC. Before Steve Jobs and Steve Wozniak, founders of Apple Computer Corporation, found their mentor and backer Mike Markkula, they approached a number of firms with the idea of a commercial version of the personal computer. Firms like Hewlett Packard and Atari turned them down, reckoning that a couple of college dropouts could hardly walk in the door with anything earth-shaking.

Kodak Corporation was appallingly slow in moving into the new technology of digital imaging. Despite holding a dominant position in the photographic film industry for decades—or possibly because of it—the company made little response as PC chips became faster, graphics software became more sophisticated, digital scanners became better and cheaper, and more and more people wanted to put pictures into their documents. By the time the company began seriously investing in digital imaging, particularly the digital camera, the field was already crowded with large and small firms offering bits and pieces of the solution.

In the early going, Kodak had a number of options, such as partnering with a firm like Apple, which was crusading to sell computer users on a visual style of operating. It could have seriously entered the scanner market. It could have made a serious foray into graphics software, possibly by acquiring one of the more promising companies in that sector. Unfortunately, by the time it came to the party, the hors d'oeuvres were mostly gone.

There is plenty of evidence to indicate that the dominant firm in an industry is seldom the one to dominate the next wave, or the technology that drives it. For example, hindsight suggests that one or more of the major telecom players, such as AT&T, MCI, or British Telecom, could have conceived of the Internet and virtually owned it as an adjunct to the transmission networks they already had in place. Instead, the Internet grew in a topsy-turvy fashion almost on its own. In the short run, the firms making the most money from the online phenomenon will be the telecoms who carry the traffic. However, they have done little to shape the development of the phenomenon itself.

Indeed, the newcomer may actually have a definite edge over the established dominant player, because its leaders are much more likely to overturn the assumptions that made the dominant firm so successful. The organization that's best at doing something for the millionth time is typically the worst one at doing something for the first time.

To the extent that your technological radar shows opportunities for exploiting new technology, you have to ask yourself how wedded your organization is to the current way of operating. Is your enterprise constitutionally able to abandon old mindsets, see the implications of new technologies, and seize the opportunities they present?

Although information technology enjoys the spotlight these days, there are many other dimensions of science and technology to consider in scanning your technology radar across the business landscape.

For example, medical research is an obvious candidate for attention; new techniques in medical practice can radically change the severity, outcomes, and costs of various diseases. Pharmaceutical research is also a strong driver of economic and social change. Lifestyle medications that treat problems such as obesity, impotence, and hair loss can create huge markets virtually overnight if they work well enough.

Research into food chemistry can create possibilities for new products and threaten existing ones. Success in dealing with various crop-threatening pests can have far-reaching effects on world supply and demand for various food products. These outcomes can change the opportunities for businesses that sell agricultural machinery, fertilizers, and food products.

Energy research may also become an important driver of economic and social change. A serious commitment by major auto manufacturers to a viable electric vehicle, combined with meaningful government sponsorship, could radically change the transportation options available to the market. Occasionally, engineers revisit the concept of long-range dirigibles as a means of transporting cargo. New technologies for construction and propulsion could make such airships feasible. A new emphasis on supersonic travel, which languished in the wake of the disappointing success of the Concorde, could change options in air travel and the industries connected to it.

Ecological research can also turn up results with important political and social impacts. The continuing debate about global warming, i.e., the gradual rise in the Earth's benchmark temperature, seems to be tilting, especially under the weight of findings such as 1998's average rise of 0.58 degrees Centigrade, the biggest change on record. Laws, lawsuits, and international policies can arise from these controversies. For some businesses, these events might seem very remote; for others, they could have a direct and immediate effect.

Technology Is Selective in Its Effect

It pays to be skeptical of glittering generalities about how this or that technology "will revolutionize such-and-such an industry" or "will completely change the way we do business." These kinds of heroic pronouncements tend to obscure more than illuminate. The simple truth about all technological developments is that they are highly selective in their effect. They help some people, set others back, and have little effect on others.

Farmers use various types of technology, including sophisticated machinery, chemical preparations, and even computers for resource planning. Yet farmers are some of the lowest-paid workers in modern economies.

Law enforcement agencies, ranging from national and international agencies down to the local level, have used advanced weapons technology, forensic techniques, and information technology increasingly in recent years. However, professional criminals and terrorists have matched them at almost every turn with advanced technology of their own.

Medical technology has reached near-miracle status in saving lives and restoring people to normal function, particularly in America. Yet the American Medical Association reports that over 120,000 people die per year in the U.S. due to simple errors in diagnosis, treatment, and medication.

Technological advances create industries and destroy others. The legendary *Encyclopaedia Britannica*, long an icon of the American culture, is no longer published as the familiar set of beautifully bound books. Now one orders the encyclopedia on a plastic disk less than five inches in diameter.

In a later discussion we shall explore some of the ways in which technological changes can open new business opportunities and close off others. Each individual business experiences the benefits and threats of technology in its own unique way. Tracking the broad waves of change in technology is important, but it is much more important to translate them into their specific effects on your enterprise.

The Age of Cheap Information

Understanding the so-called information age, or the Third Wave, is less a matter of following the latest digital technology and the latest Internet terminology, and more a matter of understanding a few very basic effects. And the most basic effect of information technology will be *cheap information*.

From the standpoint of information, and the role it plays in a developed economy, the single most influential development in world history was probably the creation of the binary number system. On a par with the wheel and axle, the binary system made possible the standardization of every kind of information into digital form, i.e., simple pulses (on/off, yes/no, one/zero) that could be manipulated, analyzed, stored, transmitted, captured, and converted back into familiar forms like numbers, words, sounds, and pictures.

The binary system rested in technical obscurity for decades until the arrival of the silicon chip, the hardware capable of doing remarkable things with it. Coupled with telecommunications, which created the capability to transmit this new digital information, the chip has created a new ecological surrounding for human beings. We now live in, and can no longer escape from, an environment of cheap and abundant information. This new information ecology will be a mixed blessing.

The so-called information revolution has become so all-pervasive and so complex in its effects that it deserves careful study by all executives as a key business topic in itself. Even a competent summary of the topic and its implications are beyond the scope of this book, and every business leader needs to undertake his or her own education on the topic. For this discussion, however, we can highlight certain key elements of the topic relevant to the environmental scan.

Cheap chips. Microchip manufacturers can now turn out microchips in huge quantities at very low prices. Indeed, cheap chips hidden away in watches, TV sets, children's games, telephones, microwave ovens, automobiles, hotel doors, and countless other everyday devices have already turned them into "things that think." Their thinking may be very primitive and limited to a single use, but indeed the gadgets around us are getting smarter. Chipmakers can now produce chips so cheaply that we will think of them as disposable. We will very soon see cheap, single-purpose chips embedded in a huge variety of commonplace objects. So-called "smart cards," i.e., simple credit-card-like devices with embedded chips will almost certainly become more widely used as identification cards, medical records, driver licenses, and other "packages" of individual information. Cheap chips could replace printed labels on cargo shipments, consumer products, and warehouse pallets, containing a complete inventory of the items inside. Requiring no electrical power, they can simply store information burned into them by simple appliances that spit them out and affix them to packages. Chips that speak, i.e., respond to a radio signal pulse, can recite their stored data to a handheld scanner passed over a package. In addition to the very sophisticated and expensive microprocessor chips found in computers, low-end cheap chips may ultimately become one of the most important drivers of information logistics.

The networking of everything. Cheap chips will mean that more and more everyday devices will exude information. The cash register that a century ago was basically a box to hold money is now a participant in a network that measures sales, forecasts demand, restocks inventory, and incidentally manages cash. The theory of the Network Economy, compellingly articulated by Kevin Kelly, editor of *Wired* magazine, holds that cheap chips and cheap ways to move information around will create a world in which just about everything can talk to everything else.[1] To the extent that someone decides to put a chip in touch with other chips, they become part of a worldwide network, driven by ever-expanding connections and ever-falling costs. The real value of a fax machine, he points out, depends on the number of other fax machines it can communicate with, as with telephones, networked computers, and the Internet. The more entities that participate in a network, the greater, exponentially, the value of the network becomes. Far beyond the familiar networks of computers, fax machines, telephones, and their companions, ordinary objects will have chips that measure things, store information, and speak their memories when asked. This view rests on the questionable assumption that every additional participant in a network has something of value to offer, but the premise calls for serious study. Intel's chairman Andy Grove speaks of the daunting intellectual challenge of understanding a world with "a billion connected computers." Kelly and other fans of the "net culture," which at times swerves unnervingly close to looking like a cult without a leader, speaks of a world with trillions of connected cheap chips.

Productivity fueled by falling information costs. Experts debate about whether the PC and its friends have actually made business more productive overall or may have actually retarded it. Some claim that the falling cost of information equipment such as PCs, telephones, copiers, and fax machines have offset rises in other costs, holding down inflation and producing greater overall productivity, as well as growth in gross domestic product without the usual growth in the labor force normally needed to drive it. Others argue that the PC and the Internet are huge time-wasters, encouraging otherwise productive workers to dawdle over routine correspondence, reports, and calculations. Does spending two days producing a report using a half-dozen type fonts, eye-catching graphs, embedded tables and spreadsheets, scanned-in photographs, and color printing actually create more value than spending a half-day getting the information right and printing it in a mundane, "vanilla" format? Those who argue that computer games, Internet porno sites, and email used to exchange jokes and recipes siphon off valuable employee time during work hours do have a point. Presumably, however, as information costs continue to fall, and handling information cheaply gets a higher priority than making it pretty, we might reasonably expect productivity benefits. However, we still have no reliable way to measure information productivity, or the productivity of knowledge workers. Until we do, the gains will be speculative, and the arguments will probably continue.

Information dependency. The U.S., as the most computerized country in the world by far, is also the most computer-dependent. The ever-increasing integration and complexity of the information infrastructure makes it disturbingly vulnerable to failures in various subsystems. Other developed countries face this problem as well, but not nearly to the extent the U.S. does. We can expect to see data outages become more common than electrical power outages, and more severe in their impact. Beyond the infamous Y2K problem, the failure of a communication satellite, a major Internet backbone system, a credit card processing center, all or part of the air traffic control system, or a major stock exchange could bring tens of thousands of businesses to their knees. Perhaps more worrisome is the threat of attack on the information structure by highly motivated terrorists or enemy states acting through third-party cyberterrorists. Historically, designers of data systems have given security and data protection a relatively low priority, typical of the perceived level of threat at the time. Now, however, a determined enemy might well be able to cause havoc with the U.S. economy, its defense system, and the public sense of safety. Ironically, since such enemies typically have rather primitive information structures of their own, the developed countries cannot reply in kind. The U.S. federal government, including the Department of Defense, the CIA, and the FBI, have launched high-priority programs to define the nature of the cyberterrorist threat and plan for the developments needed to counter it. Other advanced countries are rapidly following suit.

Information glut, garbage, and pollution. One of our biggest problems of the information revolution will be how to get rid of information, not how to create more of it. We are well past the point of information pollution in the advanced societies, and certainly in the U.S. Television, radio, magazines, newspapers, music, junk mail, bank statements, telephone bills, computer disks, CD-ROMs, email messages, data files—all swirl around us in a rising tide of dataglut. Like compulsive people who save string, we save too much information. We need to learn to dispose of information, not cherish and hoard it. The simple fact is that we don't have the capital capacity to store all of the information being produced, and we're falling further behind every second. The ecological downside of the PC is much like that of the automobile. Just as every additional car imposes costs on the transportation infrastructure, throws off pollution, and eventually requires an additional investment to recycle it to the environment, so every PC imposes costs, throws off more information—much of it polluted—and has to be recycled when it becomes obsolete in about three years. The same reasoning applies to the Internet. Every new Web site makes its creator feel a part of the cyber-revolution, but it also adds to the pollution the rest of us have to inhale. The much-vaunted Internet search engines like Yahoo!, Alta Vista, Excite, and others will become less and less useful, as they degenerate into card catalogs for useless information. Information quality will become a major issue for business in the next decade. Indeed, we may see another "quality revolution," this one focused on *information quality assurance.*

The cyberparadox: technology versus humanity. An ideological dilemma is developing that I believe will more and more shape cultural and commercial attitudes toward the information revolution. Like it or not, we will come to the point of asking: Which is more important, culture or technology? Notwithstanding the soothing assurances offered by fans of the digital future, the digitizing of society will pit human values against techno values. We will begin to see the psychological and cultural downside of the digital society once it begins to cause pain. The cyberparadox will be:

The more "wired" humans beings become, the more isolated they feel.

The notion that people who sit for hours at keyboards typing at one another around the world constitute any kind of community will become increasingly bankrupt. The increasing atomization of society and the severing of personal connections to real communities will cause psychological stress and a sense of "connected anonymity." The "digital society" is a concept embraced and promoted mostly by people with a particular psychosocial orientation, that of the *social isolate*. To the extent that the rest of us permit a minority with a particular sociopolitical ethos to dictate the design of our relationships, we will experience the stress that comes with a sense of dehumanization. We will very likely opt for enclaves of humanity, i.e., places and circumstances to which we can turn for a genuine sense of contact and community. Once we have "wired" the world, we can never "un-wire" it again.

Y2K: The Biggest Wildcard of Them All?

You would have to have been living in a cave for the past year or two not to have heard about the so-called "millennium computer bug," or the "Y2K" problem. This issue is a prominent example of a significant technology wildcard that can bring both pain and benefit, with the balance of the two very hard to predict in advance.

To recap the Y2K issue, for those living in caves or those who haven't been following information technology, many computer software systems of all types, all over the world, may malfunction when the year changes from 1999 to 2000, due to a historical flaw dating back to the mid-1950s. Early computer and software designers, particularly in IBM and also in the U.S. Defense Department, established certain standards and technical policies that have become almost universally adopted. One of these widely accepted policies has been the so-called six-digit date system, in which a date is represented in computer code in terms of a two-digit number for the month, followed by a two-digit number for the day, and a two-digit number representing the last two digits of the year.

In the mid-1950s, computers were so new that few people thought about design issues that might arise forty or fifty years later. During that period, almost all dates used in software systems were dates within the current century. Because the magnetic-core storage memory used in early computer systems was so scarce and expensive, designers decided to conserve memory by dropping the first two digits from the year component of all dates, and simply represent the dates by the last two digits, on the assumption that everyone would know that the first two digits had to be "19." The result: when the year 2000 arrives, the computer continues to interpret all dates as falling within the 1900s, so it can't tell the difference between 2005 and 1905.

The possible impacts of this date ambiguity are multifarious and generally difficult to predict. In the most extreme cases, whole programs or portions of programs could malfunction, causing a temporary shutdown of the host computer. Software with poorly designed error guard features might not respond gracefully to unanticipated errors in the data information.

At the other extreme, invalid dates on documents could be a mere nuisance. In the middle, a wide range of possible malfunctions could cause erroneous computation results or malfunctions in computer-controlled equipment. In some cases, the bogus results might go unnoticed by anyone not properly suspicious. Date-related malfunctions could be innocuous in some circumstances and disastrous in others. Further, millions of so-called embedded systems, containing date-sensitive special purpose chips, lurk in countless control systems from elevators to nuclear power plants.

History may well portray the Y2K problem as a test of national and corporate leadership, just as much as a singular issue of information technology. It will tell us much about how governments and corporate leadership teams respond—or fail to respond—to impending threats to the well-being of their enterprises.

Although computer and software designers presumably realized that the turn of the century would create major problems, it was only in 1995 that serious discussion of the problem began to rise to the level of a national agenda. The U.S. Federal government only began serious action in 1996 with the creation of a national task force. A few other major countries followed suit, and some major corporations began to mobilize for the problem.

However, worldwide response to the looming Y2K problem was distressingly slow. By the beginning of 1999, the final year before the bits were to hit the fan, only twenty-seven countries had even appointed national commissions to study the problem. A number of countries had barely finished assessments of the magnitude of the problem, and only a few had mounted major, serious efforts to manage it. Russian missile-control computers, antiquated and neglected, posed especially frightening possibilities.

Corporations in the U.S. and other countries were all over the spectrum in terms of converting anxiety into action. Progress also varied significantly from one industry to another. Remarkably, worldwide attention to the Y2K problem arose, literally, in the last days of the century.

As an author, I am in the awkward position of going to press with a book that will be released shortly before the end of the critical year of 1999, and consequently any predictions I may offer regarding the Y2K problem will come back to haunt me almost immediately after publication. It won't be long after the release of this book that we'll know the early results. It's a bit like reading those psychic predictions published in the supermarket tabloids at the end of every year and saving the paper to check their accuracy.

Consequently, the most I can attempt at this point is to offer a rationale for thinking about the Y2K issue, and outline some of the cause-and-effect dominoes that seem most likely to come into play when the computers wake up on January 1, 2000. Here are some of the major dimensions of the issue.

Scope of the Problem

If we are to believe the most popular estimates of the cost to detect and fix the Y2K bugs in all active software systems

worldwide, we have to conclude the job can't be done completely before about 2002, and certainly not by the magic date
of January 1, 2000. By some estimates, there are about eight
billion lines of computer code in the world (a figure that
instantly invites curiosity about the estimating procedure
used to arrive at it), with about half of them in the United
States. Similar estimates put the cost of finding and fixing
most of the offending lines of code at about $300 billion.

A problem of this magnitude poses not only economic and
financial issues but issues of technical resources. Many of the
long-surviving mainframe software systems, dubbed "legacy"
systems by the new breed of young information technologists,
were developed many years ago. Their builders used earlier
programming languages such as COBOL and FORTRAN, earlier programming systems associated with IBM's operating
systems, and even software from firms that no longer make
computers, such as General Electric, Univac, and Burroughs.
Not only is it almost impossible to locate enough programmers
versed in these older languages, but there may not be enough
programmers on the planet to do the sheer amount of work
that will be necessary to find, fix, debug, and test the enormous amounts of program code involved.

Bear in mind that the existing population of programmers
and system developers, already in short supply, is fully committed to the requirements of new software developments
already underway. Huge numbers of them would have to be
diverted to repair work that would add little or no value at the
expense of the economic returns previously expected of the
original projects.

The interlocking of computer systems between large corporations, government departments, and various international agencies poses a potentially huge wildcard problem, which few
experts know how to assess. Large companies may cut off business with suppliers who do not conform to their Y2K standards.
Banks in less developed countries might not be able to participate in electronic fund transfer systems and currency
exchanges. Many organizations may disconnect their systems
from others simply as a safety measure, until they can be sure
no problems remain. This could cause a significant slowdown in
some aspects of business as people revert to safer, more labor-
intensive methods of handling data between organizations.

A seldom-mentioned side effect of the Y2K fix is that fixing software bugs involves writing more code, which inevitably introduces more bugs. In other words, fixing one bug causes others. These secondary bugs will eventually cause their own problems.

Severity of the Potential Impact

The effects of the Y2K problem will certainly be selective, varying in their intensity, affecting some industries and sectors of society much more severely than others, and showing up sooner in some places than others. The U.S. is the most computer-dependent society on the planet but also probably the most advanced in dealing with the problem. This combination of dependency and relative preparedness could be fairly equivalent across a large number of countries, resulting in approximately the same degree of severity.

Experts disagree radically about the magnitude of the economic effect of Y2K. Some liken it to a major snowstorm or hurricane that causes a brief economic spasm. Others predict much more extensive and long-lasting impacts. And others seriously predict a worldwide recession with the possible loss of a percentage point or more on global economic growth. But most agree that no one really has a confident basis for a detailed prediction.

The late start on fixing the Y2K problem means that it will be solved partly by design and partly by discovery. That is, the more advanced countries and corporations will eliminate the most destructive bugs by aggressive investigation and repair, but will probably encounter many others by the simple expedient of waiting until they show up. In some software systems, containing rarely used sections of code, Y2K bugs might not show up for several years after the change-over to 2000. Presumably, those working actively on the problem will focus on so-called mission-critical systems first with fewer resources devoted to secondary systems.

Economic Effects

Y2K will make itself felt economically on two levels. The level most widely discussed in the popular press is the level of information handling itself, e.g., funds in bank accounts; employee

payrolls; investor accounts in brokerages; government payments of tax refunds, welfare, pensions, and social security;
and various dimensions of economic activity where the information itself is the raw material of commerce, such as inter-
bank fund transfers and currency trading. The effect could be
to distort, destroy, misplace, or misinterpret financial data,
possibly to the disadvantage of many millions of customers.
Major failures of banking software could actually cause the
shutdown of some banks or the temporary suspension of operations for others.

The second and less widely discussed level of impact is in
those parts of the physical economy that are managed by
information technology. For example, electrical power outages
could seriously disrupt manufacturing, transportation, business communications, and retailing of all kinds. Heavy transport, such as trucking, rail services, and shipping, could all
slow down or snarl due to the failure of antiquated information systems.

Interruptions in the flow of raw materials to factories and
the flow of finished goods to warehouses and retail outlets
could cause significant shortages. Shocks to the overall distribution system for goods and services could cause back-ups at
some points and shortages at others. This could lead to inventory overloads for some firms, consumer hoarding, and price
gouging at the retail level.

The merger of Union Pacific Railroad and Southern Pacific
offers an object lesson in logistical meltdowns. The two companies discovered, after merging, that their respective computer systems were almost completely incompatible. For
months, they struggled with shortages of cars in some areas
and pile-ups in others, lost cars, and cars traveling empty *both
ways*, not to mention disgruntled customers abandoning their
services for other carriers. Before getting the chaotic situation
under control, the new firm had lost tens of millions of dollars
in revenues and many customers.

The net economic effect of a logistical jam-up, if it happens,
will almost certainly be an overall reduction of industrial productivity and probably a measurable reduction in gross domestic product (GDP) for most advanced economies. However,
predicting the magnitude of the impact is beyond the skills of
the most expert economists and forecasters. Indeed, it may be

rather difficult to measure or estimate the impact with any degree of confidence, even afterwards.

Social Effects

Fear, combined with economic shocks caused by Y2K, could lead to significant social effects, such as the loss of jobs due to the bankruptcy of some businesses or the suspension of operations by others, especially small ones. One obvious effect could be the loss of consumer confidence in banks or the banking system with a possible run on bank cash supplies. Such a reaction could range from rather mild all the way to a major panic that would force the suspension of banking operations—a "bank holiday" as U.S. president Franklin Roosevelt euphemistically named it.

Because banks in most countries are required to keep only enough cash on hand to cover a small percentage of investor funds (typically about six percent in the U.S.), few banks could withstand a major frontal assault by depositors at the front door demanding their money. In a typical major city, the cash transport resources provided by armored car companies could easily be swamped by a modest run on major banks; the only plausible defense would be a temporary suspension of operations. A loss of confidence in the cash economy could also lead to panic buying and hoarding of food, household supplies, gasoline, heating oil, and cash itself. Heavy cash withdrawals within three to six months in advance of the magic date could create a "mattress effect," i.e., an unreported reduction in the "M1" money supply and possible liquidity problems for some banks, making less money available to lend. Interest rates could rise as a result.

A number of people planning to travel to far corners of the Earth in late 1999 to celebrate the new year will probably have second thoughts because of the risk that the Y2K bug will cause airline computers to malfunction. Airlines may have difficulty enticing customers to fly on January 1, 2000, or indeed within weeks before and after that date.

Of course, a small percentage of people will certainly "head for the hills," invoking a survivalist mindset of self-reliance and retreat from accepted sociopolitical structures. It's also likely that the "nut factor" will increase significantly, i.e., the number of cult groups, fringe movements, and individuals who exhibit behavior more bizarre than usual will increase, in part also because of the arrival of the new year 2000, which many interpret as the de facto turn of the millennium. The more violent of these people could engage in sabotage, vandalism, bombings, and acts of terrorism.

Any major disturbances caused by the Y2K problem could also invite cyberterrorists to step up their attempts to disrupt the information structures of the major economies, in particular the U.S.

Possible Legal Impacts

The litigation industry in the U.S. has not missed the significance of the Y2K problem. Lawyers by the thousands are brushing up on information technology in hopes of finding lucrative targets for lawsuits. The legal possibilities are virtually endless. Hospital computer systems that malfunction may create threats to patients' lives and well-being. Airline computer malfunctions leading to canceled flights, lost or misdirected luggage, or overcharges for fares invite consumer lawsuits. Overbilling or mis-billing by businesses of all types, failed shipments, missed tax deadlines, errors in financial data, and many other information malfunctions can all invite lawsuits for negligence.

Many insurance firms are worried that business interruption insurance, typically a fairly profitable line, could suffer enormous losses if many businesses file Y2K-related claims for loss of revenue caused by customers, suppliers, business partners, or government agencies.

Lawyers may target software suppliers as well as firms that use the software in their businesses. On the legal theory that software developers should have anticipated the Y2K problem in their designs, they may seek to hold them accountable for the effects of the malfunctions on the users of the products.

An important dimension of the legal question could involve some form of legal amnesty for software developers and users. Those seeking damages might have to prove gross negligence or malicious intent, not simply the failure of software.

Y2K and You

What should you be doing to assess the Y2K threat to your business and to defend yourself against its worst possibilities? Obviously, if your business is highly dependent on information technology, it makes sense to map out the cause and effect sequences of events—the dominoes—that will translate into direct impacts on your operation. Of course, you need to evaluate your internal data systems and make sure they are Y2K-compliant, or at least that they will be resilient to the impacts of the Y2K bug until you can improve or replace them.

But beyond those measures, you need to evaluate the possible effects of malfunctions in the data systems operated by your customers, your business partners, your suppliers, and any others with whom your systems are interconnected. This calls for careful and creative analysis, and a keen eye for connections that may not be obvious. Clearly, the Y2K issue is a game of dominoes.

Dehumanizing the Customer Interface: The Digital Moat

Many organizations, and most large ones, are making what I believe to be an important mistake in one particular use of information technology, namely the *electronic customer interface*. Beginning in the mid-1990s, many firms, particularly in America, began installing automated telephone "menu" systems that route customer calls through a series of decision points to the proper department. Some, such as AT&T, even began using digital speech-recognition technology to try to figure out how to route the customer's call by having a synthesized voice ask for a spoken response and then deciphering the possible options from the caller's statement.

Still others have attempted to manage customer calls completely by automatic response with no human contact of any kind. I recently had occasion to call a city department to arrange for an inspector to visit my home and verify that some remodeling work met with city building code requirements. When I called the proper telephone number, I was dragged through a procedure in which I keyed in various elements of information by pushing buttons on the telephone, including the permit number I had been given. After I had completed my task, a computerized voice announced the day of the week on which the inspector would visit. Then the computer hung up the phone.

I was both impressed and appalled by the experience. Confirmed digital citizens will no doubt smile approvingly at this latest triumph of technology. Others may experience a sense of dismay in knowing that one more large organization, in this case a city government, has decided that human contact is too costly and not a worthwhile investment of its resources.

There is a clear and probably unstoppable trend on the part of large organizations toward using information technology to depopulate the customer interface and reduce the costs of managing customer relations. Banks do it, insurance companies do it, telephone companies do it, local utilities do it, airline companies do it, and so do many, many others. I believe this is a pernicious and destructive trend for several reasons.

First, it's a clear statement to the customer that says, "We're too busy to bother with your particular idiosyncrasies, so we're handing you over to the computer. You will be allowed to do whatever it's been programmed to do." It tells the customer that standardization, efficiency, and cost savings are more important than any feelings or special needs the customer might have. It also says that any variation in the customer's need or problem that doesn't fit into the software algorithm is not important and will simply not be tolerated. In the case of the city inspector, the computer simply announced the date of the inspection. I would have expected a human to verify that someone would be home on that day, and to negotiate a more suitable date if not.

It's as if the executives of many companies have decided to build a kind of digital "moat" around their organizations to keep the customers at a comfortable distance. By refusing to have a human being answer the telephone, not only do they save money, but they avoid having to interact directly with an upset customer or one who has a complicated or time-consuming problem. The computer cannot—yet—hear and respond to the anger, frustration, or apprehension in the voice of the caller, so nobody at the firm has to deal with his or her feelings. Further, since nobody knows which customers are disgruntled and which are satisfied, it can be assumed that all customers are basically happy.

It's abundantly clear that many people find this digital barrier offensive, off-putting, and often frustrating when it prevents them from completing their missions. Yet, just as most people have accepted the proposition of doing part of the service employee's job themselves, such as operating the automated teller machine and filling their own gasoline tanks, most will probably passively accept the digital customer interface. Indeed, what choice will they have, if this becomes the standard? What number do you call to tell someone the computer gave you lousy service? Where do you go to complain about the complaints department?

This tendency to digitize, standardize, and depersonalize service interactions with customers will turn out to be a mixed blessing for many large companies, I believe. At the same time they are driving down their costs with information technology, they will be dooming themselves and their service products to the status of standardized commodities, which will be under constant threat of replacement by other, cheaper information processes.

When a person can call a computer and purchase automobile insurance without ever speaking to a human being, how can the firm hope to differentiate its value package from those of its competitors? When banking has become a purely standardized process of conversing with a computer, either by telephone or by online computer access, what makes any bank different from another? In this standardized, digitized world, the only competitive weapon will be a cheap infrastructure with plenty of cash flow with which to battle other low-cost, anonymous competitors.

Not surprisingly, new and inexperienced firms in the pure information industries, such as Internet service providers (ISPs), depend heavily on the digital moat to distance themselves from their customers and keep their operating costs as low as possible. With over 4,000 ISPs in the U.S. alone, all trying to lure customers with lower and lower prices, many simply do not want to face the fact that their customers need and want something more than an online sign-up procedure and a local telephone number. Curiously, Internet service and Web site hosting are industry sectors that could benefit greatly from customer-focused differentiation of their service packages. We may see more and more attention paid to the customer's state of mind as they realize that simply connecting two computers is not necessarily a high-value service.

For the smaller firm, the big-company trend toward digitizing customers may present special opportunities for competitive advantages. By creating a customer experience that is unique, differentiated, and valuable, the more service-oriented firm may be able to mark off a part of the playing field that the digital Goliaths are not interested in, or capable of, dominating. It remains to be seen whether jaded consumers would respond favorably to a renewal in personalized, individualized service, especially when the largest providers are all pushing toward commoditized products at ever lower prices. However, it makes little sense for the smaller firm to resort to the digital moat as a cost-reduction option, since it typically enjoys very few others and could well be passing up its best avenue for differentiation.

At a deeper level, we may well see a consumer backlash against the arrogant anti-customer attitudes that prevail in most of the software industry. The computer is no longer a toy, no longer an oddity, no longer a gadget. It's a necessary part of business life and a popular artifact of most economically developed cultures. Consumers are increasingly fed up with the exploitive ethos of forced obsolescence that forms the core precept of the industry. Software products have become increasingly unreliable as they've become ever more complex and ever more short-lived.

If the advocates of the software industry hope to see the computer accepted universally in the culture on a par with, say, the automobile, then they will have to live up to the same customer expectations applied to the automobile. How many people would put up with a car that stopped running at least once a day, stranding them on the way to or from work? How would they react to finding out they have to replace their car with a new one, even though there's nothing wrong with it?

The same types of government regulations and controls that apply to cars and other consumer products could well become the fate of computers. Presently, the designers of a commercial software product feel free to do just about anything they like to the customer's computer. Why shouldn't the software supplier be required to disclose exactly what the product does to the customer's computer, i.e., what files it adds to the hard disk and where, which files it modifies, and which files if any it deletes? Drugs and over-the-counter medicines come with warnings about their side effects; why not require the same of computer software?

If such a consumer backlash takes hold, it could create real problems for companies that can't adapt, and real opportunities for those that can. The computer culture will have to learn a whole set of attitudes and social skills to cope with it. Technical people will have to learn to express themselves in the language of ordinary people, not "geek-speak." They will have to learn to cater to all sorts of non-technical priorities in order to sell their products to increasingly reluctant and demanding customers. And, if the forced-obsolescence dynamic begins to fail, they will have to learn a bit of humility, as they find it necessary to focus on real customer value as the S-curve flattens out and the computer's gee-whiz phase fades into history. It will certainly do them good.

Internet Mythology: What the Internet Will and Won't Do

If you want to form your own perspective on the future of computers and the Internet and their effect on society, the first thing to do is stop listening to geeks. It's hard to imagine any source more biased and less likely to be accurate about the future than that peculiar subculture of socially disconnected souls who base their self-definition and self-esteem on a relationship with an inanimate object. That is, if you don't count the bemused journalists who mindlessly tout their agenda.

Computers and information networks are definitely here to stay, and they've brought huge benefits to business, education, and private life. The real benefits—and problems—yet to come will surely surpass our imagination. Yet few developments in our culture have enjoyed such wide exemption from logical scrutiny as the current Internet craze. Despite clear signs that the Internet will not survive as a single, monolithic information structure, the fad rolls on like some relentless juggernaut, devouring everything in its path.

The confluence of special-interest promoters of the Internet theology, better known as the "gee-whiz conspiracy," has had remarkable success in selling it to journalists, political figures, and much of the general public. But their theology is fundamentally flawed, distorted by the dual filters of technological thinking and upper middle-class values, and not informed by a broader view of culture, human needs, and business reality.

Most of the benefits touted for the current Internet structure by the gee-whiz conspiracy will probably fail to materialize. The real benefits will be different, and probably greater. The Internet craze is living on borrowed time, and the sooner we pass through the current puberty phase and into a more realistic concept of the role of the online experience, the sooner we can take advantage of what it has to offer.

In characteristic contrarian form, I offer a few assertions about the nature and future of the Internet.

Assertion #1: Internet users are segmented by motive. One of the biggest mistakes newswriters constantly make is referring to Internet users as a single category of people. The few references to demographic segmentation one reads seem carefully chosen to support one of two conclusions: either everybody is doing it, in which case they pretty well match the general U.S. population, or Internet marketing has a great future, in which case they're highly educated and affluent. Of course, every kid in America is surfing the Web every day after school, so they're also very young. The simple fact is that nobody knows who the "typical" Internet user is, what he or she looks like, and why he or she plugs in. The few serious attempts to understand people as users of the online experience seldom find their way into the media.

When you consider the chaotic nature of online activity, the fact that few Internet service providers have any kind of demographic information about their users, and that many people share accounts and log in from schools, colleges, and libraries, you can quickly conclude that any attempt to characterize Internet users statistically is little more than a wild guess. Yet busy or lazy journalists will swallow and dutifully recite just about any plausible-sounding statistic if they think it comes from someone in the know.

This concept of Internet user as everyman (and woman) tends to hijack any serious, critical inquiry about what the online experience really does for people, how it can serve different needs for different people, and what its growth prospects really are. We need a better segmentation model, based on how and why people use the online experience. I modestly nominate the following possible role-based segments:

1. *Academics*—students at all levels as well as academic researchers who use the Internet to exchange technical information and locate information related to their specialized fields. This is probably a much smaller segment than most of the others.

2. *Computer professionals*—people with computer-based occupations, such as hardware and software engineers, programmers, Web site designers, computer consultants, and many others in the actual computer industry. Many of them operate the structure of the network itself. There are probably several million of these highly specialized people, most of whom use the Internet often for specific computer-related purposes.

3. *Busy professional people*—aside from those with computer-based jobs, many professional people use the Internet, or at least the Web, as a source of specific information related to current needs or problems. They typically sign on, look for what they need, and sign off. They tend not to relate to the Internet as an all-purpose hobby shop.

4. *Consumers and "computer moms"*—people who sign up for consumer-type services like America Online, largely because they've heard it's "cool" and it's something they should know about. Parents also may want to keep up with what their children are seeing and doing on the Internet. This may be the largest group of users overall, but it may also be the most fickle. Once the first novelty of "going online" has faded, how often and for how long will they log on? As newcomers join this group, others may fade out. America Online's total membership may continue to rise, but the bulk of online use may center on new arrivals.

5. *Kids*—unbiased estimates of the number of children going online are difficult to find, although the "gee-whiz" contingent that touts the Internet implies that there are many. Younger children seem to view the computer and the Internet as a play experience; adolescents and teen-agers seem to want a combination of a game-like experience with the experience of mastering the use of the medium itself. And, of course, many teenagers find searching for pornographic material on the Internet exhilarating and engrossing.

6. *Junkies*—people with addictive personalities who use online activity as an escape from everyday life and spend a great deal of time engaging in it. These may be serious technophiles; people mildly or seriously addicted to computer games; socially withdrawn people who are more comfortable with limited contact, mostly with others like them; and pathologically isolated people who simply use their computers to occupy their time. Some Internet zombies spend hours every day in chat rooms, playing games, and exchanging messages with newsgroups of various types. This group may constitute a significant portion of the general population, say as many as five percent of adults, which would be equivalent to about ten million people just in the U.S. This category probably also includes people with eccentric political views, as well as free-speech ideologues, i.e., people who rabidly promote the Internet almost as a cult and lobby constantly to prevent control or regulation of any form of Internet activity. They may be the main reason why Internet opinion polls are notoriously unreliable.

7. *Misfits*—the socially maladjusted, disaffected, bewildered, and seriously disturbed. This group is potentially the most destructive. The Internet will amplify the "nut" factor, i.e., it allows people with socially unacceptable ideas, impulses, and behavior to find one another, and to feel validated in their pursuits. Consider that, if all the online anarchists, hate groups, militia groups, pedophiles, stalkers, hackers, and scam artists in America total only one-half of one percent of the population, we're still talking about more than a million people. For them, the Internet is not only fascinating but a useful avenue for expressing anti-social impulses.

No one knows for sure if this is a valid set of categories either, but it seems to me it makes sense to try to understand Internet users in terms of the motivations behind their activities in order to guess how they may affect the future of the medium. Of course, there is probably considerable overlap in these categories, even if they turn out to be valid. Some misfits are also junkies, and vice versa. Business people, academics, and even computer moms can also be misfits. Knowing the motivation that brings a particular type of person to the online experience may help to know how the medium may respond to their demands and interests.

Assertion #2: Internet use will obey the S-curve, leveling off, surprising many people, and ruining some. Contrary to the most sacred precept of the Internet ideologues, the whole world won't be online—*ever*. This is the hardest possibility of all for them to accept, yet it is really the least arguable. The

S-curve concept, explained in Chapter 5, "How to be Your Own Futurist—Without Getting Lost in the Ozone," dictates that the growth of anything levels off in an S-shaped pattern as the energy fueling it gets tapped out. In this case, what gets tapped out will not be the data capacity, or "bandwidth," of the world networks. It will simply be the supply of people whose mental habits and personal activities dispose them to go online. And the supply of such people is probably much smaller than many experts assume.

Internet promoters claim an online population of fifty million or more people. I don't believe that figure for a minute. Without substantiation, it's hard to validate any such claim, although most seem to accept it without question. Does it count active Internet accounts or all people who could possibly connect? What pattern of activity defines a user? Daily? Weekly? Monthly? Once in a lifetime? Anybody with a PC and modem? The whole family, if there is a PC in the house? Even Intel's chairman Andy Grove, a respected thought-leader in the digital revolution, conceded in a recent interview that he logs on "maybe two hours a month." Omnipresent news coverage conveys the impression that every adolescent and teenager in America surfs the Net. We're a long way from that.

MIT's director of media technology, Nicholas Negroponte, predicted in 1997, "There will be *one billion people* on the Internet by the year 2000." These "by the year 2000" predictions have been coming back to haunt their authors. The flawed assumption is that the ecological niche feeding the S-curve of Internet use consists of the entire population of the Earth. As a practical matter, not more than one-tenth of the Earth's people will even qualify economically for at least twenty years, and only a fraction of them will actually have the necessary interest. Of those, very few will ultimately average more than a few hours online per month.

The first noticeable effect of the S-curve will be that most users, except the base population of junkies, will spend less and less time connected, as the novelty fades and as they locate their favorite sources of the specific information they want most. A large number of business users, for example, typically log on to a service for a matter of seconds, retrieve stock market data or certain news items, and then hang up. As the rate of new, high-time users joining the online services slows

down and existing users reduce their time, total message traffic on the network will level off and actually decline. This will
come as a huge shock to the Internet ideologues. Internet-only
marketing firms such as the legendary amazon.com and others, whose business plans rest on the assumption that the population of active users will rise almost without limit for many
years, will be hung out to dry.

   *Assertion #3: Internet marketing will be the big failure story
of the decade.* The information superhighway will be littered
with the remains of firms that bet their investors' assets on
the "TV model" of online marketing, i.e., selling things cheaply
or even giving them away in order to draw enough users to
sites subsidized by paid advertising. By early 1999, some
start-up firms were announcing that they would sell products
online at cost and would make fabulous profits from the advertising revenues supplied by firms eager to sell other things—
presumably for a profit—to the hordes of users who
stampeded to their sites. One firm announced that it would
give away thousands of computers for free; all the recipients
had to do was agree to accept advertising messages that could
not be removed from their screens. Journalists knowingly
hailed this move as "a brilliantly conceived strategy," and "the
logical next step in Internet marketing."

   Driven by these kinds of *kamikaze* marketing ventures, the
Internet has already become a no-profit zone. Indeed, the
Internet will be a destroyer of profits as new firms rush head-
long to lose money under the presumption that an infinitely
rising volume of users will somehow make them whole. Many
naive investors have already parted with their skins by gam-
bling on over-hyped stock offerings for "profitsomeday.com"
businesses, as one analyst dubbed them. Many more investors
will be caught when the bubble bursts. Indeed, the volume of
money being thrown at Internet start-up firms, and the
atmospheric prices paid for their stocks, will work out to a
fairly sizable wealth transfer across the U.S. economy. Every
share of an Internet-only marketing firm should come with a
tulip bulb.

   The autopsy of the Internet marketing model will eventually reveal death by fatal assumption—three fatal assumptions, in fact. The first is that the number of people online will
rise to the sky, or at least vastly higher than current levels.

Without this assumption, the necessary advertising revenues won't be attracted away from other channels.

The second critical assumption is that a large enough universe of advertisers will bring a large enough total investment to this channel to make the give-away model profitable. Conversely, successful sites will have to attract an enormous population, not just junkies who visit Web sites for fun but actual buyers. Few will succeed; most will go broke trying. Even assuming that only a small number of sites will survive as the channels of choice, those sites will have to cannibalize enough advertising investment from other channels to cover the costs of attracting the buyers. Ironically, they will probably have to use conventional channels of advertising, i.e., print and television, to attract buyers to their sites; the Internet itself is a notoriously poor advertising medium for Web sites.

And the third critical assumption is that the advertising messages on the "magnet" sites, e.g., giveaway businesses, search engines, portal sites, and the like, will be phenomenally productive. Presumably, the firms paying for advertising time will see irrefutable evidence of greater sales and profits from the users who see their ads. There is no reputable evidence available, so far as I know, that Web site ads pull more sales for the money invested than conventional channels, except for the traditionally successful products of pornography and software. Without this assumption, they will concentrate their investments in those channels that do show adequate results.

If any one of these three critical assumptions fails to pan out, the model collapses.

Assertion #4: Most businesses will use the Web site to support existing methods of doing business. The "page" concept for presenting information over networks, based on the Hypertext Markup Language, or HTML, has gained phenomenal acceptance. The Web page structure, which includes online forms and embedded mini-programs such as Java, has become a useful standard model for packaging ideas. It's hard to imagine that it will not become even more widely used. As Web software technology develops and becomes easier to use, creating a Web page layout of information will likely become no more difficult than using a word processor or graphics package.

In 1989, when Hewlett Packard decided to become the most "wired" company in the world, its experts chose the Internet technical protocols as the basis for its internal network. When the Internet's World Wide Web became popular and the Web page concept caught on, the company was already matched to the world information environment. Employees there have long been comfortable filling in online forms for reimbursement of travel expenses, and exchanging documents with their counterparts all over the world. This trend will almost certainly take over in more and more corporate environments. Eventually, many firms will operate with information structures that are virtually indistinguishable from the Web.

As an intelligent alternative to trying to force an entire business operation onto the Internet, more and more firms will use the Web site concept as an extension of the basic business structure. Online ordering works very well, once you can attract the customer to your site. Customer-service procedures can often be implemented more effectively online than through service employees answering telephones. You can make almost infinite amounts of information available to your customers online, once they know where to find you.

Customer-service Web sites offer a way to share labor with customers. Just as the ATM allows the bank to have the customer do part of the teller's job, the Web site can put the customer in charge of tasks that used to require a telephone call to a service clerk. In some cases, the interactive Web page may even involve fewer errors and better solutions than those provided by a human operator.

A conversation with a human is typically a *linear, sequential procedure*, i.e., asking one question at a time and getting one answer at a time. For example, the telephone company's customer who calls seeking a change in service may not know what services are available or how to describe what he or she wants. Working with the *two-dimensional* visual structure of a Web page, the customer has a multi-dimensional view of the possibilities and works through menus and pathways of his or her own choosing. Further, if the Web page contains the correct version of the price list, policy, or procedure, it's correct for every customer. Employees who don't have the proper job knowledge or misunderstand the policies will make mistakes or give some customers the wrong information.

Assertion #5: Content segmentation will reduce the appeal of brute-force search engines. Although the physical structure of the Internet will probably continue to be monolithic, i.e., an enormous distributed network of transmission lines, its information structure will become ever more compartmented. The segmentation of users by motivation described in Assertion #1 above is driving the segmentation of information. In other words, pedophiles know where to go for the information they want. Medical people learn where to find the information they need. Stock market investors learn which sites suit their needs best. Kids find out where the best games are. Students and academic researchers learn where to find the data they need.

As Internet users evolve from curious newcomers to routine users, they will probably have less and less need for brute-force methods of finding information. This may mean that search engines will remain the method of choice for junkies and others who surf the web for amusement, and become less appealing to others who have specialized needs. Once an attorney, for example, discovers the Web sites of the various legal associations, law schools, and legal databases, he or she is less likely to start searching for information at a general-purpose search engine.

We will probably see a proliferation of special gateway sites, i.e., portals to certain kinds of subject matter of interest to certain kinds of people. This could mean less "high-quality" traffic for the general search sites, and less justification for their advertising charges. Those who have been adopting the "pay for position" policy, i.e., moving certain sites up the list in exchange for listing fees, could find their practices less and less salable as the listed sites find their way into the architecture of special-interest areas.

These assertions, admittedly contrary to the prevailing popular view of the Internet, may intrigue some people, confirm others in their suspicions, and enrage others. In any case, I'd prefer to base my guesses on some definitive form of logic rather than the "gee-whiz" proposition that has exempted the Internet craze from critical scrutiny for too long.

CyberPolitics: The Battle for Control of the Desktop

A funny thing happened on the way to the computer revolution: it got hijacked by big business. What began in the mid-1970s as a technical oddity of interest to a small band of hobbyists and technophiles slowly caught on with normal people, went uptown, and spawned a constellation of lucrative industries. In the early days of the computer revolution, "entreprenerds" set up small firms with clever names and hawked all kinds of gadgets and software programs, typically to one another but increasingly to business people who began to see their possibilities. The computer business then virtually epitomized the entrepreneurial free market. However, as a few of these firms grew to alpha size, the game began to change.

There is now a fierce battle underway for control of the look and feel, and the basic functioning, of the software on the desktop. Every firm directly connected to the information industry will be affected, and many others will be hit by stray bullets from the battle. Even those who think of themselves as merely software users have a big stake in the outcome of this ideological war. The use of information technology is now so all-pervasive that no firm can afford to ignore the implications of the competitive developments that will play out over the next five years.

In recent years, the phenomenal growth and profitability of Microsoft Corporation, under the direction of cybercult hero Bill Gates, has made it a favorite target of resentment, as it has increasingly become characterized as a corporate bully. The technophile culture came to see Microsoft, and by implication Bill Gates himself, as representing the epitome of Big Business greed and arrogance. The firm earned a reputation as not only a ruthless competitor but an unfair one as well. Rivals accuse Microsoft of using the monopoly market power of its Windows operating system to twist the rules for competition to favor itself at every turn. With its corporate headquarters outside of Silicon Valley, far to the north in Redmond, Washington, the company increasingly diverged from the original culture and ethos of the Valley.

The source of the growing animosity toward Microsoft and its cofounder Bill Gates lies in the basic ideology of the computer culture. As Microsoft's Windows product steadily displaced the Apple Macintosh as the computing concept of choice and went on to become virtually the only plausible choice for the vast majority of computer users, software products of every kind became heavily dependent on the design of Windows. The market began to center around Microsoft's operating system, and other entreprenerds found their innovative options sharply limited.

Silicon Valley entrepreneurs developed a cynical expression to describe those who embraced Microsoft's all-encompassing Windows-based world view, to the exclusion of contradicting ideologies. "That guy," they would say, "drank the Kool-Aid." This macabre reference to the legendary Jim Jones cult, which committed mass suicide in Guyana by drinking cyanide-laced Kool-Aid describes a person considered unable to think independently and overly willing to buy the "Microsoft solution."

With the dominance of Windows, Gates and the other Microsoft executives soon realized that they held the ace card in the battle to control what the computer screen of the future would look like. And the holder of the ace card, they also realized, could dictate the terms of the competition to virtually everybody in the game.

Each new version of the Windows operating system, released by Microsoft with great fanfare and enthusiastic promotion by computer magazine editors and even consumer media such as *USA Today*, brought millions of dutiful customers to the computer stores to "upgrade" their systems. It also brought more and more software firms, including Microsoft's potential rivals, to their knees, as they had to rewrite their products to keep them compatible with changes in Windows. Soon, Microsoft was driving virtually the entire PC software industry, and to a great extent the hardware industry as well.

PC makers wanted to offer their products with pre-installed software and, since all of the most popular programs required Windows, they began to purchase the Windows system directly from Microsoft. Once all PC makers were offering a Windows-based software setup on their products, none could turn back. Microsoft now had the entire PC hardware industry in thrall. Large and powerful firms like IBM, Compaq, Dell, NEC, Hewlett Packard, Gateway, and Packard Bell all dutifully accepted Microsoft's terms and prices for the right to market Windows to their customers.

When the Internet and the World Wide Web burst into the public consciousness about 1995, Microsoft began to move aggressively and ruthlessly to dominate this new world of computing as well. Its alleged attempt to exterminate Netscape Corporation, the creator of the Web browser and one of the most admired pioneer firms of the Internet, became for many in the industry the last straw. They concluded that Microsoft intended to dominate and control all aspects of the computer industry, including the Internet, and that it would stop at nothing to achieve its ends.

As anti-Microsoft fervor began to build, more and more stories came to light, involving alleged attempts to destroy, cripple, or take over smaller companies who seemed to have products or technologies that might threaten Windows' dominance. The U.S. Justice Department filed an unprecedented lawsuit in federal court, claiming that Microsoft had used its monopoly position as practically the only supplier of operating systems to bully both PC manufacturers and software makers into yielding the competitive turf.

Further, various members of the powerful Silicon Valley fraternity of business founders, such as Oracle's Larry Ellison, Sun Microsystems' Scott McNealy, and Netscape's Jim Barksdale began to gang up on Bill Gates, Microsoft, and Windows. All participated enthusiastically as witnesses in the Justice Department's lawsuit. Indeed, executives from Apple, Compaq, Hewlett Packard, Intel, and America Online all testified, or hinted, that Microsoft had tried to bully them into abandoning various products and developments that might weaken the Windows hammerlock on the industry. They also began to support alternative technologies such as Java and Linux, which were promising software alternatives to the Windows style of computing.

Ultimately, if Microsoft falls from its lofty perch as the alpha firm in the software industry, it will probably be because it lost touch with the culture, ideology, and value system that put it there. Bill Gates has become, to many in the Silicon

Valley subculture, a traitor to his own kind. In his rise to fame, legendary fortune, and unbridled corporate power, he violated one of the most sacred canons of the geek culture: *inclusiveness*. The early culture of computers cherished the notion that anybody with an idea and a garage could make it, and make it big. Some of them obviously did, and Bill Gates and his cofounder Paul Allen were two of them. But somewhere along the way, Gates parted with the geek value system and went over to the Dark Side. He joined the aristocracy. They saw him as a destroyer of opportunities instead of a creator, and for that he can probably never be forgiven.

Notes

1. Kelly, Kevin. "New Rules for the New Economy: Twelve Dependable Principles for Thriving in a Turbulent World." *Wired*, September 1996, p. 140.
2. For a feisty, contrarian view of the Internet and the whole "wired" philosophy, see Clifford Stoll's *Silicon Valley Snake Oil* (New York: Doubleday, 1995).
3. For a review of the impacts of the "connected economy," see Stan Davis and Christopher Meyer's *Blur: The Speed of Change in the Connected Economy* (Reading, MA: Addison-Wesley).

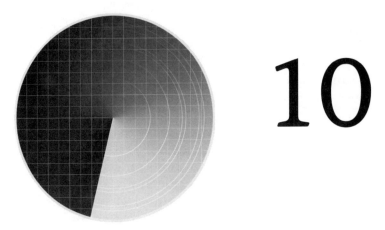

Your Social Radar

*Every man is a creature of age in which he lives;
very few are able to raise themselves
above the ideas of the time.*
—Voltaire

The purpose of the social radar is to understand the social dynamics that shape the intentions of those whose actions can enhance or impede the growth of your business.

Cultural and Social Factors That Shape Customer Intention

Just about everybody knows that if a firm is going to do business outside its home market, its leaders have to understand the social and cultural factors in each local market that can affect demand for its products or services, customer attitudes toward the firm, the practices of its competitors, and a whole host of considerations unique to each particular business culture.

However, even if the firm stays mostly within its home market, it is still critical for the leaders to understand the key *social drivers*—attitudes, values, beliefs, emotions, ideologies, styles, trends, and preferences that affect the market acceptance of its particular value package.

And in either case, the social dynamics that shape your opportunities may originate far beyond your customers. You may find it easier or harder to do business as a result of various social, political, and legal macrotrends beyond your control.

Using your social radar necessarily involves a certain amount of subjective judgment, speculation, and hypothesis about what's going on in the hearts and minds of the humans in your business environment. Trying to make any confident declaration about the implications of a complex set of social dynamics is foolhardy at best, and potentially suicidal at worst.

However, whenever you make your decisions about various socially sensitive business issues, you are unavoidably proceeding from some set of assumptions or conclusions, or at least from some basic frame of reference that reflects your own beliefs and biases. So, you may as well make the premises for your decisions explicit, rather than leaving them submerged in your own mind or in the collective unconscious of the members of your leadership team. By identifying the social factors to which you choose to adapt, you can at least have intelligent debates, evaluate your strategies against some agreed criteria, and rethink the premises if they prove to be invalid.

As imperfect as it is, your social radar can enable you to take a rough inventory of the social factors that can affect your firm the most, focus on the most critical of these, and make some important decisions about how the firm should present itself in its marketplace. This counts for a great deal, even if it can never be more than educated guesswork.

The first thing we must do in making our scan of the social dimension is to scale down our ambitions to something reasonable. Otherwise, we'll be seduced into trying to write a comprehensive encyclopedia, covering every possible social trend or issue we can think of. The social radar must give us a focused, distilled, essential understanding of the forces that are shaping our particular opportunities. We don't have to define all dimensions and all forces for all businesses. We need to limit our inquiry to an intelligent snapshot of the issues we must realistically face. As with all the radar scans, it's just as important to know what not to study as it is to know what you should study.

Focusing your social radar requires some judgment, experience, creative thinking, common sense, and—frequently—

input from a fresh point of view. This dimension in particular is one in which you can trap yourself in your own narrow perceptions, preconceptions, and life experiences. For example, if you want to sell to teenagers, it's important to learn how teenagers think, feel, and view the world. Many adult marketers simply assume that they understand teenagers because they themselves were once teenagers. However, there is very little support for this presumption.

If you're accustomed to marketing your products in developing countries, you may have adopted an unconscious mindset about markets and customers that may not work properly in the larger and richer economies. This principle also applies in reverse: what sells in the richer economies may not fit with the social definition of value in developing countries.

Even moving up-market or down-market from a particular position on the product scale may not be as easy as you think. The basic social definition of the product in the mind of a particular buyer may not extend to the mind of a buyer at a different point on the scale. Not everybody wants to eat Big Macs and not everybody wants to drink champagne. The quintessentially American product Kentucky Fried Chicken didn't go over well in Switzerland. Why? The memorable slogan "It's finger-lickin' good" was repulsive to the Swiss, who don't eat with their fingers. Chevrolet's Nova met with amused indifference in Central and South America. Why? Because in Spanish, the term "no va" means "doesn't go."

One of the largest and most glaring marketing failures in recent history has been the inability of computer and software companies to move the focus of their products from the technophile to the consumer. Despite all the talk about computers becoming consumer products, and all the hype about the Internet being the democratizing influence that makes all users equal, they persist in victimizing their customers with terminology, procedures, and product features created for the technically minded. Computer and software suppliers, with a few exceptions such as game makers, still don't understand how to move the computer from technical toy to everyday tool.

The phenomenal acceptance of the computer comes more from the tolerance and perseverance of non-technical customers than from any strategy for reaching them in their zone of experience. Indeed, it is clear to anyone who cares to view it objectively that the social acceptance and use of the Internet is being paced more by the hype in the popular press than by its practical usefulness or its appeal to non-technical people. The technical people who develop computers, software, and online technology tend to be highly introverted sociophobes with limited verbal skills and limited understanding of the "civilian" world. Their personality traits, social values, and limited communication skills act as pacing factors in the development of information technology, just as strongly as do the physics, chemistry, and engineering knowledge involved in chip design and manufacturing.

At the risk of oversimplifying the exploration of the social forces, we can subdivide the task into three general lines of inquiry: driving values, driving trends, and driving conflicts. Again, focusing on the prospects of your particular enterprise, you can explore the social aspects of your business environment to identify the first-order influences that deserve the most attention.

Driving values. Some values are so primal, dominant, and accepted that they are seldom even mentioned, but mentioning them sometimes helps us to understand them. Sometimes we become starkly aware of a certain driving value only after we give it a name and an identity. Then we may see clearly, perhaps for the first time, how pervasive its influence is. For example, personal mobility is a fundamental value in the American culture. Virtually every American from the age of sixteen onward feels entitled to own and use an individual unit of transportation. Americans own and drive more cars than citizens of most of the rest of the world combined. A huge part of the U.S. economy involves the production, sale, movement, operation, and maintenance of automobiles. In the more socialized countries of Europe, the responsibility of the government to provide services to the needy is so deeply embedded as to be taken for granted. The role of government in leveling economic opportunity and protecting the have-nots from the haves is, in many countries, an article of faith. Yet in other countries, notably the U.S., "welfare" tends to be considered a necessary evil, a form of institutional failure. The mercantile values of consumption and personal convenience are deeply embedded in most English-speaking cultures, yet they are often explicitly rejected in some of the more orthodox

Islamic cultures. In reviewing the driving values that relate to your business, you have to be able to detect and identify the obvious. Which of the dominant values are both relevant to your enterprise and strong enough to shape your opportunities?

Driving trends. Trends are driven by values. A newly rising value, as it gains wider and wider acceptance across a culture or a segment of a culture, gives rise to accepted ways of behaving. One dominant trend in American popular culture for the past two decades has been a steadily increasing emphasis on sexuality in all forms of public expression. Advertising, entertainment, music, and the news have all been subject to intensive sexualization in language and imagery. The intense desire of young people, especially young males, for sexual experience and exemption from parental controls creates an enormous appetite for sexual symbology of all kinds. This becomes a consumer appetite to the extent that those who create and market media products of all kinds search for the response mechanisms that will make their products successful. As a more mundane example, the trend toward privatizing government-owned corporations is gaining momentum around the world. It seems driven largely by a practical ideology that considers competitive enterprises based on economic reward superior to subsidized government operations. As the scorecard progressively favors privatization over government ownership, the trend intensifies, because it satisfies the needs of multiple constituencies. As with driving values, reviewing the driving trends that relate to your business requires detecting and understanding the most obvious. Which of the driving trends are both relevant to your enterprise and strong enough to shape your opportunities?

Driving conflicts. Sometimes the measure of a culture is in its social conflicts—the issues of value which it fails to resolve. In most of the wealthier, media-oriented cultures, a person can easily get the impression that major social conflicts are becoming more numerous and more rancorous. In any case, they seem to be the raw material of which the news is made. Debates rage about abortion, the death penalty, and euthanasia. In the poorer cultures, simple ethnic hatred is often the most common form of conflict. More complex cultures have more complex conflicts, which often center on differences in values and perceptions of entitlements. In the American culture, few issues have been so divisive as that of abortion, characterized as a conflict between a "right to life" and a "right to choose." The conflict is not only one of values but of basic paradigms. Each of those slogans invokes an entirely separate, self-consistent set of explanations about the relationship between a pregnant woman, her unborn fetus, and the rest of society. Canada has for years struggled with a conflict between people in Quebec, who seek to secede from the country and establish a separate republic and those who favor continuing as a multi-cultural state. Australia has an ongoing debate about the issue of declaring itself a separate republic, free of its traditional position as part of the British Commonwealth. The debate could hardly be said to be tearing the nation apart, but nevertheless it expresses deeper-lying differences in values that are beginning to surface in the culture. As with driving values and trends, understanding the conflicts that relate to your business means detecting, describing, and analyzing them. Which of the major conflicts arising in your business environment are both relevant to your enterprise and strong enough that their outcomes can shape your opportunities?

Sometimes the best way to get a grip on the driving values, trends, and conflicts most relevant to your business is a simple brainstorming discussion with people who can contribute special insights and perceptions that you may not have. This is truly an area where a multi-disciplined approach can bear fruit.

Consider assembling a cross-disciplinary team, including such disparate specialties as sociologists, psychologists, economists, historians, artists, entertainers, and philosophers. Pose a simple question such as "What's happening in the X culture?" i.e., the particular culture or segment of a culture you want to understand better. Let the discussion range far and wide, while you and your experts take notes. Head off arguments and debates, capture the most provocative ideas, and assemble them for analysis later. During the analysis, you may discover a few key considerations that establish a useful point of view for assessing the potential impacts.

Careful consideration of a wide range of ideas, together with good judgment in making sense out of them, are the two most important factors in getting a picture on your social radar that you can both trust and put to use.

The American Culture: Prototype for the New World Order?

Some commentators believe that the American socioeconomic structure and culture is the basic point of reference for predicting what most of the developed or developing countries will look like over the next few decades. They believe that America's political influence, its virtually unequaled economic power, its command of information technology, the success of its economic infrastructure, and its highly consumerized lifestyle will make it the model of choice for developing nations to copy. Some go so far as to say that even the economically successful nations of Europe and Asia will move closer to the American model, particularly in privatizing government enterprises, loosening government controls on business, and generally reducing the economic control and influence of government on everyday life.

Others are not so sure. Some see evidence of alternative lines of development appearing in various cultures, particularly non-English-speaking and non-Christian cultures. Japan has for years maintained a peculiar brand of feudal capitalism, based on complex ties between corporations and their suppliers, lenders, and government overseers. China seems to have been cooking up its very own brand of communistic capitalism, which seems to confound many Western entrepreneurs. A number of the Islamic countries base their economic models on the assumption that Islamic religious law is paramount and that all secular activity, including the conduct of business, must operate under its directives. Not all governments accept the American social ideology or its view of economic Darwinism, preferring to take a strong hand in the process of allocating wealth and diminishing what they see as an unfair advantage achieved by certain corporations and social classes over others.

In any case, the American socioeconomic model deserves careful study for a number of good reasons. Whether or not any particular country or corporation chooses to adopt, emulate, or adapt it, or parts of it, useful lessons can be learned from the model and perhaps useful features can be considered.

One reason for analyzing the American model is that it tends to present a picture of what may be in store for similar societies, i.e., English-speaking or Judeo-Christian cultures. Economic structures, political structures, legal systems, social norms, and popular styles are sufficiently similar across these post-European cultures that business practices that arise in America are often readily applicable in similar countries.

Secondly, the American economy is so vast that it can support an enormous amount of research and development, experimentation, and trial-and-error learning in almost all sectors, and particularly in business practices. People in other countries, even those with very different socioeconomic structures, can benefit by observing the success and failure of many new theories, practices, institutions, fads, and fashions, and adopting only those they find appealing. In a sense, America serves as a huge laboratory for the testing and selection of ideas.

Evidence of this is the regular attendance by foreign delegations at major American conferences in almost all fields—science, technology, medicine, business, and many more. The better-known American experts draw large turnouts when they lecture in other countries, partly because they come from America, aside from their particular qualifications and credentials. This is certainly not to assert that the best ideas come only from America, merely that the sheer size of its economy makes it the source of more intellectual raw material. The size of the American publishing industry also plays a part in the rapid migration of American business concepts around the world.

In recent years, the U.S. has been a destination for what some call "industrial tourism," i.e., the trend for executives from other countries to visit and study the major American companies that are legendary for having solved certain critical business problems, or for having developed management approaches that others find appealing. I have often been asked to participate in these kinds of study tours, particularly to help executives sort through and integrate the overwhelming input of ideas and models, some of which contradict others. Many of the management associations in other countries have taken up the role of industrial tour guides, organizing special excursions to America for their members and for executives in their business communities.

From the angle of view of your social radar, the American environment has a number of important characteristics that tend to shape the conduct of business. Understanding these dominant features can help to set a framework for business strategy, either for doing business there or for extrapolating your strategy to other business environments.

For the sake of this discussion, we should acknowledge the following key characteristics of the American socioeconomic environment, as it exists at about the beginning of the second millennium.

America has a two-channel culture. With the arrival of television in the early 1950s, America became a country with two parallel cultures, now coexisting in the minds of a quarter of a billion people. One, which we might call the *personal culture*, or the natural culture, is the long-existing culture of personal experience and local community. Experiences within the family, neighborhood, community, school, church, and at work constituted the raw material for a shared understanding of what it meant to be American, and what values and standards for behavior prevailed. The second culture, arising with television, and reinforced by movies, radio, and to some extent the print media, is one we might call the *popular culture*. The popular culture is the set of ideas, images, impressions, icons, slogans, brands, and stories shared amongst a large number of people as a result of transmitted imagery, not as a result of direct individual experience. In other words, much of what people think about, talk about, debate about, and fantasize about is the substance of *synthetic experience*. Images and feelings associated with war, violence, drama, adventure, and romance seen on television and in movies take their place in the mind in and among the images built from direct personal experience. For most Americans, the idea of living in America is a collage of personal and synthetic experience. Inexorably, the popular culture has been shaped by the demands of television production, which increasingly favors an amusing style of presentation due to the very nature of the experience of watching it. This bifurcated culture explains some of the quandaries faced by political leaders who try to promote various ideas and points of view. In many respects, the popular culture is a set of ready-made slogans, catch-phrases, and visual clichés, which may not always represent the actual substance of thought and feeling. Many Americans, for example, agree emphatically with statements such as "Senators and Congressional representatives are motivated only by their own political interests," while at the same time registering general approval for their own local representatives. One response may simply be a learned slogan—the popular culture—while the other may be an expression anchored in direct experience—the natural culture. Certainly, the values and responses of the popular culture tend to perfuse the experience of the natural culture, but it can be a grave mistake to confuse one with the other.

America is a commercial society. A visitor from Mars, viewing the entirety of the American experience, could hardly avoid the conclusion that the production and exchange of goods and services is the primary dynamic of the nation's existence. Americans are consumers above all else, and even as producers they participate in a never-ending effort to stimulate more and more demand for the fruits of their labor. Social status is largely defined by the ownership of purchased goods, and by the capacity to purchase more. The capital value of the infrastructure for distributing products to all corners of the country dwarfs the entire net worth of most other nations. American firms spend billions of dollars to promote demand for their products. The entire broadcast industry, both television and radio, most of the periodical publishing industry, and increasingly the Internet, pay their operating costs by transmitting advertising messages for pay. Advertising is virtually ubiquitous in the society—on billboards, in radio and TV ads, embedded in movie scenes, woven into children's cartoon shows, on hamburger wrappers, on ATM screens, on T-shirts and hats—virtually any space visible to a large number of people. The brand names of products form the common vocabulary of everyday conversation. Children learn to speak the language of brands from a very early age. The right to market a product is one of the most primal of entitlements in the American culture, and politicians seldom oppose it in any general way, typically only when a particular corporation or industry has been politically demonized and is especially vulnerable to attack. American children, from the earliest ages, are considered a distinct set of consumers and fair game for the promotion of virtually all products that might appeal to them. Many would argue that this consumerist ideology has done more than any other factor to create prosperity for Americans. Others would argue that it has created an economy dangerously dependent on discretionary consumption and "push" marketing rather than natural demand, and consequently is prone to emotionally driven recessions. In any case, it is unrealistic and even foolish to deny the power of this production-consumption ideology in shaping the business environment.

America is an atomized society. America has always been a nation of diverse social and ethnic groups, more than most others on the planet. But for several decades, a combination of factors has been at work loosening, dissolving, and severing the meshwork of social connections that form the macroculture commonly identified as American. Mobility is one of the strongest forces; at least fifteen percent of American households move each year. Families relocate to bigger and more luxurious houses as their means improve. Professional people are willing to move to other parts of the country to advance their careers. The small-town model of neighborhoods previously romanticized in popular literature now exists only in the smallest of towns. Few people know their neighbors well. While Hollywood movies have typically portrayed American life as white, urban, and middle class, the rise of television news programming has emphasized differences of all kinds. Racial, ethnic, political, religious, and economic differences are the raw material of TV drama. News shows, talk shows, and "real-life" dramatizations portray conflict across virtually all dimensions of culture. Increasingly, America is becoming a collection of microcultures, even as the media images of the popular culture portray a world driven uniformly by what some critics call "Hollywood values," i.e., materialism, sexualism, narcissism, and rejection of traditional values of family, community, and society. Paradoxically, as America's media-based culture reaches to all parts of the society every day, ethnic and social divisions are becoming more pronounced, not less. The curious effect of the avalanche of information seems to accentuate differences in the culture, not pave them over. This ever-increasing diversity and differentiation is a distinct feature of the American culture and has profound effects for all companies doing business there.

America is a minimal-control society. One of the most deeply held of all American values is the right, as Supreme Court Justice Louis Brandeis put it, "to be left alone." Within broad limits, a person living in the U.S. has the right to be anonymous if he or she likes. The privacy and sanctity of one's home is considered unarguable. The authority of police and other law enforcement agencies is strictly circumscribed. Increasingly, Americans perceive governments at all levels as necessary for certain social and economic missions and to be kept out of all others. Two doctrines, enshrined in the U.S. Constitution, work to limit the intrusion of government into the lives of individuals. One is the doctrine of "separation of church and state," which dictates that Congress may not pass laws related to the practice of religion. The other is the doctrine of "states' rights," which dictates that all political powers not specifically granted to the U.S. federal government by the Constitution remain with the fifty individual states. Although government bodies at all levels have the power to regulate various business activities, it is generally accepted that regulation should focus on preventing illegal or unethical practices, not on enforcing various social values. In recent years, government programs aimed at *forced parity*, i.e., creating artificial advantages for various groups considered socially disadvantaged, have steadily lost support. Contrasting the American sociopolitical environment with a very different one can highlight the differences in the way governments are allowed to influence the conduct of business. In a country governed by Islamic law, such as Iran, religious precepts are fundamental to commercial decisions. In a country with a highly socialized government, such as Sweden, social values impose very heavy constraints on the actions of corporate leaders. In the U.S., commercial values are virtually on a par with religious values.

America is a knowledge-based society. Information, in virtually all its forms, has always been a basic raw material for American business and in the everyday life of many of its people. America has the largest number of telephones per hundred people than any other country. The number of people with a full secondary education is higher in America than in all but a few other countries. American colleges and universities turn out millions of people with degrees each year. Almost thirty percent of the adult population has one or more college degrees. A greater fraction of the female population is college-educated in America than in almost any other country. The number of patents, trademarks, and copyrights granted in the

U.S. swamps those in the rest of the world. The U.S. book publishing industry dwarfs those of all other countries combined.
The number of American newspapers and magazines is mind-
boggling. Americans see or hear more advertising messages
per person in a typical day than any other citizens on the
planet. American media producers churn out an endless tide of
movies, TV shows, and music albums, which sell in markets all
over the globe. In recent years, American television networks
have developed the capacity to gather news from all over the
world and transmit it all over the world as it is happening,
twenty-four hours a day. American universities and trade
associations host conferences on a bewildering range of eso-
teric topics. The personal computer was developed in America,
and the proportion of its population who use computers is far
higher than in any other country. It seems unlikely that any
other country will overtake the U.S. in computer technology,
largely because of the huge acceptance of the phenomenon in
the society.

Social Values: Rising, Declining, Conflicting

Certainly the dominant national values of the country in
which you seek to do business will affect the opportunities
open to your firm and will set certain rules of engagement.
Doing business in a country with a democratically elected government is usually much different than in a monarchy, or one
with a socialist or communist ideology. Doing business in a
predominantly Islamic country can be radically different than
in more secular cultures. And, of course, extreme versions of
political or religious practice may completely rule out some
countries as attractive business opportunities.

Obviously, also, the level of economic development can
shape the social factors that affect your business, quite aside
from the economic constraints themselves. For example, government bureaucracy, the lack of clear laws for commerce,
higher levels of corruption, and unsophisticated business partners in developing countries can create a completely different
set of constraints than you might face in the more mercantile
cultures.

As the developed countries and most of the developing ones shift toward more media-based social environments, the effect of television, movies, radio, and to some extent periodical publishing is to bring an ever wider array of social issues, causes, conflicts, dilemmas, agendas, and conflicting value systems to the public attention. To the extent that television, in particular, follows the American commercial model, i.e., "free" programming paid for by advertisers, its content gravitates strongly toward an amusement orientation, with conflict, sexuality, scandal, violence, and a focus on the peculiar and aberrant. This forms a natural nutrient medium for the argument of the most extreme social issues and agendas. For nations with state-controlled broadcast industries, this evolution of content will generally be slower.

Some of the more volatile social issues can directly affect your business, others can represent milder or more long-term impacts, and others may have little effect. Your social radar should be carefully tuned to identify those issues or developments that can act either as primary drivers or as dominos, i.e., drivers of your drivers, changing the opportunities available to your business. A fair treatment of even the most dominant social issues would require more space than available here, but the following topics can serve to illustrate the kinds of issues that should show up on your social radar.

Ecological issues, for example, pose direct impacts to the cost structure of certain industries. The extractive industries, such as oil, natural gas, coal, lumber, metals, and minerals, all face increasing pressure to reallocate ecological costs along the resource chain. The social premise that the builder or the buyer of an automobile should pre-pay or co-pay the costs of its pollution and its eventual recycling into the environment can radically change the pricing structure for all participants in its lifecycle if the premise finds its way into law and government tax policy. Social issues that affect companies at one end of the resource chain can work their way to the other end, affecting all players involved.

Unpopular products also draw significant attention because of their social impacts. In recent years, the U.S. tobacco industry has become a favorite demon of Congress and the news media, as the evidence of tobacco's health effects has become virtually undeniable. Although the deadly effects of tobacco have been known for several decades, only in the 1990s has the social and political tide turned against smokers, and consequently the firms that sell their addictive products to them. Australia has also had strong anti-tobacco regulations for a number of years. This trend will almost surely spread to many other countries, although probably at a slower rate.

Other consumer products may be in for similar treatment, such as the junk food category with its sweet colas, high-fat snacks, and candy, much of which is marketed directly to children. Class action lawsuits have wrung hundreds of millions of dollars from companies that make products such as asbestos materials, birth control devices, and breast implants. In 1999, the cities of New York, Chicago, and New Orleans filed lawsuits against the major American gun manufacturers, seeking to hold them financially accountable for accidental deaths involving their products. When social causes become popular, they sooner or later become the raw material of litigation and legislation.

Issues of social justice are very attractive to media producers, and none makes better news than the specter of a greedy, heartless corporation exploiting helpless little people. This model easily fits companies operating in industries such as waste management, where the location of a landfill or processing center will always upset someone; smokestack companies that close money-losing manufacturing operations in cities that have become economically dependent on them; and healthcare providers that deny expensive care to individuals who need it.

Corporate greed and exploitation are indeed facts of life in all industries, but unfortunately too many firms get painted with the same brush. Even the most reputable and ethical firms still have to manage the public perception of their operations.

Exploited workers in third-world countries also make excellent news clips, especially when they make products marketed in the wealthy countries by famous companies such as Nike. In recent years, several Hollywood stars have been burned by lending their names to fashion products marketed in the U.S. but produced by "slave labor" in other countries. The real news angle is the idea of a glamorous, wealthy, and admired beauty getting rich on the backs of poor people suffering in despicable conditions.

Although slave labor, child exploitation, and abominable working conditions are much too common in developing nations, the sad truth is that they seldom find their way into the flow of TV images unless there is some dramatic hook such as the involvement of a movie star or a big corporation. One could argue that there is more cynicism in the editing bay of a typical TV studio than in the boardroom of a typical corporation.

In the U.S., and increasingly in other developed countries, the status of women is a major social issue. Sexual harassment in the workplace and the denial of equal opportunity for advancement ebb and flow in the media as issues affecting the public perception of corporations. In countries such as India and others, feminist activists are fighting their way up from a much lower level of social justice than their counterparts face in America and the richer economies. Japan and certain other Asian countries, as well as many South American countries, tend to fall at the middle of the scale of opportunity and social activism by women. In the U.S. especially, issues of sexual harassment and gender equality have crossed over into the political and legal realms with strong government involvement.

Issues of law and order have been gaining more public attention in most developed countries lately. In the U.S., a number of states have passed stringent laws dealing with sex offenders, drunk drivers, stalkers, and habitually violent people. As the interests of the haves are increasingly pitted against those of the have-nots, we may see a trend toward curtailment of certain civil liberties long taken for granted. For example, several U.S. states have introduced procedures for chemical castration of rapists and child molesters, i.e., injection of medications that reduce libido. The rights of convicted sex offenders to move about freely and anonymously in the society have been sharply curtailed. The right to procreate may eventually be denied to women who clearly cannot cope with child raising, such as drug addicts and homeless teen-agers with multiple children. A number of other developed countries have used a variety of these measures for some time.

The insatiable appetite for social conflict on the part of American news producers and talk shows has contributed to an atmosphere of hyper-sensitivity to anything that could possibly be construed as critical of any supposedly disadvantaged interest group. Statements or actions by public figures or corporations draw fire from special-interest advocates for blacks, Latinos, gays, lesbians, feminists, disabled people, and almost every group that can be portrayed as categorically victimized. Media producers hungry for provocative content are eager to give screen time to even the most obscure or trivial of these supposed atrocities when they cannot find enough other material.

The effect of this attack-dog reporting is a form of press censorship—not censorship *of* the press, but censorship *by* the press. As the media sniper fire intensifies, public figures and corporations guard what they say and do ever more self-consciously, taking great care not to present a target for public attack. In some cases, this stifles valid points of view and distorts public debate about important issues such as race politics, gender politics, and the politics of economic opportunity.

In one peculiar case, Taco Bell Corporation broadcast commercials for its fast-food restaurants showing basketball star Shaquille O'Neal suffering from "taco neck syndrome," caused by tilting his head to eat so many tacos. Newspapers reported a blistering attack from the National Spasmodic Torticollis Association, accusing it of making fun of people afflicted with a rare neurological disorder.

In a more troubling episode, the administrators of a midwestern American university imposed sanctions on a male student for making derogatory comments about female students in a campus newspaper. He was required to apologize publicly and attend a course on "gender sensitivity," or face expulsion. The school's administrators apparently decided it would be less stressful for themselves to sacrifice the male student's right to free speech—however uncivil his message might be—than to face the wrath of the rabid feminists on the campus, some of whom were on the faculty. This event, and others like it, have profound implications for the role of the media in the developed societies, particularly America.

This self-censorship, in the face of the "political correctness" social dynamic, is much more pervasive than many people might believe. I recently noticed it in a very unlikely setting. Living in southern California, I have visited the Disneyland theme park in Anaheim many times. One of the theme displays, visible from the old-style train that circles the park, is a wilderness scene depicting the life of early American settlers.

A settler's cabin is ablaze, presumably illustrating the hazards of early life in the American West.

For years, the scene included the body of a settler, lying in front of the cabin with an arrow in his chest. A year or so ago the settler's body disappeared. I can only speculate that Disney designers made the change so as to avoid a public spanking from any advocacy group that objected to character- izing American Indians as violent. Without the dead settler, the only hazard to be portrayed was that of having your house burn down, which is hardly enough to warrant a special scene.

Some social agendas, although pushed by very small con- stituencies, can generate a great deal of noise when their advo- cates figure out how to capture the attention of news producers. Some animal rights activists, for example, have developed dis- ruptive and even violent methods of stating their case, which vir- tually guarantees them time onscreen. Anti-abortion activists, in some cases, have resorted to threats, physical assault, sabotage, bombings, and even murder to get camera coverage.

And increasingly, the "nut factor," i.e., the fringe segment of society that seems to prefer the more unusual and highly spe- cialized issues, gets its share of attention whenever its meth- ods are provocative enough to become news. The key point for businesses of various kinds is not that these obscure agendas threaten to gain broad acceptance, but that their advocates can be capable of harassment, sabotage, and violence in pur- suit of their causes. Any agenda that makes it to the TV screen deserves to be reviewed in terms of its overall potential to affect the interests of your business.

Social values and attitudes such as patriotism tend to rise and fall over time, as world events make military conflict more or less likely. Since the end of the Vietnam war, young Americans have shown less and less interest in military ser- vice. Coupled with a strong economy and the availability of good jobs in the civilian sector, the U.S. military services have lost much of their appeal.

In 1999 the U.S. Air Force, for the first time in its history, resorted to a $75 million advertising campaign in an effort to recruit the needed number of new people. Enlistment bonuses of several thousands of dollars failed to lure enough enlistees, and attractive civilian jobs lured away record numbers of highly trained technical people. The U.S. Navy fell short of its required strength by 7,000 people in 1998, leaving some ships without full crews. Even the U.S. Army was in peril of falling below the 480,000 level of soldiers mandated by Congress.

Another significant rising social issue, particularly in the new age of cheap and abundant information, is data privacy. This will almost certainly broaden into a major legal issue and a companion political issue, as different standards come into conflict across national boundaries. The U.S. and Europe seem to be at opposite ends of the spectrum regarding views about data privacy. This philosophical gap will certainly have a major impact on international commerce, and particularly Internet commerce.

The U.S. has for years permitted corporations to do almost anything they liked with customer data, within the bounds of commercial activities. The huge MetroMail database, for example, contains data on about ninety million American households. A constant flow of consumer data updates each household record, to the extent that every household can be classified in terms of the number of occupants, children, cars, approximate income, number and brands of credit cards used, rent or own status, mortgage balance, and a host of other variables.

The American commercial view seems to be that, once a person makes a purchase, any identifying information captured as part of the transaction becomes the property of the firm that sold the product. The firm considers itself perfectly entitled to use that information in its further efforts to market to that customer, and to sell it to other firms for the same purpose. In particular, the credit history of most American citizens is accumulated, packaged, and marketed by a small handful of companies, with relatively little control or oversight. In most cases, U.S. citizens have little or no recourse against a credit bureau that distributes erroneous data, except to force the firm to correct it in the future.

Most European countries, on the other hand, have long viewed commercial data as the property of customers, not corporations. Germany, for example, has established a commission for data protection, the Datenschutz, which audits major corporations to make sure they are handling data according to German law. It has the power to restrict the commercial activities in Germany of even the largest global financial firms, for example, if they do not comply with German requirements.

In late 1998, the European Union Directive on Data Protection went into effect, with stringent requirements and legal procedures, including provisions for restricting commercial activities and blocking the Web sites of offending companies. It requires companies who want to use a person's individual data to get permission from that person, and to limit its use to the specified purpose. Individuals can take legal action to determine what information a firm has about them, find out where the firm got it, and require that it be corrected or deleted if it is objectionable under the Directive.

A politically significant provision of the Directive, Article 29, specifies that foreign governments are expected to enact equally stringent provisions of their own, or face controls on data flows into and out of the EU nations. This, and other political efforts within the U.S., may help to kindle a new wave of interest in privacy, but the gap between American and European practices is still quite wide. Closing it or reconciling the two views will probably require considerable time, effort, and conflict.

Even as representatives from government and commercial sectors in the U.S. and Europe work to bridge the philosophical gap regarding data privacy, both sides seem to be moving further in their original opposing directions. American Web site operators and software designers, for example, insist on implanting "cookie" files on the computers of those who view their sites. A cookie is a small file that can record data about the visitor's computer, software, email address, and Web sites he or she has visited. Many European privacy advocates consider the cookie a quintessential example of an exploitive mindset that is distinctly American.

In early 1999, Intel Corporation set off a firestorm of protest and debate when it disclosed that its newest Pentium microprocessor chips would be serialized, and that each one would have a distinct digital identity. Upon interrogation by a program on a Web site, the user's software could transmit the identity of the computer to the Web site. The benefit of this feature was presumably that the Web site could customize its response to each individual visitor, based on stored information about that person's preferences. The Orwellian downside was the prospect of losing one's privacy and anonymity while browsing the Web.

With the rising concern among computer users about viruses that can destroy their data, hackers that can destroy Web sites and steal critical business data, and diabolical Web sites that track their activities and bombard them with unwanted marketing messages, this issue of data privacy will probably grow to the proportions of a major social and political issue in the U.S. as well as in Europe and elsewhere. The romance of the Internet is steadily giving way to the practical realization that brings its own set of problems, issues, and threats.

Your social radar may detect other social issues, trends, events, dilemmas, or agendas not mentioned in this discussion. Some may be unique to your line of business; others may be domino effects of other social forces. In any case, it is important to have a reasonably clear concept of the social factors that are shaping your business, and to think through the major contingencies that might arise as they play themselves out in your environment.

Cultural Imperialism and Protectionism

The economic dominance of the U.S. has led to worldwide acceptance of many of the artifacts of the American culture, in addition to the products of its enterprises. Sitting in a cocktail lounge in a Copenhagen hotel, I was startled to hear the piano player play and sing an astonishing variety of American popular songs, from show music to pop-rock tunes. Walking by the beach in Tel Aviv, I passed Hilton and Sheraton hotels, McDonald's hamburger shops, and Pizza Hut shops. In Singapore I saw young people wearing T-shirts displaying the names of American sports teams. In Tokyo I visited a distinctly American-style pizza parlor, complete with employees wearing roaring twenties costumes and singing old popular tunes like "I've Been Workin' On The Railroad." American culture, it seems, is everywhere.

Notwithstanding the anti-American fervor so aggressively displayed in certain countries, the simple fact is that America ranks as the most admired country in the world. The wealthy, consumerist American lifestyle is the envy of all but the most ascetic cultures. American media firms virtually dominate the music and movie business worldwide. American news networks such as CNN, FNN, and MSNBC broadcast the Americentric view of world news on a twenty-four-hour schedule. American computer and software products are used all over the world. American medical practice is widely regarded as the state of the art. American books are commonly translated into other languages. American management thinking and business practices are once again the model for international study.

This wide acceptance of the images of the American culture, if not necessarily the substance of it, can obviously work to the advantage of American firms seeking to market their goods and services overseas. However, in recent years a kind of anti-American cultural counter-trend has been rising in some countries, particularly in the developed economies. There seems to be a growing feeling among some national political establishments that the world has become too Americanized.

With American products so omnipresent, particularly fast-food restaurants, movies, music, videos, fad toys, and sports gear, more and more people seem to feel that their own national cultures are being somehow invaded or polluted by American logos, brand names, and symbols. They see this as a form of cultural imperialism, or even perhaps cultural colonialism, as American firms dominate their respective sectors in other countries. The distinctly American language and style of the Internet also troubles a number of cultural advocates in other countries, who would like to see it internationalized, or at least "de-Americanized."

The French government, for example, has made several efforts to limit the import of American entertainment products, particularly music, videos, and movies. Some political figures have floated proposals to limit the number of hours of non-French television that can be broadcast.

Trade barriers such as quotas and tariffs have been in effect for many years as part of the normal political competition between nations, but recently other, more subtle barriers have been arising to impede the presumed takeover of world commerce by American products.

Japan, for instance, has long employed the *keiretsu,* an intricate system of interlocking relationships among firms in certain industriesthat has the effect of passively resisting the incursion of foreign firms into the Japanese business environment. These well-rationalized subtle barriers have been giving way in recent years, particularly under the pressure created by the Asian financial crisis that began in 1997, but they are still largely in place and effective.

A revealing case study in cultural defensiveness lies in the exclusion of rice imports to Japan. Key Japanese political leaders have long been dependent on the support of the country's rice farmers, who number a relatively small part of the population but wield enormous political power because of a historical quirk in the apportionment of legislative seats to farming districts. For years they rationalized various "soft" regulations and unspoken restrictions on foreign rice with the polite explanation "Japanese consumers prefer the taste of Japanese rice, and don't want to buy foreign rice." As the lack of competition kept Japanese rice prices embarrassingly high, pressure mounted to allow imported rice into the country. Stubbornly, the Japanese government imposed steep tariffs on imported rice as recently as 1999, especially from the U.S., with the effect that rice from California sold, in Japan, for more than twice its price in America.

In China, the state-owned news media have played a lead role in fostering "buy Chinese" sentiments, largely by a barrage of negative reporting about foreign products and companies. In a highly publicized incident, Northwest Airlines took a sustained and concentrated media beating in major newspapers, as well as on China Central Television and China National Radio, over an alleged on-board incident between a Chinese passenger, en route to Los Angeles, and a flight attendant.

In a particularly aggressive move, the Chinese Electronics Industry Ministry joined forces with the State Technology Supervision Bureau to hold a press conference denouncing the quality of electronic products made by foreign firms such as Sony, Samsung, and Sharp. Even the American retailing giant Wal-Mart ran into a brutal press campaign, charging false advertising and illegal business practices. Chinese consumers and retailers have apparently reacted strongly to this "reverse advertising," as the ministries hoped. This is one of the more unusual, and perhaps distinctly Chinese, forms of cooperation between government and industry, and provides an object lesson in the kinds of thinking companies can encounter in developing economies.

Some political analysts argue that the Western model of internationalism, largely expressed in the American philosophy of global commerce, is by no means enthusiastically embraced by a majority of third-world regimes. According to UN Secretary General Kofi Annan, "Throughout much of the developing world, globalization is seen not as a term describing objective reality, but as an ideology of predatory capitalism."[1]

Commerce, whether international or domestic, is every bit as social and political as it is economic. No firm can afford to proceed in ignorance in an environment where social activists, pressure groups, protectionist governments, and entrenched competitors are working constantly to shape the conditions under which business gets done. Even if certain forces in the social environment seem to have little direct effect on your business, you may still find that their domino effects on your customers, partners, or competitors can change the opportunities available to you.

Notes

1. Speech by Kofi Annan at Harvard University, September 17, 1998. Excerpted in *The Futurist*, March 1998, page 27.

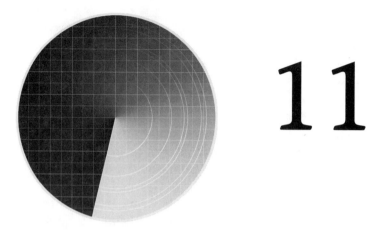

Your Political Radar

*Politics, n. A strife of interest masquerading
as a contest of principles.*
— Ambrose Bierce
The Devil's Dictionary

The purpose of the political radar is to understand the intentions of those who can influence the rules for success in your business.

As with the economic radar, the social radar, and others, we find that many presumably political trends and issues spill over into the other radar sectors. It is hard to imagine an issue that is solely political in its implications, without social and economic effects, for example. Again we must remind ourselves that the eight strategic radar "sectors" are simply useful guides for our thinking processes. There is no need to try to force-fit any finding into a single, "correct" category.

There's More to Politics Than Politics

When business people think about the political environment and its possible effects on their enterprises, they often tend to think strictly in terms of the legislatures and regulators who set the rules that affect their industries. The terms "politics" and "political" tend to trigger standard ideas and images associated with governments of various levels, or similar bodies that exercise formal authority. But politics, as it affects businesses, is a more complex and interesting proposition than just lawmakers and laws. Your political radar should include all of the key influences on the lives of your customers and competitors, as well as your own.

My favorite definition of politics is:

the study of the control systems of a society, and the people, agendas, and methods that influence them.

Politics is all about influence. It's about how a person, group, or coalition can gain access to the control systems, or access to the people in charge of the control systems, and have their desires drive the rules for behavior.

What's a control system? It's a set of structures, rules, and relationships that people allow to influence their behavior, whether because of need, greed, or fear of punishment. The structure of a national, provincial, or municipal government is a control system. A system of criminal laws is a control system. A code of civil law is a control system. A military command structure is a control system. A corporate structure is a control system. A regulatory agency and its mechanisms for influence over corporations in a certain industry, such as healthcare, is a control system. The structure of a university is a control system.

But the most important feature of any control system is the *organizing principle*, or political ethos, that governs it. Even the most highly structured government can't function without a set of motives that activate its machinery. A monarchy, a dictatorship, an oligarchy, a junta, an elected government, a church, a corporation, or a sports team operates from an *ideology* of some kind. The people who have the most influence over that ideology, and sell their ideas for implementing it, can be said to have the most political influence in the situation.

Their motives may be noble or venal, altruistic or selfish. The ideology may be more or less consistent, more or less palatable to others, and more or less applicable to the objectives of the organization. It may range from highly consistent to completely fragmented, with various factions contending for dominance. The behavior of the institution, and its influence

on the lives of those it controls, will depend on the nature of its
ideology and its competence in implementing it.

To analyze the various "control systems" that can influence
your business, you need to think very broadly about what's
being controlled and how. There is a wide spectrum of influence in human life, ranging from formally constituted governments, to social institutions such as churches, associations,
and universities, all the way to the power structures that
define how a particular industry might work and the unwrit-
ten rules for behavior in a certain profession.

Since the beginning of the twentieth century, the press has
emerged as a kind of invisible control system, a kind of shadow
government in its own right. Those who refer to the publishing
and broadcasting establishment as the Fourth Estate want to
call attention to its powerful role in human life. In some ways,
the firms who create and regulate the flow of information in
the society act as governing bodies, promoting some ideologies
and squelching others.

Some elements of the political environment are obvious and
easy to identify. National governments pass laws and create
regulating bodies that set up rules for doing business. State,
provincial, or local governments do the same. The influences of
one may contradict or conflict with the influences of another.
Every executive team should clearly understand the implications of the formal laws and regulations that govern the right
of their enterprise to conduct business. The framework of
trade laws and regulations is usually a good starting point for
the political scan, because it helps you identify the constraints
on your actions. It tells you what you can't do and what you
must do. In between is the range of action open to you.

But once you understand the formal structure of the key control systems that dominate your opportunities, you must go
further and learn as much as possible about the ideologies that
animate them, and the source of those ideologies. Then you
may be able to guess what kinds of changes might be coming in
the political environment that affects your business. You can
speculate more intelligently about possible strategic options
you may be considering, and whether the developing political
climate is more likely to favor them or oppose them.

Case in point: The European Union, and the set of plans and
structures for implementing it, signals a clear ideology with

clear economic, social, and political implications. An integrated Europe has a lot of support, although not all countries are equally enthusiastic and not all have yet signed on completely. Doing business in Europe, whether your firm is home-based there or elsewhere, will increasingly depend on working within the ideology of an integrated continental financial system, trade system, and business culture.

Case in point: Doing business in Japan, for foreigners, has always involved an element of complexity and enigma. Japan's peculiar brand of feudal capitalism, with its interlocking corporate structures known as the *keiretsu,* the heavy hand of government ministries, and a dash of xenophobia, presents a unique set of political considerations for any foreign firm. Does one team up with an established Japanese firm and play the silent partner? Does one go it alone and try to build a new brand concept? Does one buy up an existing player? Is it wise to advance the foreign identity, brand concept, and corporate logo, or is it better to impersonate a Japanese business entity as much as possible? These are fundamentally political questions whose answers may drive a whole variety of related issues of finance, product development, marketing, and infrastructure.

Case in point: The city of Brisbane, in Australia's state of Queensland, has for a number of years operated on an enterprise model rather than the standard bureaucratic pattern of a municipal bureaucracy. A series of progressive mayors and a strong executive branch have taken many pages from the book of business and have applied the methods of customer research, strategic planning, marketing, and process improvement to guide the development of one of Australia's largest and most prosperous political entities. Changing the ideology of government from one of regulation to one of empowerment changes the design of the control systems. What a government organization does, and how, reflects the values and views of its leaders.

The Heavy Hand of Government: Unanticipated Consequences

One of America's famous legal philosophers, Supreme Court Justice Oliver Wendell Holmes, remarked "Nobody with a weak stomach should watch either sausage or the law being made."

I must confess to belonging to the *laissez-faire* intellectual camp, at least mostly, when it comes to the question of whether and how government should try to shape commerce. Many business people do as well, although some are rather selective in their preferences. "The government should stay out of business!" an executive thunders. But in a footnote to the conversation, he amends his view slightly: "But the government should definitely keep cheap foreign products from flooding our market and stealing jobs from our people." It seems everybody wants something a bit different from government.

And government leaders, being human, are enormously tempted to try to give people what they want, particularly those who have some part to play in returning them to political office. Some governments tinker with money supplies and exchange rates. Others buy and sell commodities on the open market, hoping to stabilize volatile trading. Others own and operate corporations that compete—usually ineptly—against firms in the private sector. Government attempts to fix the problems of society by bullying business enterprises range from the merely annoying, to the comical, to the downright destructive.

Case in point: The city government of San Francisco has long supported various aspects of the gay and lesbian political agenda. Under the mayorship of former state legislator Willie Brown, a noted social activist, the city passed an ordinance in 1997 requiring all firms doing more than $5,000 per year of business with the city to provide the same health and insurance benefits to partners of gay workers that they offered to "straight" workers. This put the city squarely in the position of recognizing gay partnerships as equivalent to heterosexual marriages, and using the city's political influence to force companies to do the same.

However, getting some 16,000 firms to comply with the political agenda turned out to be a bit more difficult than they had expected. Managers of city departments had to stop doing business with both Federal Express and United Parcel Service, two of the largest international package transport firms, when they refused to comply with the demand. They had to pay smaller, less qualified firms up to ten times as much to ship items to Europe. News of poorer service and higher prices on everyday items such as toilet paper caused grumbling among many managers, but few were bold enough to speak against the ordinance in a city long known as a center of gay and lesbian life. The city did, however, continue doing business with the U.S. Postal Service, even though it does not offer domestic-partner benefits to gays and lesbians.

Case in point: In a similar spasm of social responsibility, the state government of Hawaii mandated that all businesses offer healthcare plans to their workers and that the firms pay part of the costs. Hailed on the U.S. mainland as a forward-looking program, the state's plan had a number of significant unanticipated consequences. The most serious result was that employers capitalized on a part-time provision in the law, which applied only to employees working twenty hours or more per week. The result: a big reduction in the number of full-time jobs, and a huge number of workers with nineteen-hour part-time jobs. It became very common in Honolulu to find workers traveling to two different jobs in the same day to work their weekly total of thirty-eight hours, if they could succeed in coordinating their work schedules between two different employers.

In his classic little book, *Economics in One Lesson*, Professor Henry Hazlitt advanced a very simple proposition:

> **Virtually every time a government intervenes in a free-market economy, it causes exactly the opposite of its intended result.**[1]

For example, Hazlitt points out the folly of the minimum wage, so popular with socialist or social-activist administrations. If the government pegs the minimum wage rate close to the market price for unskilled labor, it has little or no effect. If it sets the wage well above the market price, employers eliminate or don't fill as many low-end jobs as they can, driving up unemployment among the very people who can least endure it. If it sets the wage well below the market price, it has no effect because employers are already paying higher wages to get the employees they need. Hazlitt offers a number of other examples to support his argument that help from the government is usually worse than no help at all.

Management expert Dr. Peter F. Drucker makes a similar point. "Sooner or later," he maintains, "just about every government program, with the notable exception of warfare, accomplishes exactly the opposite of its stated objective."

With a wide range of government entities operating in a typical fair-sized country, there is a spectrum of sociopolitical ideologies. These varied ideologies find expression in all manner of legislation, social programs, and regulatory policies. Some local and mid-level officials operate according to their own homemade ideologies, while others prefer to study the theories of various professional ideologues in universities and think tanks.

Some political parties bring their ready-made ideologies with them when they come into power. Europe recently has seen a widening conflict between traditional socialist views of guaranteed wages and benefits, and the "destructuring" rationale recently popular in America. The French government tried to cope with the country's intractable unemployment problem by legislating it out of existence. It tried to push through legislation reducing the standard work week to thirty hours, while requiring employers to continue paying the same gross wages for the work. This, presumably, would cause them to need and hire more workers. *Voilà!* the unemployment problem is solved. *Mais non.*

This economically naive line of reasoning, tried in various other desperate regimes, works on the assumption that employers will not respond by immediately looking for ways to limit their rising labor costs. Job cutting, replacing low-skill jobs with automation, and outsourcing tend to follow directly as unanticipated consequences. The two contrasting governmental views of the corporation, either as an economic mechanism for growth or a political cow to be milked, are at the core the difference in economic success from one nation to another.

Many governments, particularly in Europe, try desperately to avoid the terrifying "tractors driving down main street" syndrome, i.e., the prospect of mass strikes by workers in various industries, disgruntled at the prospect of losing this or that fringe benefit. For many, it is too convenient to demonize Big Business and deflect the rage of the disaffected toward the corporations as a way to avoid the political hard work of dismantling the parasitic governmental constraints on the economy.

And in some cases, the people running a government are simply too backward and ignorant for their own good. For years the country of Zaire, recently renamed the Democratic Republic of Congo, has dozed on top of one of the world's largest deposits of industrial grade diamonds. Yet, because of the greed, hunger for power, and sheer economic ignorance of one government after another, mining of diamonds has nearly come to a standstill. No reputable firm has found a way to make a reasonable return on its investment, knowing that corrupt governments will confiscate most or all of the revenues from the operation. The people living under these regimes pay a terrible price for the economic ignorance of their leaders.

In more politically benign environments, many firms choose to employ lobbying efforts, both formal and informal, to inform and influence key political leaders. Although a treatment of lobbying methods and goals is beyond the scope of this book, it is certainly advisable to know which legislators and regulators are most involved in the primary issues for your business, and to understand the ideologies that guide their actions.

The Age of Agendas and Dilemmas

Your political radar must also be able to detect critical social issues through the informational fog created by a media environment obsessed with drama. We seem to be coming into a period in which, increasingly, we find the interests of one particular sector of society pitted against those of another. Perhaps this has always been the case, economically at least, but the daily news seems more and more taken up with the theater of agendas, dilemmas, and conflicts. Issues affecting the interests of a particular business enterprise are very likely to be embedded in highly dramatized stories, with their meanings obscured by the reporting techniques used to emotionalize the content.

An issue like food safety and sanitation, for example, is less likely to be presented in the context of experts explaining the dangers and costs, and more likely to be presented in the context of a dramatized story about people dying from eating food sold by one particular company, which becomes a one-dimensional villain in a morality play. The content becomes subordinate to the drama, and experts, if there are any, get relegated to the role of supporting actors.

More worrisome is the tendency of newswriters to blur or eliminate the distinction between journalistic opinion—the slant—and content. A very strong trend in "issues reporting" over the past decade or so is to dramatize and sensationalize coverage, with content becoming ever more scarce and implication becoming ever more prominent. In the process of emotionalizing the presentation, newswriters unavoidably make choices that push viewers and readers toward certain interpretations and moral judgments.

Journalists, particularly in America, have for years tried to delude the public, and often themselves, that there is such a thing as "objective journalism," and that they practice it. In recent years, with the media-led destruction of one public figure after another, this charming fiction has become ever more difficult to promote. The impeachment trial of U.S. president Bill Clinton in early 1998, and the media orgy which centered on the most salacious details of the allegations of his sexual misconduct, brought U.S. public opinion of America's news establishment to an all-time low. A record number of Americans now believe that the companies, newswriters, and newsreaders who populate the core of the media industry have virtually no meaningful code of ethics regarding the making and selling of their product.

Certain social issues tend to expose journalistic bias better than others. When the slant of a story tends to match the pre-established ideology or values of a majority of viewers or readers, i.e., the presenting journalist shares the views of most readers, he or she tends to emphasize the moral tone of the story and minimize attention to conflicting views. But if the journalist prefers an alternative ideology to the one currently popular, he or she tends to portray the issue as one of conflicting ideologies, with roughly equal coverage given to both. This creates the impression that the citizenry is about equally divided, or at least that the matter does not enjoy a significant consensus.

Statistical surveys of American journalists and many others involved in news production indicate they are decidedly liberal in their personal political views. Surveys of those living and working in the Washington, DC market indicate an overwhelming personal preference for Democratic candidates, causes, and objectives over those of Republicans. Certainly, every journalist should be entitled to his or her political views as an ordinary citizen, and there is no guarantee that one's views will taint his or her perceptions, choices, and explanations. However, the possibility is real and cannot be ruled out as a general matter. Issues such as physician-assisted suicide, abortion, same-sex marriages, and many others tend to challenge the ability of journalists to exclude their personal biases.

The issue of the death penalty in the U.S. shows more clearly than most others the differences between the personal social views of many journalists and those of the general public. Surveys over a number of years have indicated that a very large majority of Americans favor the death penalty for certain crimes, with the number in favor ranging from about seventy-five percent to as high as eighty-five percent. This level of approval has consistently stayed roughly the same for many years. However, whenever a newsworthy execution takes place, most newspapers apply exactly the same slant: the controversial execution has once more dramatized the fierce debate in the country about the desirability of capital punishment.

The execution story focuses on the fear, apprehension, and suffering of the person about to be executed—the victim—and displays that pathos as the background for the calls of the aggrieved family for justice and the calls for compassion by those who oppose the death penalty. Regardless of the division of opinion on the issue—any issue—the 50-50 treatment of two opposing views raises or lowers both to the level of implied parity. The design of any news story is a decision rooted in some ideology or other. Most educated people have little trouble understanding this point, although they may be distracted from its effects if the dramatic presentation is effective. Journalists seem to be the only ones who still deny it.

The purpose of this discussion is not to dwell on the problems of the news industry but rather to form a realistic view of how the issues affecting a particular business enterprise find their way to the attention of those in a position to influence the consequences. Many executives become frustrated by the stories they see in newspapers and on television, portraying corporations as typically cynical, exploitive, heartless, and arrogant. Often their lack of understanding of the news industry leads them to victimize themselves with their own naive expectations.

These days, every senior executive needs a practical understanding of how the news gets made and the way in which companies and their leaders are cast into the roles defined for them by the story line. And certainly, every executive must expect, sooner or later, to participate in an important media interview. Knowing how to manage these opportunities has become an indispensable leadership skill.

Media expert John Wade, who trains executives to manage media interviews, says:

> The agendas of the media and business are not naturally compatible, even though the media are themselves businesses with the same ultimate motivation of making money. There has always been distrust between the two entities, even before the advent of television. There is now a wary coexistence with each willing to use the other for possible benefit.[2]

A discussion of the techniques for dealing with the media deserves a complete book in itself, but a few key points may be useful here.

Probably the first realization every executive needs to make is that news companies seldom have any interest in making life difficult for any particular company or its leaders. They have no innate desire to make businesses look bad or good. In general, they are neither against the interests of your firm, nor in favor of its interests. Their interest is in selling news, not doing battle with the corporate world.

To realize this, you only have to watch your local news for the occasional "isn't that sweet" story about how a local company helped a school, or rescued a stranded whale, or allows its delivery drivers to check in on little old ladies confined to their homes. They are quite willing to assign a company to a positive role in a news story. The key point is: *there must be a story*. If you don't understand this, you risk descending into a state of permanent paranoia. The fact that the corporation as the evil empire is a more popular choice for typecasting than the benefactor of the community says something about the market, not about the motives of news producers.

The second key realization is that news companies are basically addictive organizations. Just as some small firms become totally dependent on the business of one large customer, news organizations have become totally dependent on advertising revenues, at least to the extent that they operate on the American model of "free" information. This means that they have no choice but to design their products to capture the increasingly fickle attention of people who are bored, inattentive, and jaded by an oversupply of drama. This is the reason that terrorists resort to ever more horrific acts to gain attention for their agendas; they understand that yesterday's drama is today's boredom.

Newsroom veterans have an old and revered maxim: "If it bleeds, it leads."

The third key realization for executives who hope to understand the political treatment of agendas and issues in the press is that most journalists don't like to work hard, either mentally or physically. Providing them with *interesting* information, which can become the substance of a provocative treatment, can often reduce the temptation for them to conjure up conflicts, crises, and moral dilemmas. To be fair, the job of digesting and interpreting complex concepts, facts, and figures is intellectually fatiguing. Many news people have a hard time keeping a high standard of inquiry, analysis, and synthesis as they deal with one story and deadline after another. It only makes good sense to help them do a good job.

As an author, I've been interviewed countless times by broadcast and print journalists. I have met with many who are bright and capable, and some who displayed a remarkable grasp of the concepts I've presented in my books, and who have clearly invested time and mental energy to prepare for the interview. Others, however, are just plain lazy. And a few are not even very bright. Just as the capable and diligent journalist can build a quality information product based on an interview, the lazy or incompetent can do great damage. This is why the PR departments of publishing firms provide a kit of simple materials to interviewers, including the actual text of interview questions they can use.

Anti-Corporate Politics

When T.J. Rodgers, founder and CEO of Cypress Semiconductor, received a form letter from Sister Doris Gormley, representing a Catholic order of nuns, he read it carefully. Then he went through the roof. Sister Gormley, it seemed, was putting him on notice that her order was planning to vote against the re-election of the entire corporate board, including him, at the next shareholders' meeting. Her reason: the board had no female or minority members.

Rodgers immediately drafted a reply to the Sister, which he later included with the company's annual report to the shareholders. In his letter, he informed her that the primary qualifications for board membership were knowledge of the semiconductor industry and its problems, and a solid grasp of business principles. Since he had not yet found a woman with those qualifications, he felt no obligation to appoint someone to any of the five critical positions on the board solely on the basis of reproductive status. He further informed her that her proposition was indeed *immoral*, in that she was asking him to disadvantage the thousands of people who had entrusted the board with their funds, for the sake of making an empty political gesture.

Rodgers' letter triggered hundreds of responses, over ninety percent of them in favor of his action, including a number from self-identified feminists. The *Wall Street Journal* ran a front page article on the controversy, including interviews with Sister Gormley and Rodgers. Members of Congress, other CEOs, and none other than Nobel economist Professor Milton Friedman expressed views on the matter. Friedman referred to an article he had written for *The New York Times* in 1970, titled "The Social Responsibility Of Business Is To Increase Its Profits."

The core of Rodgers' argument, and the views of others in business who have spoken out against special-interest snipers who advocate "socially conscious investing" is that trying to penalize a corporation is simply a case of choosing one interest group over another. In the Cypress case, the advocate was claiming that the social good of appointing an unqualified member of a presumably disadvantaged group to the board outweighed the financial interests of thousands of shareholders.

Corporations have always been the target of assaults and accusations by socially motivated people, many perfectly well-meaning in their zeal, who feel they should be expected to solve the social problems of the society. "After all," they reason, "they have all that money. Why can't they use it to help this or that person, this or that cause?"

A few years ago, a displaced factory worker named Michael Moore achieved his fifteen minutes of fame by producing a movie titled *Roger and Me*, based on the plight of people in the town of Flint, Michigan. They had depended on the nearby General Motors car plant for their livelihood, and GM planned to close the plant because of excess capacity and high operating costs.

Moore built his film as a slice of life, showing the struggles of ordinary people left out of the American dream by a big, greedy, heartless corporation. His special touch was a series of cinematic ambushes on Roger Smith, then CEO of the company, portraying himself as an innocent reporter just trying to get the all-powerful mogul to stop and explain why he'd kicked all these people out of their jobs. The film made great cinema, especially for those who need to see life in terms of justice and injustice, but it added little to our understanding of the problems of cities, families, and communities. And it certainly offered no plausible rationale for corporations helping communities by operating plants that are no longer needed.

At the risk of launching off on a personal political rant: it seems to me that the corporation, as an economic invention, is one of the few things we have in the developed world that works extremely well. When it fails to create value for human beings and benefits for the society at large, it is usually when we try to twist it into something it can never be. A corporation is an economic creature and nothing else. The board of directors of a corporation, at least in Western law, has one and only one responsibility: to safeguard the assets of the firm's owners, the shareholders. No one else looks after that interest. No one else can. And, if they fail to do it, the corporation fails to deliver the only valuable outcome of which it is capable: focusing human energy to achieve worthwhile objectives.

A corporation is a marvelous invention, the social equivalent of the wheel and axle. When we try to make it into something other than what it is, an economic structure for organizing resources, we are insisting that it serve a purpose for which it was not invented. We are not disavowing the critical importance of poverty, inequality, and tragedy in human life simply by acknowledging that a corporation is not the mechanism of choice for solving them. But when we understand that corporations are adaptive creatures, shaped by the decisions of the officers and directors, who are the only stewards of the shareholders' interests, we can arrange the playing field so that corporations contribute to the objectives of the society through the very process of competing with one another for resources, for which they are so marvelously well designed.

Of course, every civilized society must demand that the leaders of its corporations behave responsibly and ensure that their enterprises operate within the accepted boundaries of honest competition, respect for human rights, and concern for the natural environment. Further, the "social marketplace" tends to reward those firms that treat their employees well. Many firms have distinguished themselves as good places to work and good corporate citizens. But it makes little sense to expect corporations to take up social causes as their primary motivations.

In short, if you really want to eradicate poverty, figure out how to make the absence of poverty profitable, and it will disappear quickly. But don't waste time and energy condemning Big Business for not doing what it was never designed to do. Corporations can only achieve results valuable to the society by amplifying human energy, not by allocating it to social agendas.

Notes

1. Hazlitt, Henry. *Economics in One Lesson*. New York, Crown Publishing Group, 1981.
2. Wade, John. *Dealing Effectively With the Media*. Los Altos, California: Crisp Publications, 1992, Page 15.

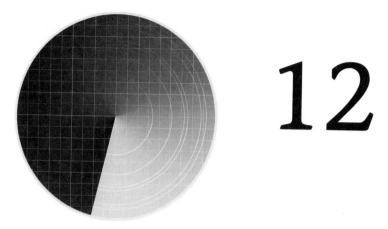

12

Your Legal Radar

Lawyer, n. One skilled in the circumvention of the law.

Litigant, n. A person about to give up his skin for the hope of retaining his bones.

Litigation, n. A machine which you go into as a pig and come out as a sausage.
—Ambrose Bierce
The Devil's Dictionary

The purpose of the legal radar is to understand the legal constraints, processes, and events that can create or destroy opportunities for growing your business.

Trade: Laws and Lawlessness

Certainly the leaders of any business have a responsibility to know and abide by the laws that govern their particular industry, as well as the general legal requirements of the national culture in which they operate. But having a good, working legal radar requires more than simple compliance. It requires thoughtful consideration of a whole range of legal considerations that can make or break your business. Each company must come to terms with a unique set of legal truths, trends, and issues that define its legal environment.

If you're doing business in one of the advanced economies, you'll probably be less vulnerable to illegal behavior on the part of others, such as unscrupulous competitors or corrupt government functionaries. In legally immature societies, you may face a whole range of handicaps, including theft, sabotage, extortion, and terrorism, as well as more socially benign crimes such as fraud, violation of contracts, and theft of intellectual property.

Indeed, you may find yourself seriously considering whether to do business at all in certain environments, in view of the risks associated with inadequate legal protection. Locating a plant in a third-world country might seem like a great idea, if you consider only the financial factors such as ultra-low real estate costs, construction costs, and labor rates. But a host of other factors could make it a bad deal overall. Consider, for example, the availability of reliable labor with the required skills; infrastructure issues such as transportation; the availability of fuel and raw materials; the availability of financial support services, and the physical security of the facilities.

In the category of legal issues, which we are considering here, you need to make a careful review of the legal codes where you plan to operate, and particularly the laws that apply to trade. This is not a subject for learning by accident or trial and error. Failure to detect or avoid certain legal landmines *before* you open a business can set you up for a very negative experience. You may find that the legal code in a less developed country is weak, vague, or even nonexistent. In nondemocratic societies, what passes for a legal code is typically a hodgepodge of restrictions and definitions of punishable offenses, with the primary purpose of enabling the ruling regime to squelch its political enemies and snuff out dissent. There may be very few legal constraints on the ability of government officials to impose punitive or exploitive taxes, fees, or fines on foreign businesses, or even to confiscate their assets. Getting expert advice and assistance in this area can be very important.

You also need to evaluate the structure of the legal process wherever you plan to operate. Legal codes in many third-world countries tend to favor indigenous businesses outrageously over foreign enterprises doing business there. The associated body of case law and legal practice is often heavily distorted toward victimizing foreign firms and allowing local firms to renege on legal and financial obligations. Wherever corruption is rampant, a pattern of bribes and payoffs can pit both the government and the local firm against the foreign operator.

Even if the country of interest has a reasonably stable political and social environment, with a reasonable code of laws, you may still find various difficult issues appearing on your legal radar. For example, protecting copyrighted material, trademarks, logos, brand names, computer software, patents, trade secrets, and a whole range of intellectual assets can be a nightmare in some countries. A number of Asian countries, for example, have no legal or political tradition of protecting copyrighted material. Piracy of music and computer software runs rampant in China, Hong Kong, and Taiwan. Copyrighted periodicals, books, and other publications have virtually no protection in the Philippines.

On the Kowloon side of Hong Kong, a tourist can't walk a full block without being accosted by an entrepreneur trying to sell a "copy watch," a cheap knock-off of a brand-name timepiece such as Rolex, or Cartier. Entrepreneurs in these cultures do not view the creator of an intellectual product as having any special rights or entitlements. There is very little moral stigma attached to copying the work of others. Westerners, long accustomed to the legal and social concept that a person who invests time, talent, effort, and money in creating an intellectual asset is entitled to a legal advantage that allows him or her to profit from the creation, and to prevent others from doing so, are often appalled at the simple disregard for these rights.

The U.S. Department of Commerce, and increasingly trade ministries from the developed countries, have made intellectual property a focus of aggressive lobbying with other governments. In recent years, the World Intellectual Property Organization (WIPO), has served as a tool for the developed nations to press the undeveloped ones to respect intellectual property rights, and to create laws governing the issues. The U.S. and China, in particular, have engaged in a long and tedious exchange, with slow but significant progress.

Theft of intellectual property, however, is not confined to the third world. With the phenomenal growth of the Internet, and the feverish activities of the anarchist subculture of the Web, copyright theft has become much more widespread and much more difficult to combat. Outlaw Web sites appear and disappear, as their operators move from one hosting service to another. They offer pirated copies of commercial software products, illegally acquired photographs and other graphic images, and digital copies of popular music, all for downloading at no charge by others of their kind.

Legal sanctions against Web pirates are rather weak, and governments have so far been slow to act against them. Government attempts to regulate or police the Web, or to hold online behavior accountable to conventional legal standards, routinely meet with noisy political opposition from the defenders of the Web as an anarchic medium, many of whom argue that "free speech" should be the only criterion for the Internet's operation.

Some businesses may have relatively little vulnerability to theft or destruction of intellectual property, while others may live or die based on the continuing market value of these types of assets. Aside from the protection of legally defined intellectual property, a firm must carefully guard its business information, financial data, and customer data from theft and exploitation.

Another growing issue, especially for firms based in developed economies and operating in the developing ones, is the problem of ethical standards for doing business in certain legal gray areas. For example, the difference between a bribe and a "commission," paid to a commercial go-between in a third-world country, is often a matter of interpretation. Small monarchies, for example, seem to abound with business agents, brokers, and consultants, all of whom seem to trace their bloodlines to a king, shah, emir, sultan, or other grand poobah. Red tape magically disappears and approval cycles suddenly accelerate after they receive their commission payments.

Corrupt customs agents, police officers, import-export officials, and government regulators view bribes as a normal part of their compensation. Indeed, police officers in countries such as Mexico are so underpaid that the temptation to supplement their salaries with other sources of income is almost irresistible. Indifferent government officials at the top of the bureaucracies are actually encouraging corruption at the front lines by their management practices.

This issue of commissions and bribes is often a very difficult one for businesses in developed economies. In some cases, a corporate representative who pays a bribe to clear away an obstacle to doing business in a developing country may be violating the law of his or her home country, with potentially serious consequences. In any case, a reputable firm needs a clear and ethical policy for dealing with foreign go-betweens, even if it sometimes involves a competitive disadvantage.

Liabilities, Lawsuits, and Legal Nightmares

Another critical aspect of your legal environment is liability. Depending on your industry, your products and services, and your methods of doing business, your firm may face a range of legal risks if things go wrong. Obviously, some firms operate with a much greater risk of product disasters or environmental disasters than others. Events like Exxon's Alaskan oil spill in 1989 or Union Carbide's chemical catastrophe in Bhopal, India in 1984 create legal nightmares for the firms involved, which can drag on for years. The crash of an airliner, a fire on a cruise ship, or the collapse of a soccer stadium can trigger a firestorm of lawsuits that can impose enormous legal fees, to say nothing of the cost of damages or punitive judgments. An incident of food poisoning can devastate the revenues and earnings of a fast-food company.

Particularly in the U.S., legal attacks on "deep pockets" institutions are widespread. Any large, profitable corporation is more vulnerable to attack simply because of its greater ability to pay. The contingency fee structure of the American legal industry's liability sector, combined with legendary money settlements in famous cases, creates an enormous appetite for litigation. The class-action lawsuit, a legal mechanism that allows a law firm to sue on behalf of a large number of aggrieved individuals, whether they have complained or not, can create an enormous economic liability if a firm is found guilty of negligence or violations of the law.

In many cases, plaintiffs sue large firms in hopes of gaining settlements out of court. A firm may be unwilling to endure the legal costs, negative media attention, and distraction of the executives' attention, so it simply pays off the attacker.

Increasingly, especially in America, the lawsuit has become a competitive weapon. When one company copies the product or technology of another, or misuses another's intellectual property in some way, the aggrieved firm may seek to limit the competitive advantage its rival can gain from the assets. It may be able to block the competitor from using its proprietary assets, or it may be able to recover all or part of the profits generated by the use of the assets. In some cases, the aggrieved firm is satisfied to settle on a licensing agreement of some kind, in which it gets a share of the competitor's profits.

In other cases, a firm may use a lawsuit to block a competitor's market momentum, sometimes with little or no legitimate proof of harm. Several years ago, Polaroid Corporation used the courts to force Kodak Corporation out of the market for instant cameras and film, collecting an $800 million settlement in the process. More recently, Kodak sued Japanese film maker Fuji, charging that it used unfair practices to prevent Japanese retailers from selling Kodak's products. A number of Silicon Valley firms have willingly testified in the U.S. government's antitrust lawsuit against Microsoft, charging that Microsoft routinely used unfair business practices to squelch competitors.

A corporation, or a whole industry, can find itself on the wrong end of a lawsuit used by a government for political purposes. In recent years, both the federal and state governments in the U.S. have launched punitive lawsuits and legislation against the tobacco firms, charging that they cynically exploited smokers, knowing for decades that their products were addictive and deadly. Prospective settlements totaled over $300 billion. Tobacco companies have enjoyed enormous influence over legislation in past decades, but more recently have been thrown completely on the defensive by a change in public sentiment. Media support for the anti-industry campaign has strengthened the public reaction and almost certainly emboldened legislators to demand ever more severe financial remedies.

Regulations: Defining the Playing Field

Some industries and some lines of business involve oversight and regulation by government bodies that is so stringent that it amounts to a significant fraction of a firm's operating costs. Companies whose business activities or products represent potential threats to health, safety, and environmental integrity usually face a wide array of regulators, often with no sign of coordination or cooperation amongst them.

Primary industries like mining, construction, and heavy manufacturing operate under the supervision of health and safety agencies and pollution control agencies. Pharmaceutical firms require extensive government review and approval of their products before they are eligible for release to the market. Consumer products of many types require safety approval to ensure they are not flammable, toxic, or breakable in such a way as to threaten the user. Food products, especially meat and dairy products, involve thorough inspections during various stages of preparation. Hospitals have to comply with many reviews and standards imposed by agencies that control their licenses and other authorizations to do business.

Many analysts believe that the overall, long-term effect of government regulation of various aspects of business activity tends to promote safer and better products, while fostering fairer competition based on a minimum standard of quality. At the same time, many business operators argue that excessive or overly stringent regulation drives up operating costs and eventually disadvantages the consumer. This balance between quality and cost is a key issue in virtually all sectors of trade.

In the U.S. financial services industry, for example, a long history of federal control and regulation has produced a hodgepodge of distorted business structures. Banks are allowed to enter into certain lines of business but not others. Brokerage firms can sell some kinds of products but not others. Mergers between certain types of firms are encouraged by the regulatory structure and mergers between other types are prevented.

Choosing how and where to do business must involve, to some extent, making choices about the regulatory environment in which the firm will have to operate. In a country such as the U.S., for example, the choice of any of the fifty states can make a big difference in terms of operating costs imposed by regulatory compliance. In the early 1990s, the state of California earned a reputation as hostile toward business, and a number of businesses relocated to nearby states such as Arizona, Utah, Nevada, Oregon, and Washington.

Conversely, a number of U.S. states have revised their regulatory structures to attract new businesses, and some even use high-profile national advertising campaigns to tout their "business-friendly" environments. By a quirk of various state laws, a huge number of U.S. firms have incorporated themselves in the tiny state of Delaware, which is primarily an agricultural state.

Since 1993, U.S. Vice President Al Gore has spearheaded an aggressive campaign to reduce paperwork, eliminate unnecessary regulations, and streamline approval processes in many aspects of the U.S. federal government's operation. His Re-Engineering Government initiative, or "REGO," earned considerable respect for its accomplishments.

Deciding where in Europe to locate an operating headquarters has always involved careful consideration of regulatory controls and barriers. Marked differences in political viewpoints and attitudes between various national governments and regulatory bureaucracies have led some businesses to favor one area of the continent over others. The same is true for Asia and South America.

In recent years, more and more European firms have embraced the European quality standard known as ISO 9000, published by the International Standards Organization in Geneva. ISO 9000 defines a set of methods for describing and auditing manufacturing processes to encourage the building of high-quality products. ISO 9000 has achieved the status of a *de facto* regulation, to the extent that many large firms require their suppliers to provide evidence of formal registration and compliance.

In some cases, your legal radar should include a scan of the legal issues facing your customers as well as your own. You might not find the regulatory environment uncomfortably complex, but if your customers are businesses, their issues become your issues. Understanding the pressures they face can sometimes enable you to build solutions that offer greater value than those of your competitors.

Contracts: How Not to Victimize Yourself

Many firms, especially small ones and one-person operations, have learned the hard way that some people they do business with don't always keep their word. Those who haven't been severely burned in a business deal at least once tend to rely on trust, good faith, and the expectation of fair play. Those who have tend to use contracts and written agreements to clarify and enforce the deals they make.

However, any experienced business person can tell you that even the most specific written contract is often of very little value if your business partner decides to double-cross you. Why? Because enforcing a contract, under the legal systems of most developed countries, usually costs more than it gains. Entering into an agreement, a business person will typically say, "We've got a written contract on this; we can't lose, because if they back out, we can take them to court." However, the right to take someone to court is usually the right to throw good money after bad.

Disclaimer: The following discussion is not intended to be, nor should it be interpreted as, legal advice. It is merely a set of conclusions arising from long and painful experience doing business with people who are skilled at impersonating ethical business partners. The reader is advised to consider it for its educational value.

The ugly truth is that most legal systems make it almost impossibly difficult for a person who has been cheated in business by another to recover what he or she has lost. Virtually all legal proceedings are ponderously slow. The municipal courts in my home town take pride in what they call a "fast track" system, which requires that ninety percent of civil suits go to trial within *one year* after filing. God only knows what the "slow track" standard is.

The prospect of feeding your attorney's children for a year or more, in hopes of recovering a loss from someone who may have gone out of business, left town, declared bankruptcy, or simply passively resists and delays the legal attack, usually exhausts the patience and determination of the aggrieved party. My firm has found it necessary to abandon several legal proceedings against business partners who defrauded us out of considerable sums of money simply because it was not cost-effective to proceed, even though we could have undoubtedly won the judgments.

If the legal action involves another country, you can multiply the frustration factor a hundredfold. You will probably need lawyers in both countries, and you may find that the defendant can easily delay, confuse, and impede the process at little cost, while your legal costs mount rapidly. Differences in the laws of the two countries, as well as differences in the way legal proceedings work, can sometimes confound all attempts to put together a sensible litigation strategy.

Even if you manage to get the matter into a court of competent jurisdiction, you have no guarantee that the terms of the contract, which seem so absolutely clear to you, will seem the same way to a judge. Indeed, if a contract dispute goes to litigation, then your contract really means whatever a judge says it means. People who renege on their business commitments are often quite creative at rationalizing their behavior as well.

For many business people, especially those with small businesses, the greatest cost of a legal dispute is emotional. Their sense of outrage at being cheated is compounded by ever-increasing frustration as they discover, at every turn, that they have very little real power in the situation. They become even more frustrated when they learn that the legal "system" is not really a system at all, and that it does almost nothing for the aggrieved and almost everything for the plaintiff. A feeling of impotence and rage is quite common for people in these situations, as they gradually begin to face the fact that the contract they considered such a key asset is just another piece of paper.

The foregoing discussion does not mean that contracts are worthless, or that you should forget about using contracts and written agreements in your business activities. It does suggest, however, a different view of the role of a contract, and a different focus on making sure your business partners comply with their commitments. Let's review some key practices in the art of "partner compliance."

1. Use a contract or letter of agreement primarily to *define* the commitment each party is making. Just as locks on houses and cars keep honest people honest, contracts keep honest people aware of their obligations. Misunderstandings and misperceptions can arise, even between honest and ethical people, especially as time passes. Avoiding disagreements is the most valuable benefit of a written agreement. Of course, trying to enforce the agreement legally is even more difficult if it's vague, confusing, or has terms that conflict with one another.

2. Make the agreement as *simple and concise* as possible, consistent with covering all important points of agreement. Regardless of what some lawyers may tell you, the strongest agreement uses plain language that the proverbial person on the street can easily read and understand. I prefer, in the majority of cases, to use a plain-language letter of agreement, written in conversational language, that defines with simple bullet points what my firm and the other firm are agreeing to do. Both parties sign two copies of the letter, and each party gets a copy.

3. Define the *"exit strategy."* Two of the most important items in an agreement are the ones most often omitted by people who trust the party they're doing business with. One is the means for canceling or terminating the relationship between the parties. If circumstances, change, can you get out of the agreement legally and morally? Many people agree to business arrangements assuming they will work out fine and they will endure forever. It's important to spell out the conditions under which the agreement will terminate, expire, or be canceled by either party. The second most common missing ingredient is a penalty for failure to comply with the terms of the agreement. Surely we hope and believe the other party will keep their promise, but what happens if they don't? Including a form of compensation for failure to comply means that, if you do litigate successfully, or the other party thinks you can, you have a pre-agreed remedy. Otherwise, you'll be in the position of asking a judge to decide how much the other party's misbehavior should cost them. Also, every agreement should include a provision that requires the losing party to pay the costs of litigation in case legal action is necessary. Without this, in most cases, your legal costs come out of your own pocket, not the pocket of the other party.

4. *Review the terms* of the agreement periodically with the other party to keep everybody mindful of their obligations. Don't allow time or inattention to diminish the status of any of the elements of the agreement.

5. *Keep the financial see-saw tilted in your favor.* Avoid paying for anything before it is delivered, and avoid partial or advance payments unless you have custody of something of value that justifies the payment. My firm lost a substantial sum to a small software developer who went out of business without completing the product we contracted for. We had paid development fees and advances on royalties, but never received a usable product. Particularly with software and other intellectual products, half of the job is no job at all; it is almost impossible for one programmer to take over and complete a project begun by another, without starting almost from scratch. In this case, litigation was futile because even if it was successful, he was insolvent and could not have repaid the funds.

6. *Consider binding arbitration* as a way to avoid litigation and still protect your right to a settlement.

The gist of this advice is not to neglect the use of well-designed contracts and agreements but rather to manage your business relationships in such a way as to make litigation unnecessary. If you operate on the basis of trust, spoken agreements, or assumptions about how people will perform, you're asking for trouble. If you depend on a written agreement, assuming it will cause unethical people to behave ethically, then you're dangerously reliant on a legal system that deserves little trust. But if you keep the financial see-saw tilted in your favor, as mentioned above, then even if the arrangement fails, you should be able to minimize your loss.

Your legal radar will probably display many other issues and factors that are specific to your business. This discussion can, of course, only point out some of the main features to be considered in the review of the legal environment. Bear in mind that the legal issues of your customers, and even your competitors, can present both opportunities and obstacles for your firm.

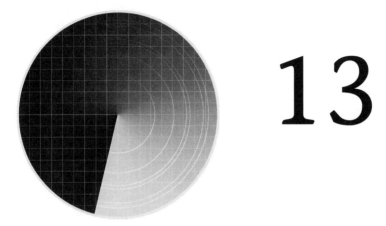

13

Your Geophysical Radar

Civilization is a race between
education and catastrophe.
—H.G. Wells

The purpose of the geophysical radar is to understand the geographic, geopolitical, and ecological factors that can affect the growth of your business.

Infrastructure and You

The strategic thinking process can sometimes get so abstract, complex, and sophisticated that we risk overlooking the ordinary but critically important aspects of everyday business. While you're busy plotting your next brilliant competitive move, a major electrical power outage can disable your entire customer service operation. The strategic picture can change significantly if your competitor's plant burns down. You may not be able to execute your clever strategic plan if you can't hire enough qualified technical or professional people to do the work. A communications satellite that falls from orbit could bring your business down with it.

Your geophysical radar can help you see what's happening in the physical, tangible world around you, spot potential threats or problems, and hedge your strategies with alternatives and backup options. In some ways, the geophysical radar involves more creative thinking and careful perception than the other radars, even though it may first seem rather mundane in scope. When you start to think about the many aspects of the tangible environment that can affect your business, you begin to see that this dimension of the environmental scan can rank as high or higher than the others for some businesses and under certain circumstances. And certainly, geophysical factors can have economic, political, and social consequences.

Get a large sheet of paper and make a cartoon sketch of your firm embedded in an ecological business system, with which it interacts and on which it depends to achieve its mission. Start sketching in the various players, resources, and elements of infrastructure that are crucial to your business. How many of them do you take for granted?

How does weather affect your business, both directly and indirectly? Do weather differences in different geographic areas of business make a difference in your opportunities? How does it affect your customers? Your competitors? Do weather catastrophes like hurricanes, earthquakes, or floods affect demand for your products and services? If you operate ski resorts, you probably prefer to see long winters and lots of snow. If you operate a construction business, you might prefer milder weather.

Some firms have made niche businesses out of weather-driven marketing opportunities. For example, Paul W. Davis Systems, Incorporated, a company in Jacksonville, Florida, specializes in insurance restoration, which is the reconstruction of homes and commercial properties damaged by natural disasters. The firm operates several franchises throughout the U.S. and Canada.

When the government of Kuwait faced the formidable challenge of putting out several hundred oil-well fires set by the retreating Iraqi army in the 1991 Persian Gulf War, it chose Red Adair because of his legendary reputation for this rare but crucial line of business. You may have never heard of him, but if you have an oil-well fire, he's the guy you call.

Conversely, insurance companies around the world have been concerned lately that the purported rise in Earth temperatures, and weather-related phenomena such as *El Nino*, could bring unprecedented occurrences of weather disasters with very costly damages. This brings in firms known as reinsurers, who manage large pools of capital used to syndicate major risks beyond the capability of an individual carrier.

What about the simple but crucial components of everyday logistics on which businesses and consumers depend? In an advanced economy, people seldom have to think much about the availability of food, clean water, electrical power, public transport, and telephones. But when a regional disaster befalls such a country, or if a business is located in a developing country where such things are considered luxuries, its problems change radically. In the future, data outages will become more frequent than electrical power outages, and surely more costly.

In fact, infrastructure issues can completely invert the competitive picture and change your market dynamics radically. I was stunned to learn from executives of TeleRJ, the telephone company in Rio de Janeiro, that the firm had a waiting list of 1.1 million customers who wanted to buy cellular telephone service. In a developed economy, a million customers on a waiting list can only be a dream; in a developing country, it can be a nightmare. If your company is one of the customers waiting for service, you'll have to find a way to do business without it. If you're the company with the list of customers, the opportunity comes dressed in a straitjacket.

The simple issues of moving goods to the market or moving raw materials to the necessary locations become special problems for some kinds of firms. If you manufacture and sell a product that is unusually heavy, perishable, hazardous, attractive to criminals, or otherwise in need of special attention, the costs and risks of moving it about can become a major factor. Depending on the country where you place your operation, the availability of dock facilities, security measures, storage, and commercial transport can become critical issues. Strikes or other industrial actions by dockworkers or transport drivers can play a key part in your plans.

Sociological issues such as crime, physical security, and social disorder can rise to first-order significance on the geophysical radar screen of some firms. A number of corporate headquarters operations have migrated out of large cities in order to retain highly qualified professional people, particularly women, who refuse to face the daily risks in coming to work and going home. The costs of theft, sabotage, and other property crimes becomes a significant factor for some firms located in high-crime areas. Executive security is a growing concern for many firms.

Local utilities in many parts of the U.S., such as gas and electric companies, telephone companies, and waterworks, have recently had to review and reinforce their physical security measures with the rise of militia groups with anti-establishment agendas. The Southern Poverty Law Center in Montgomery, Alabama, founded and directed by attorney Morris Dees, maintains a database of over four hundred identified hate groups and militias that identify themselves with disruption of the social order in the U.S.[1] Over half of these actively use the Internet to recruit members and promote their causes. Of course, businesses operating in developing countries have long had to cope with radical and sometimes violent political groups, who often view foreign corporations as both enemies to be attacked and ready targets for terrorist acts that get good television exposure.

Making good use of your geophysical radar involves fully engaging your mind with the diverse aspects of the real world in which you operate. The factors discussed here are only a sample from which to start. Your firm may experience others that are unique, peculiar, or specifically related to your line of business. You need to identify and prioritize those that offer the greatest opportunities and the most serious threats, and think carefully about how to cope with them.

Natural and Unnatural Disasters

In early December, 1998, environmental scientists claimed to have documented for the first time that industrial pollution and dust from Asia travels thousands of miles, contaminating the air as far away as Texas. Massive forest fires in Indonesia spread clouds of smoke over several thousand miles of territory in Asia in 1997. The clear-cutting of Brazilian rainforests creates weather effects detectable throughout North and South America. Ecologically speaking, all countries now share the same backyard. Debates and dissertations about greenhouse gases and global warming, depletion of ocean fisheries, reduction of rainforests, and falling water tables punctuate the growing international concern about the physical environment.

Although this is not the proper occasion for a polemic about man's inhumanity to nature, it is legitimate to include the range of ecological issues in a review of the geophysical radar, regardless of one's personal stance on this highly politicized topic.

Nor is it necessary to rehash the legendary ecological disasters of the past few decades, such as the Exxon Valdez oil spill off the coast of Alaska, the Iraqi oil fires in Kuwait, the Union Carbide chemical release in Bhopal, India, or the nuclear reactor meltdowns at Chernobyl in the Ukraine and Three Mile Island in Pennsylvania. But we must acknowledge that each imposed an enormous cost, not only in money, property, and sometimes lives, but also in a sense of anxiety and concern about the possibility of similar events in the future.

We don't have to review here the long list of firms and industries whose activities have brought lawsuits based on real or alleged environmental abuse, such as heavy manufacturing, mining, logging, whaling, oil transport, and waste disposal. But those firms and industries have had to cope with heavy legal costs and intense social pressure, as well as the reparations many of them have had to pay. Now all firms need to review and understand the levels of risk they face in regard to the impacts of their operations on various parts of the ecosystem and the social and financial pressures that can accompany irresponsible corporate behavior, as well as mishaps over which they have little or no control.

Geopolitics: The Power of Place

Simple geography can obviously have a huge influence on a firm's options for doing business. However, many of us fail to notice the most obvious facts of geographic relationships, because they've always been right in front of our noses. For example, a simple but profoundly important geographic fact is that the U.S. shares only two borders with other nations, Canada and Mexico, and its relationships with both of those neighbors have been friendly for many decades.

Contrast that with the fact that Israel, for example, shares
no border with any nation friendly to its existence. Commerce
between Israelis and Palestinians, as well as nearby Arab
states, does exist, but firms do business in an atmosphere of
tension and mistrust. Australia has no borders with other
nations at all. It stands alone as a continental nation.
Australians have long debated their status and relationship to
other nations in the world economy. Some Aussies think of
themselves as more oriented to Europe and the U.S., while
others argue that the country should consider itself part of
Asia. New Zealand, a modern economy on an island nation of
only three million people, shares many of the same issues.

Obviously, political strife or the prospect of outright war
between countries casts a dark cloud over the business prospects
of firms doing business in or with any of the protagonists. The
political status of Taiwan has long elevated tensions between
China and its trading partners, particularly the U.S. But in a
distinctly Chinese style of accommodation, trade between
Taiwan and the mainland has grown steadily, and wealthy
Taiwanese business operators invest heavily in mainland
businesses.

The return of Hong Kong to Chinese control in 1997, after
ninety-nine years of British rule, took place without incident
despite dire predictions by many of a military-style subjuga-
tion of the island. Most observers lately give the Chinese high
marks for its handling of the new Hong Kong Special
Administrative Region, as it was renamed. A peaceful accommodation of Hong Kong and Taiwan by China can have enormous implications for firms doing business in and with those
political entities.

The long standoff between North Korea and South Korea, in
an uneasy state of limbo since the Korean armistice in 1953,
has dampened possibilities for commerce between the two
countries and has certainly retarded the development of the
north's economy. Foreign firms doing business in South Korea
are always mindful of the background of tension and potential
conflict on the peninsula.

The sudden revolution in Iran that toppled Shah Reza
Pahlavi—"the Shah," as he was affectionately known by
Western supporters—immediately changed the fortunes of
hundreds of foreign firms doing business there. American and

European firms that had sold arms and various weapon systems to the Shah's regime were suddenly out of favor. Some lost money and had their assets confiscated. That sort of thing tends to happen routinely on the African continent, but most experienced business operators have long ago learned not to gamble on fragile political regimes.

Going further back in history, the creation of the Panama Canal in 1914 was a distinctly geopolitical event, and a disreputable one at that. American president Theodore Roosevelt strongly favored the idea of a canal bisecting the continental mass of North and South America. When the government of Colombia balked at the terms offered for access to the territory needed to build the canal, Roosevelt mounted political support for a breakaway insurrectionist faction in the affected area. With military and economic assistance, he supported the creation of a new country, which he and his backers immediately recognized as having sovereignty over the canal. Of course, the government of the new republic of Panama was quite willing to accept the terms offered.

A less political but still very important issue in your geophysical environment can be the population itself. Social and religious practices in some countries enjoy higher priorities than the day-to-day requirements of business. In strongly Islamic countries such as Saudi Arabia, for example, men and women do not work together in the same room. Imagine the social, political, and cultural adjustments that must be made when a female representative of another country, such as U.S. Secretary of State Madeleine Albright meets with the top leaders of such a country. The first Islamic country I lectured in was Malaysia, and I was surprised when my hosts asked me to extend the usual schedule of the one-day seminar by two hours. The extra time allowed for a break so the Muslim participants could attend prayer services.

Geographically, all firms depend on the availability of qualified labor. Gateway 2000 Inc., a computer maker headquartered since its birth in the rural state of South Dakota, found it increasingly difficult to grow with its market without the highly specialized designers, engineers, and manufacturing experts needed to build its products. It moved its headquarters to San Diego, California, where the living conditions attracted a large number of the young professionals the firm needed.

On a more subjective level, certain industries tend to cluster in certain geographic areas, and locating a firm's headquarters in the preferred area can affect its access to the kinds of services and market opportunities it needs to thrive. For instance, New York has long been the center of the U.S. publishing industry. One can operate a successful publishing firm in another city, but must do so without the benefit of easy access to authors' agents, publicity experts, printers and graphic service firms, book reviewers, retail distributors, book clubs, and banks that understand the peculiar financing needs of publishers.

California's legendary Silicon Valley became the hotbed of choice for launching new firms in the computer and information technology industry, largely because established firms such as Hewlett Packard, Sylvania, and Fairchild Semiconductor were there. The arrival of Intel Corporation, with its microprocessor chips, and the launch of Apple Computer Company brought the area into the world limelight. New firms, often launched by emigrants from the established firms, naturally chose to settle in the same area to take advantage of the established culture and infrastructure of the emerging industry.

Incidentally, America also has a "chocolate valley," which is home to a number of firms that make chocolate products. Hershey Foods Corporation and M&M Mars Incorporated are located virtually a stone's throw from each other, in a rural region of Pennsylvania. Hershey, Pennsylvania bears the name of Milton S. Hershey, the founder of the company. Nearby, Mars turns out millions of chocolate products in Elizabethtown.

Of course, some countries get to be known as centers for certain types of commerce, and their reputations tend to become self-reinforcing over time. Switzerland has long been known for watches, cheese, and, to some extent, chocolate. Of course, Swiss banking is legendary for its mystique of secrecy and service to the great and the near-great of the world. Israel has long played a key part in the cutting and polishing of diamonds. A few European capitals quickly come to mind with regard to the fashion industry: Paris, Rome, and Milan. Hong Kong has served for many years as the commercial hub of Asia, organizing imports and exports as the storefront for

China and an easy access point into and out of many other countries in that region.

Geo-Economics: World Supply and Demand

What does the price of tea in China have to do with your business? Increasingly, more than you may think. With the steadily increasing *population pressure* caused by rising levels of consumption in China and a number of developing countries, we are getting ever closer to the time when many businesses will routinely have to consider the effects of consumption patterns in other parts of the world.

We've become accustomed to considering the effects of global supply and demand for oil. But what about food? What about water? Most of the developed economies have managed to keep their resource infrastructures roughly matched to their consumption levels, if not by producing raw materials, then at least by importing them at reasonable prices. This is not always the case for the developing economies.

The oil shock of 1972 and 1973 caught many oil-dependent economies unprepared, and it took a number of years for the adjustments to take place. Nevertheless, new sources and new technologies developed steadily and had the effect of mostly disarming the oil-producing cartel, OPEC, and gradually eroded its pricing power. By late 1998, the combination of depressed world demand, especially in Asia, and greater production efficiencies sent oil prices to a post-war low, as adjusted for inflation.

For years, unabashed capitalists and aggressive business planners have been ridiculing the dire threats of the environmentalists about world oil supplies, the loss of rain forest and timberlands, population growth, and global warming. Many of the somber predictions simply haven't come true.

However, we may be the last generation that will have the luxury of plowing ahead with aggressive economic development without feeling the direct ecological side effects. The phenomenal growth of third-world populations and economies over the past decade, and the likelihood of continued rapid growth, even though punctuated by occasional disruptions, is putting more and more pressure on the resource environment.

Even those who feel no empathy for the environmentalist cause may find themselves experiencing some economic repercussions that may affect their businesses directly.

Experts at the Worldwatch Institute, a group admittedly committed to an environmentalist agenda, predict that China's continued rapid industrial growth, coupled with a lagging infrastructure and the virtual absence of resource planning policies, will cause supply and demand problems that spill over into the developed economies.[2]

Russia also represents a serious eco-economic problem, due to the disintegration of much of its historically weak infrastructure. Even though Russia has plentiful oil supplies, its aging railroads, leaking pipelines, and inadequate storage and docking facilities make it difficult to move the oil to markets. Serious oil spills over land have contributed to major ecological problems across much of the Ukraine. Further, its primitive and aging transport system causes waste and spoilage of a major portion of its agricultural output, with shortages and high prices in the cities.

With a population greater than one billion people, even a small proportional change in China's level of material consumption will have a large net effect on demand for resources of all kinds, and subsequent pressure on supply. For example, as the Chinese rush to urbanize and industrialize, farm land is being steadily sacrificed to non-food purposes. The area of land that can produce grain crops is shrinking, while the demand for food of all kinds is obviously rising.

This rising demand for food is compounded by two related trends. The first is the tendency for people in developing countries such as China to aspire to the living habits of their wealthier counterparts in other countries. As their incomes increase, one of the first things they want is meat and other foods characteristic of the diet of rich countries. A rise in meat consumption causes a dramatic rise in grain consumption; it takes an estimated four pounds of grain to produce one pound of beef, for example. For every pound of beef consumed, four pounds of dietary grain will have to be replaced from some other source of supply. Of course, raising cattle requires much more land area, proportionally, than raising grain.

The second trend of major significance in China is the deterioration of its water supply. With heavy industrialization and rapid urbanization, non-farm water usage has skyrocketed. Falling water tables due to heavy irrigation have forced Chinese farmers to drill deeper and deeper for water. The Yangtze River, known for centuries for its abundant flow, now dries up before it reaches the sea more than one-fourth of the days in a typical year.

China is not the only developing country with a water problem. Parts of India, Pakistan, and much of Africa face continuing problems with water. Worldwide, an estimated two billion people are without an adequate, stable supply of water.

Just a few years ago, China crossed over the balance point at which it could no longer produce enough grain domestically for the demands of its population. As domestic grain production actually falls due to urbanization and loss of cropland, and consumption continues to rise as a result of lifestyle changes, China will progressively consume more and more of the world's exportable grain.

So what? It means that China will be soon an aggressive buyer of grain, beef, and a number of other limited-supply foodstuffs on world markets. This is likely to force prices of those items higher and higher. Citizens of grain-exporting countries such as America, Canada, Australia, and France may find themselves paying more for these food products as they follow the path of greatest profit.

The same thing may happen for oil. As world oil demand surges again, the rising lifestyles of developing countries will put them into competition with other heavy-consuming nations, probably with significant political impacts.

With other large developing countries such as India and Indonesia contributing to the population pressure on food resources, we may find that food politics and water politics join with oil politics as a basis for conflict among countries. Developed nations such as America have never used food politics as part of foreign policy, but with the steady pressure of foreign consumption on their supplies, they may very well do so, particularly if China's leaders show little appetite for reforms that allow foreign products equal access to the country's internal markets.

Food politics may also respond significantly to weather disasters such as hurricanes, widespread drought and flooding, and also to earthquakes. Many environmental scientists warn that the past four or five decades may not be typical of the kinds of weather we should expect worldwide. If the global warming hypothesis turns out to be accurate, we may well see greater extremes of weather, with an increase in major disasters such as hurricanes, destructive snowstorms, and droughts. A number of the largest firms in the insurance industry are studying with great concern the possibility of heading into a period of several decades in which natural disaster costs may spiral out of control.

Eco-politics could result in rising and falling waves of trade protectionism, as countries seek to shield their consumers and businesses. Your firm may not feel these forces directly, but it is quite possible that they can affect the general economic environment in which you operate.

Notes

1. The Southern Poverty Law Center publishes studies, reports, and a monthly newsletter about the activities of groups that violate the civil rights of others. You can contact them through their Web site at splcenter.org.
2. The Worldwatch Institute conducts studies, sponsors conferences, and publishes articles and a monthly bulletin dealing with specific issues related to sustainable development. You can contact them through their Web site at worldwatch.org.

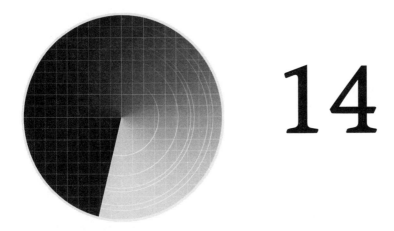

14

What Good Is a Radar If You Can't Read the Screen?

Men stumble over the truth from time to time,
but most pick themselves up and hurry off
as if nothing happened.
—Sir Winston Churchill

Bifocal Vision

At least once a year, and perhaps more often for some firms, senior management should conduct a complete strategic review of the business. Almost all successful companies call some kind of annual "time-out" for a retreat in which the top team puts aside the cares and concerns of the daily struggle and pays attention to the big picture. For many executive teams, this is an opportunity to clarify their focus, reset key priorities, rebuild their sense of teamwork, and rekindle their own energy and enthusiasm for the mission of the enterprise.

Too many executive teams, however, never quite get around to the strategic review. Hypnotized by the daily problems and pressures, they feel "We don't have the time," or "It's too much of a hassle to get everybody together," or "We pretty well know what our issues and problems are; we discuss them every day, so we really don't need a special meeting." By passing up the opportunity to rethink and rededicate, they are basically assuming that the strategic direction will somehow evolve from the sum total of the decisions they make every day. This is a dangerous assumption.

In *The Northbound Train: Finding the Purpose, Setting the Direction, Shaping the Destiny of Your Organization*, I presented a strategic planning model based on the idea of "bifocal vision." This is the ability to look beyond the day-to-day issues and think strategically, and also to pay attention to the immediate priorities for action.[1] Every executive and every leadership team needs bifocal vision.

The whole purpose of your corporate radar is to make this bifocal vision as acute as possible, and to make sure it results in a clear understanding and consensus on the challenges and opportunities facing the enterprise. Assuming we have all eight radars tuned up and working—imperfectly, to be sure—we now need a way to extract meaning from their messages, and to share that meaning with everyone in the organization who needs or deserves to know it.

Assembling the Radar Data: The Basic Annual Strategic Estimate

Eight channels of information are too many for most human beings to follow at one time. Trying to pay attention to all eight of your corporate radar screens at once, and for any length of time, would be about like trying to listen to eight radio talk shows or watch eight TV documentaries at once. It may be fascinating, but eventually mental fatigue will set in.

You need a way to reduce, distill, simplify, focus, and interpret the critical messages of the environment so you can take advantage of the lessons they have to teach. You must keep your radars scanning all the time, but you also need to "freeze" the picture from time to time so you can share it with your people. The better the managers and staff understand the business environment, the better chance they have of aligning their efforts to the strategic direction of the firm.

I believe that any business larger than a handful of people should document and distill the results of the environmental scan, in a readily readable form; let's call it the Basic Annual Strategic Estimate, or "BASE." This is a very carefully prepared, thoughtfully written statement of "what's going on out there." The content and presentation of the BASE will depend on management's interpretation of the various radar channels, and the preferences of the top team for digestible information. It could range from a single page for each of the eight radar channels, plus a simple summary, all the way to an extensive analysis and discussion of the findings.

In general, it helps to keep the BASE reasonably concise; otherwise reading it becomes a chore. Often, less information creates more value. Drowning the executive team in facts and figures, charts and graphs, and detailed analyses makes it difficult for them to find the few critical insights that can help them shape the business. Also, the act of distilling the radar information leads to valuable insights. Explaining something in very concise terms forces you to get to the core of the idea.

By the way, who should actually prepare the BASE? Answer: The executives of the firm. I hold some very strong views about the way strategic thinking, planning, and marketing should be done. I maintain that the process of transforming the radar data into valuable insights about the future of the business is an inseparable part of the intellectual leadership the firm's executives must provide. I recommend against delegating the BASE to a particular department or task force. The executive team should serve as the task force.

In the next section I will describe two methods for having the executive team divide up the work of interpreting the radar inputs and combine their results to create the BASE. One way is to prepare a draft of the BASE before the strategic retreat, and refine it during the meeting. The other way is to devote part of the meeting to defining the content of the BASE, in a workshop setting, and having the BASE finalized and published as part of the follow-up to the retreat.

In designing the actual content and layout of the BASE, we need to consider the various ways we might use it and the various people who need to have it. Issues of confidentiality and trade secrecy come into play here, but being overly secretive about the information can limit its value unnecessarily. A competent and insightful description of the business environment could be valuable to your competitors, but so long as the BASE deals only with the business environment and does not disclose your competitive thinking, a high level of secrecy is probably not useful.

The BASE should, above all, be simple and readable. It is the distillation of a large amount of evidence, speculation, projection, and insight, not a dump of the raw radar data. It does not need long, rambling philosophical dissertations on various business issues. If these are necessary, consider putting them into a separate backup document. Likewise, put in-depth factual material into a backup source. A few critical facts and observations, plus a sense of what they might mean, is usually adequate to present an issue for executive review.

Interpreting the Big Picture: The Annual Strategic Retreat

As I've mentioned, I strongly recommend a formal annual strategic conference or retreat as a way to focus executive attention on the business environment and build consensus about what the signals are telling us. The format and agenda for the retreat will vary according to the overall approach the firm takes to its strategic planning process. The timing of the retreat may relate to other major parts of the planning process, such as a managers' conference that brings all department or field managers together for two or three days. A published strategic plan, plus any operational planning process or budgeting process, all have to come together in an effective planning methodology.

Specific methods for conducting the annual strategic retreat are beyond the scope of this discussion, but we can summarize a few key points that deserve careful attention. First, the BASE is just one of several key inputs to the strategy formulation process. The top team also needs to consider the *organizational scan*, which is a review of the firm's capabilities, culture, and leadership. The organizational scan tells us what the real strengths of the firm are, aspects that need development, and issues the top team needs to deal with for the firm to carry out the mission successfully. The retreat may also include the results of an employee opinion survey, and perhaps a review of the top team's leadership, using a technique such as a 360-degree feedback survey of leadership skills.[2] All of these inputs, together with the BASE, go into the strategic review.

To see where the BASE fits into the annual strategic review, let's review a typical strategic planning process. I modestly offer the process presented in my book *The Northbound Train*.[3] In summary form here, the steps in the model are:

Scanning—the environmental scan, the organizational scan, and the opportunity scan.

Model Building—defining the strategic success model for the enterprise.

Gap Analysis—defining the difference between the current state of affairs and the state of affairs we want to move to, as defined by the success model.

Action Planning—setting a few key result areas and specific outcomes for actions needed to close the gap.

Strategy Deployment—putting the strategic concept to work throughout the organization, teaching, preaching, and realigning resources as necessary.

As portrayed by this process, the BASE is part of the scanning phase, i.e., the environmental scan.

Now let's consider how the executive team can don their thinking caps and put together the BASE. Whether they create the BASE before or during the strategy retreat, the process is roughly the same. Of course, they might choose to devote considerably more time and effort to the process if they do it in preparation for the retreat. If they do it as part of the retreat, they must have adequate information at hand, or else the process will degenerate into speculation, assumptions, and opinion swapping.

A successful executive retreat requires careful planning and preparation. Typically, the consulting team or a task force from the organization prepares a resource book for the executives' use in the retreat. This usually includes information on current financial results, forecasts, estimates, and various summaries or "backgrounders" on specific topics that might arise during the retreat process. If the team puts together the BASE as part of the retreat, then the resource book should contain the information necessary to support their work.

An effective way for the executive team to tackle the job of creating the BASE is simply to divide into small working parties of about three or four people. Each group takes one of the eight sectors of the environmental scan, i.e., Customer, Competitor, Economic, etc., and prepares its interpretation of the radar data. Unless the overall team is quite large, each working party will probably have two sectors to evaluate.

Each sector team reviews the available radar information for its assigned category, arranges the findings by relative importance or significance, and identifies critical trends and issues for discussion by the whole team. Using some pre-agreed format, each sector team organizes its results into a form that allows the whole team to understand and work with them. This might be a simple written document, especially if they prepare the BASE before the retreat. Other methods could include simple cartoon-like posters that present the key findings in easily digestible form.

Executive teams that enjoy using creative or off-beat methods may like to present the results in unconventional ways, such as skits, rhymes, or songs. In one case, my firm had the uneasy task of presenting some rather disturbing results to the executive team of a large Australian firm. Working with several of their people, we created a mock news conference, using the metaphor of a medical team reporting to the press on the results of the examination of a well-known person. With a junior executive playing the part of a local TV host known for his surliness, our consultants played the parts of the doctors.

They reviewed each aspect of the "patient's" health, analogous to the vision, hearing, digestion, muscular fitness, and nervous system, relating each to an aspect of the firm's capability for coping with the threats in its environment. The irascible interviewer asked aggressive, probing questions to make sure the team could back up its findings. The comic element of the situation enabled the executive team to face the uncomfortable findings without feeling defensive, angry, or discouraged.

During the retreat, the whole team can assemble a composite picture of the business environment by integrating the individual sector results. This becomes a very creative process that deserves adequate time, energy, and thought. This part of the retreat, in particular, can benefit immensely from the participation of a professional facilitator. Further, if the firm has engaged outside experts to help assemble the environmental scanning information, they should participate in this part of the retreat.

One useful and stimulating method for consolidating the radar results is to use an interactive "storyboarding," or cartooning process. With an entire wall of a large conference room covered with newsprint or other drawing paper, and each team member using colored markers, the group engages in a "free-for-all" drawing process. Each sector team draws symbols, sketches, diagrams, icons, phrases, or other ways to represent their findings. Anyone can add his or her own little modifications, comments, or ideas to the picture. There is no need to try to make the picture artistically appealing; in fact, the messier it is, the more useful it will probably be.

During the process, debates or differences will emerge about various aspects of the radar findings. As the team members work through their picture of the business environment, they may challenge the sector teams' findings or interpretations. Although these discussions can become complex and even heated, they tend to be very useful overall.

It is common during this process for two or more sector teams to identify the same issue in their respective areas. These "crossover" issues, i.e., trends or problems that weave through several sectors of the radar picture, may become significant to the overall interpretation. A particular technological issue could also create social, political, and economic issues. It's less important to force-fit an issue into the "correct" category and more important to understand how it weaves throughout the whole strategic picture.

There are various other interesting methods for consolidating the results of the radar sectors into a coherent picture of the overall business environment. The key point, however, is to make sure all members of the executive team participate on a personal, intellectual level in forming a consensus about what's going on. If they create it, they own it. It will become a key part of their thinking process, and it will guide the decisions they make. Further, they will be much better able to communicate its meaning to everyone else in the organization.

Refining the Business Strategy

The process of using the results of the environmental scan to create or revise the overall strategic direction of the business is, of course, well beyond the scope of this discussion. However, for the sake of keeping the concepts clearly linked, we should review some key aspects of the strategy formulation process.

First, strategy formulation is not an annual event or a one-time decision. It is an ongoing process, which develops and mutates as experience teaches us more and more about our business. We should really think of it as strategy evolution, because it is never finished, always changes, and responds to the forces of the environment.

Similarly, creating the strategic estimate is a continuing process of observation, reflection, and learning. Even if we formalize it on an annual basis for the benefit of the management process, we need to keep the radars in operation all the time. It's not as if we activate them once a year, scan the environment, and shut them down for the rest of the year. We should have our eyes and ears open all the time, and we should be constantly alert for the first signs of important new developments.

And, most important, our eight strategic radars are not machines, as the metaphor suggests. They are people. They are the executives, managers, customer contact people, researchers, advisers, suppliers, business partners, and all other people who can spot significant events in our business environment and help us understand them.

Each executive, manager, or professional staff member has a responsibility to keep abreast of developments in the firm's industry or sector, and to learn as much as possible about how its business environment operates. It is also perfectly plausible for employees at the front line to notice changes in customer behavior or actions by competitors before executives detect them. Voices from all levels can serve as the radar systems of the enterprise.

And finally, I hope I've successfully avoided creating the impression that the environmental scan is anything like scientific, systematic, or precise. It's guesswork at best. The events, trends, issues, and opportunities in the business environment are ultimately whatever we interpret them to be. Intelligent people may disagree completely about what a particular development means. We may spot critical truths of the environment that our competitors have missed. We may draw more insightful conclusions about the behavior of our customers. We may prioritize the significant issues in our environment more competently than others. But we will never fully understand the strategic environment. The best we can do is study it with intellectual innocence, humility and honesty, and learn as much as possible of what it has to teach us.

Ultimately, maybe that's what makes the job so interesting.

Notes

1. Albrecht, Karl. *The Northbound Train: Finding the Purpose, Setting the Direction, Shaping the Destiny of Your Organization*. New York: AMACOM, 1994, page 104.
2. To locate executive development materials, including 360-degree leadership assessment methods, contact the American Society for Training & Development through its Web site at astd.org. Also try *Training Magazine*'s site at trainingsupersite.com. Also evaluate the wide range of educational materials offered by the American Management Association's publishing division, AMACOM, at amanet.org. You may also wish to see Albrecht Publishing Company's Leadex/360 profile system; contact the author's Web site at albrechtintl.com.
3. Albrecht, Karl. *The Northbound Train: Finding the Purpose, Setting the Direction, Shaping the Destiny of Your Organization*. Page 69.

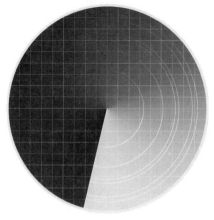

Index

Adair, Red, 232
age cohorts, age distributions, 73–74, **74**
"Age of Paradox," 33
agendas and political issues, 42–43
Airbus Industries, 48
AirFoyle, 116
Albright, Madeleine, 237
Allen, Paul, 179
alpha competitors, 100–101
Alta Vista search engine, 154
America Online, 178
America West Airlines, 79
American Airlines, 94–95
American culture, 186–192
American Express, 110, 111
American Medical Association, 117, 150
Americentric view of business, 11–13
amusement model, communications technology, 40
Andersen Consulting, 97
Annan, Kofi, 203
anti-corporate political movement, 215–218
Antonov Design Bureau, 116
Apollo electronic reservation system, 95
Apple Computer Company, 95, 99, 101, 147, 178, 238
Applied Magnetics Corporation, 2
Asea Brown Bover, 99
Asian financial crisis, 2–3
AT&T, 103, 110, 148, 163
Atari, 147
atomization of society and markets, 36, 41–42, 82, 190
Austin, Kevin, 90
Australia, 185, 207, 236, 241
Australia Telecom, 53–54
automotive industry, 4, 27, 49, 82, 85, 99–100, 105, 110, 111, 182
Autopsy/Post Services, 117
averages, masking effect of, 59
aviation and airlines industries, 3, 48, 65, 79–80, 84, 94–95, 116, 130–131, 161

"baby boom" generation, 74
balance sheet mergers, 104–105
banks and financial institutions, 2–3, 39, 41, 65, 66, 79, 80, 84, 110, 111, 103–104, 124–127, 131–132, 161, 225
Barksdale, Jim, 178
Barnevik, Percy, 99
Basic Annual Strategic Estimate (BASE), 244–249
Battelle Memorial Institute, 145
bell curve of human possibilities, 37–38
Berra, "Yogi," 69
bias, 49
Bierce, Ambrose, 204, 219
binary logic, 151
binding arbitration, 230
Black Orchid restaurant, 113
"blind side" events, 4–5
Blockbuster Video, 100
Boeing Aircraft Corp., 3, 48, 65, 126
Bookstar, 100
Boy Scouts of America, 128
brand envelope, 113
Brandeis, Louis, 190
brand preference, 11–12, 84, 97, 101, 108–115
Brazil, 10, 126–127, 234
breakthrough thinking, future-trend prediction and, 50
bribes, commisions, 222–223
British Commonwealth, 185
British Telecom, 148
Buffet, Warren, 84
Burroughs, 158

C.P. Pokphand, 126
Callaway Golf Company, 3
Canada, 143, 185, 235, 241
capacity mergers, 106
Carlson, Chester, 145
Cartier, 221
cartooning, 64

cash flow, in evaluating competition, 96
Casio, 146
Castro, Fidel, 46
celebrities as "brand names," 112–115
census information, 53
Charles Schwab & Company, 111, 129
Chernobyl nuclear disaster, 235
China, 42, 46, 76, 98, 186, 202, 221, 236, 239–241
Churchill, Winston, 243
Circuit City, 100
Cisco, 97
Citibank, 103–104
clothing industry, 95, 110
CNN, 201
Coca-Cola Co., 25, 42, 84, 97, 101, 111
"collective suicide", 26–29
Colombia, 237
communications technology, 31, 36, 39–40, 46–47, 97, 103, 104, 110, 148, 153–154, 191–192
Communism, 46, 186
Compac Computer Corporation, 107, 178
competition, 6, 17, 24, 25–29, 92–117, 223–224
conflict, driving cultural conflicts, 184–185
consolidation, 99–102
consumerism, rise of, 23–24, 118–119
continuity products, 85
contract law, 226–230
cost-oriented strategies, 24–25
Crisis Management for Corporate Self-Defense, 5
crown jewel mergers, 105–106
Cuba, 46, 66
cultural imperialism, Americanization of world, 200–203
currency exchange rates, 135–143
customer base, 6, 15–17, 36, 41–42, 53, 56–57, 69–91, 100, 108–115, 163–167, **74, 86, 88, 90**
customer service, 77–81, 100, 115, 163–167, 174
cyberpolitics, 176–179
cyberterrorism, 31, 153–154
Cypress Semiconductors, 215–216

Darwinism, economic, 186
Datenschutz, 198
DeBeers, 98
declining products & industries, 128–132
deconstruction, 33
Dees, Morris, 234
delayering, 8, 33
delivery and freight services industry, 127, 208–209
Dell Computer Company, 178
Delta Airlines, 94–95

"demand" vs. "push" economies, 26, 190
de-mergering, 33, 104
Deming, Edwards, 81
Democratic Republic of Congo, 210–211
demographics, 10, 11–12, 15–17, 33, 70, 72–77, 85, 90, 239–242, **74**
Deng Xiao Ping, 46
developing countries, 75–76, 192–195, 239–242
developing stage of product market life-cycle, 26–27
Devil's Dictionary, The, 204, 219
DHL, 127
differentiation of products, 27–28, 115–117
digital electronics, 145
Digital Equipment Corporation (DEC), 62–63, 107
digital imagining technology, 148
disaster planning and, 234–235
diverse perspectives, 50
diversification, 26
domino theory of trends, 32, 63–68, **67**, 126–128
Dow Jones Industrial Average, 58
downsizing, 8, 33
drivers of change, 63–68, **67**, 180, 183–185
Drucker, Peter F., 1, 34, 209

e-business (see also Internet & World Wide Web), 56–58, 80, 95, 129–132, 172–175
ecological issues, 149, 193, 234–235
economic Darwinism, 186
economics as behavioral science, 122–126
Economics in One Lesson, 209
economic trends, 2, 8–9, 11–13, 17–18, 23–33, 44–68, 118–143, 152, 161, 172–175, 184, 186–192, **27, 30, 61, 67, 120**
Economist, The, 121
educational issues, 76, 121–122
efficiency mergers, 107
electronic customer interfaces, 163–167
electronic polling, 90
Ellison, Larry, 178
employment programs, 209, 210
employment/unemployment rates and, 55, 133–134
energy research, 149
England, 141
entertainment industry, 38–40, 41, 111–115, 117, 201
envelope, brand envelope, 113
environmental scanning, 5–7, 14–22, 63–68, 244–251, **16, 67**
euro, 141–143
European Central Bank, 142

European Union (EU), 33, 141–143, 199, 206–207, 226
Excite search engine, 154
exit strategies, in contracts, 229
extermination mergers, 106
Exxon, 107, 223, 235

Fairchild Semiconductor, 238
Federal Express, 78, 127, 208
Federal Reserve, 124–125
filtering or censoring, 49–50, 51–59
Finland, 10
fire sale mergers, 105
First Wave of human development, 35
FNN, 201
food service industries, 4, 25, 82, 97, 104, 111, 112, 182
Foodmaker Incorporated, 4
forced parity in U.S. society, 191
France, 201, 210, 241
Frazier, Robert, 96–99
Friedman, Milton, 216
Frito-Lay Incorporated, 97
Fuji, 224
future-trend prediction, 10–11, 44–68, **61, 67**
Futurist, The magazine, 63

Galbraith, John K., 59–60, 62
Gates, Bill, 66, 99, 176, 177, 178, 179
Gateway 2000 Inc., 178, 237
GATT, 10
"gee-whiz conspiracy," 167–168
"gee-whiz" vs. "gee-won't" futurists, 47–48
General Electric, 66, 99, 145, 158
General Motors, 4, 111, 126, 216–217
generalizations and averages, future-trend prediction and, 50
geophysical location issues, 20–21, 76, 231–242
Germany, 198
Ginsberg, Allen, 43
Girl Scouts of America, 128
global marketplace (see also European Union; sociocultural issues), 2–3, 10–13, 18, 24, 25, 32, 33, 35–37, 46, 121, 126, 141–143, 220–223, 239–242
global-tribal paradox, 36–37
Gore, Al, 226
Gormley, Doris, 215–216
government (see political issues)
government statistics, 53, 55, 133–135
"greater fool theory," 61–62
Greenspan, Alan, 124–125
gross domestic product (GDP), 133, 160
Grove, Andy, 1, 8, 29, 99, 128, 152, 171
"growth psychosis" and mergers, 102
gun manufacturers, 194

Haloid Corporation, 145
"handcuffing" the customer, 84–85
Harley-Davidson, 111
Harrods, 115
hate groups, 234
Hayes Corporation, 2
Hazlitt, Henry, 209
healthcare industry, 2, 48–49, 64, 75, 149, 116–117, 150, 225
hedging, 140
Herrera, Vidal, 117
Hershey Foods Corporation, 238
Hewlett Packard, 146, 147, 174, 178, 238
Hilton, 200
Holmes, Oliver Wendall, 207
Home Depot, 106
Homo iconis, 34–35
Hong Kong, 10, 98, 221, 236, 238
Horizon Health Corporation, 2
humanity vs. technology, 154–155
hypercompetition of post-1980s and, 25–26

IBM, 99, 101, 147, 155, 158, 178
icons, 42
ideology vs. politics, 205–210
image-oriented cultures, 39–40, 42, 43
import/exports, 24, 25, 120–121
increasing returns phenomenon, 100
India, 42, 195, 223, 241
Indonesia, 3
industrial tourism, 187
industrialization, 35
inertia of customers, 84
inflation rates/inflation index, 55, 134–135
inflection, points of (see also economic trends), 8, 29–32, **30**
information, 49–59, 90, 128–129, 154, 211–215
Information Age, 32–33, 34–35, 128–129, 150–154
infrastructure, 231–234
Intel Corporation, 1, 8, 29, 99, 101, 128, 152, 171, 178, 199, 238
intelligence gathering, 14–15, 31
interest rates, 125, 134
Internet & World Wide Web (see also e-business), 27–28, 31–32, 36, 38, 40, 45–47, 50, 56, 59, 93, 94, 95, 129–132, 153–154, 165, 167–175, 178, 199, 221–222
Internet Service Providers (ISP), 165
investment services industry, 31, 64, 76, 86–87, 93, 111, 123–124, 129, 225
Iran, 236–237
ISO 9000 standards, 226
Israel, 10, 66, 236
issue futurists, 47–48

Jack-in-the-Box, 4
Japan, 2–3, 8, 10, 11, 25, 75, 195,
    201–202, 207
Java, 173, 178
Jobs, Steven, 101, 147
Jordan, Michael, 113

keiretsu, Japanese trade barriers,
    201–202, 207
Kelly, Kevin, 152
Kentucky Fried Chicken, 182
key-person security, 5
Kodak Corporation, 101, 111, 148, 224
Korea, 236

labor issues, 4, 38, 55, 119, 121–122, 127,
    133–134, 194–195, 209, 210
Lao Tzu, 44
legal issues (see litigation and liability)
Levi Strauss, 95, 110
lifestyle products and services, 75
lifetime customer value, 81
line extensions and branding, 110
Linux, 178
Lion King, The, 112
liquid crystal technology, 145–146
litigation and liability, 4–5, 20, 162,
    219–230
location (see geophysical location issues)
logistical issues, 233
logos and symbols in branding, 111, 221
long-range planning, 8, 41
Lynch, Peter, 6

M&M Mars Incorporated, 238
MacArthur, Douglas, 89
macro-trends, 32
Mahathir, Mohammed, 66
Malaysia, 66, 237
management, 2, 4–6, 10–13, 24–26,
    77–78, 99
manufacturing (tangible) vs. service
    (intangible) economies, 118–122, **120**
market share (see also customer base),
    69–70, 97
marketing, 70, 72–77, 172–173
Markkula, Mike, 147
Marriott Corporation, 1
Marriott, Bill Sr., 1
maturing stage of market lifecycle, 27
McDonald's, 25, 42, 111, 112, 200
MCI, 148
McNealy, Scott, 178
medical research, 149
mega-branding, 110–111
Mercedes-Benz, 98
mergers and acquisitions, 33, 102–108
MetroMail database, 198

Mexico, 143, 222, 235
micro tiger economies, 10
microchips, 151–152
Microsoft, 66, 84–85, 93, 96–97, 99, 101,
    106, 147, 176–179, 224
military enlistment, 197–198
minimum wage laws, 209
misery index, 55
MIT, 171
Mobil, 107
Modis, Theodore, 62–63
molecular customer, 70–72
money supply, 125, 161
Moore, Michael, 216–217
Motorola Corporation, 3
MSNBC, 201

Naisbitt, John, 37
narrowcasting vs. broadcasting, 36
National Spasmodic Torticollis
    Association, 196
natural disasters, 234–235, 241–242
NEC, 178
need context, value vs. products or ser-
    vice in, 85–91, **86**
Negroponte, Nicholas, 171
Nestle Incorporated, 97
Netscape Corporation, 178
Network Economy, 152
network technology, 152
New York Times, The, 216
New Zealand, 11, 236
niche markets, 115–117
Nokia, 97
Nordstrom Corporation, 117
North American Free Trade Agreement
    (NAFTA), 143
Northbound Train, The, 15, 244, 247
Northrop Grumman, 3
Northwest Airlines, 80

oil crisis of 1972, 8, 239
oil industry, 8, 107, 232, 235, 239
O'Neal, Shaquille, 196
online commerce (see e-business)
Only the Paranoid Survive, 8
OPEC, 239
operating costs, in evaluating competi-
    tion, 96–97
Oracle, 178
Organization of American States, 143
organizational culture, 99
outsourcing, 8, 33

Packard Bell, 178
Pahlavi, Reza, 236
Pakistan, 241
Palestine, 66, 236

Palo Alto Research Laboratories, 147
Panama, 237
partnerships, 8, 228–229
Pasteur, Louis, 92
Paul W. Davis Systems, Incorporated, 232
Pediatrics, 51–52
Pepsi, 84
personal computers, 27, 31–32, 40, 45,
    129, 147, 182–183
Phillipine Airlines, 65
photocopiers, 145
piracy, 221–222
Pizza Hut, 200
Planet Hollywood, 113
Polaroid Corporation, 224
political issues, 2–3, 19–20, 29, 31, 42–43,
    45, 66, 126–127, 193, 204–218,
    235–239
"political correctness," 195–197
population pressure, 239–242
population pyramids, 73–74, **74**
Post-Capitalist Society, 34
precision, myth, 54
preference vs. loyalty, 83–84
price wars, 25, 26–29, 26
Price-Costco, 100
primary industries, 225
privacy issues, 198–200
Procter & Gamble, 97
product market lifecycle, 4–5, 26–28, **27,**
    41, 84–91, **86, 88, 90,** 98–99, 108–117,
    128–132, 193–194
productivity, 38–39, 119, 153
profits, 24
psychographics, 16, 85
push economies, 26, 190

quality control, 24, 78
Quebec, 185

racial discrimination litigation, 5
RCA, 145, 146
Reagan, Ronald, 55
real estate finance industry, 131–132
Re-Engineering Goverment (REGO) ini-
    tiative, 226
regional business areas and, 237–238
retail sales, 96, 100, 106, 115
reversal of trends, indicators of, 30
Ries, Al & Laura, 109
Ritz-Carlton Hotels, 78
RJR Nabisco, 104
Rodeway Express, 127
Rodgers, T.J., 215–216
Rogers, Roy, 112
Rolex, 98, 221
Roosevelt, Franklin, 161
Roosevelt, Theodore, 237

Russia, 46, 240

Sabre electronic reservation system, 95
Samsung, 202
Sarnoff Research Center, 145
saturating stage of market lifecycle,
    27–28, 41
Saturn Company, 82
Saudi Arabia, 237
Scandinavia, 78
S-curves, 57, 59–63, **61**, 170–172
search engines on Web, 154, 175
Second Wave of development, 35
security, 127, 233–234
Seiko, 146
selectivity of technological change, 150
self-reinforcing advantage, 100
semantic profiling, 114
service (intangbile) vs. manufacturing
    (tangible) economies, 118–122, **120**
*Service America: Doing Business in the
    New Economy*, 77
"service management," 26
"service revolution," 77
sexual harassment, gender-based
    inequalities, 5, 195
Sharp Electronics, 146, 202
Sheraton, 200
Short History of Financial Euphoria, A,
    59
Shouldice Hospitals, 116
Singapore, 10
singularity and branding, 111
"smart cards," 151–152
Smith, Roger, 217
Smith-Corona Corporation, 3–4
social drivers, 180
sociocultural issues, 12, 16–17, 19, 36–37,
    41–42, 46, 82, 127, 154–155, 161–162,
    180–203, 237
Solzhenitsyn, Alexander, 57
Sony, 202
Sotheby's, 115
Southern Pacific Railroad, 160
Southern Poverty Law Center, 234
Soviet Union, 98
sports equipment, 3, 75
Standard & Poor's 500 Index, 58
standardization, 151, 226
stock indexes, 58–59, 123–124
strategic customer, 77
strategic planning, 5, 49–50
strategic value hiearchy of, 87–89, **88**
Suharto, President of Indonesia, 3
Sun Microsystems, 178
SuperQuinn, 82
suppliers and manufacturers, 71–72
supply and demand, 24, 25

surveys and statistics, 51–56, 90,
   211–215
Swatch, 146
Sweden, 191
Switzerland, 182, 238
Sylvania, 238
symbol-users vs. symbol-makers, 37–38
synergy mergers, 106–107
"synthetic experience," 188

Taco Bell Corporation, 196
Taiwan, 10, 221, 236
technology issues, 2–4, 12, 18–19, 31, 32,
   36, 39–40, 45–47, 128–129, 144–179
technology industries, 2–4, 25–27, 32–33,
   63–64, 84–86, 93–101, 106–107,
   128–129, 146, 147, 165–167, 182–183
Telecommunications Incorporated, 103
"Thing Economy," 119
Third Wave theory, 34–43, 82, 154–155
3M Corporation, 99, 126, 145
Three Mile Island nuclear accident, 235
Titanic, 112
tobacco industry, 193–194, 224
Toffler, Alvin & Heidi, 35
trade barriers, 201
travel as driving force of Third Wave, 39
travel industry, 92–93, 130–131
Travelers Group, 103–104
Treaty of Maastricht, 1991, 141–142
trend hypnosis, 59
trends (see economic trends)
tulip bulb mania of 16th century
   Holland, 59–60
tuning your corporate radar, 7–9
Twenty Two Immutable Laws of
   Branding, The, 109

U.S. Bureau of Census, 53
U.S. Department of Commerce, 221
U.S. Department of Defense, 154, 155
U.S. Justice Department, Microsoft
   antitrust litigation, 178
Ukraine, 235, 240
uncertainty as part of predicting future,
   50, 53–54
unemployment rates, 55, 133–134
Union Carbide, 223, 235
Union Pacific Railroad, 160
United Airlines, 94–95
United Auto Workers, 4
United Parcel Service, 126, 127, 208
United States Postal Service (USPS),
   127, 209
Univac, 158
USA Today, 51–52, 177

value packages, 71
value proposition, 89–90
value-oriented strategies, 26
values, driving cultural values, 183–184
vanity mergers, 104
Verne, Jules, 45
Viacom, 106
Vietnam, 10
Voltaire, 180
Volvo Svenska Bil, 85, 110, 111
von Goethe, Johann Wolfgang, 14

Wall Street Journal, 216
Wal-Mart, 96, 202
Walt Disney Corporation, 66, 78, 98,
   111–112, 117
Warhol, Andy, 42
watch manufacturing, 146
Waterford Crystal, 98, 111
Way of Life, 44
weather's effects on business, 232–233,
   241–242
web pages/web sites, 173–175
Welch, Jack, 66, 99
Wells, H.G., 231
Westinghouse, 145
wildcard factors in trends, 63–68, **67**
Wilkie, Wendell, 82
Winchester, 111
Windows operating system (see
   Microsoft)
Wired magazine, 152
Wizard of Oz, The, 23
working capital, in evaluating competi-
   tion, 96
World Future Society, 47
World Intellectual Property Organization
   (WIPO), 221
World Wide Web, 27
WorldWatch Institute, 47, 240
Wozniak, Steve, 147

Xerox Corporation, 111, 145, 147

Y2K problem, 98, 153, 155–163
Yahoo search engine, 154

Zaire, 210–211
Zemke, Ron, 77